JOHN CHAMBERS

A

My true story of
life and death in
the Troubles

Belfast
Child

JB

JOHN BLAKE

Published by John Blake Publishing,
an imprint of Bonnier Books UK
80-81 Wimpole Street
Marylebone
London
W1G 9RE

www.facebook.com/johnblakebooks 🔘
twitter.com/jblakebooks 🔘

First published in paperback in 2020

ISBN: 978 1 78946 274 6

British Library Cataloguing-in-Publication Data:

A catalogue record for this book is available from the British Library.

Design by www.envydesign.co.uk

Printed and bound in Great Britain by Clays Ltd, Elcograf S.p.A.

1 3 5 7 9 10 8 6 4 2

Every reasonable effort has been made to trace copyright-holders of material reproduced
in this book, but if any have been inadvertently overlooked the publishers would be glad
to hear from them.

John Blake Publishing is an imprint of Bonnier Books UK
www.bonnierbooks.co.uk

A
Belfast
Child

This book is dedicated to my father, John Chambers.
I miss and love you every single day.
To my siblings, Mags, Jean and David – this is also your story.
To my wife, Simone, and my kids, Autumn and Jude – you fill my
life with joy and happiness.
To all other members of the Chambers clan no longer with us, as
well as all the innocent victims of the Northern Irish Troubles.
And finally, of course, to my mother.

CONTENTS

INTRODUCTION

'Historically, Unionist politicians fed their electorate the myth that they were first class citizens . . . and without question people believed them. Historically, Republican/Nationalist politicians fed their electorate the myth that they were second class citizens . . . and without question the people believed them. In reality, the truth of the matter was that we all, Protestant and Catholic, were third class citizens, and none of us realised it!'

HUGH SMYTH, OBE (1941–2014). UNIONIST POLITICIAN.

Although I was raised in what is probably one of the most Loyalist council estates in Belfast, I was never what you might term a conventional 'Prod'. Don't get me wrong – coming from Glencairn, situated just above the famous Shankill Road and populated by Protestants (and their descendants' who fled intimidation, violence and death in other parts

Belfast at the beginning of the Troubles, I was (and remain) a Loyalist through and through. I was unashamedly proud of my Northern Irish Protestant ancestry (still am) and couldn't wait for all the fun and games to be had on 12 July, 'The Twelfth', or 'Orangeman's Day' (still can't). Even after thirty-plus years of living away from the place my dreams are populated by bags of Tayto Cheese & Onion crisps, pastie suppers from Beatties on the Shankill and pints of Harp lager. I cheer on the Northern Ireland Football team (though I'm not a massive football fan, I watch all the big games) and I bitch frequently about the doings of Sinn Fein.

I'm a working-class Belfast Loyalist through and through and very proud of my culture and traditions. Yet from an early age I sensed that I was somehow different. As a child I couldn't quite put my finger on it and when I discovered the truth in my early teens, I was embarrassed, mortified and ashamed – but maybe not particularly shocked. I always knew there was something not 'quite right' about me. The secret was that I wasn't as 'Super Prod' as I thought; there was another strand of Northern Irish tradition in my background, one that was equally working-class Belfast, but as diametrically opposed to Protestantism as you're likely to get. There's a comedy song that probably still does the rounds in clubs across Ireland, North and South, called 'The Orange and The Green', the chorus of which goes something like *'It is the biggest mix-up that you have ever seen/My father he was Orange and my mother she was Green.'* In other words, a Protestant father and Catholic mother. This song could have been written about family directly, so closely did it match our dynamic.

Now, if you're read CHAMBERS

country than Northern I[reland] from the comfort of any other Scotland, you'll be (just about) r..e Republic of Ireland or the fuss is about. Catholics marrying for wondering what all big deal, surely. No one cares. But in a c..ants? So what? No Ireland, where tribalism still reigns suprem.. y like Northern people can sniff out a person's religion just by lo..ng at them, and the local the prospect of the 'mixed marriage' is still cause i.. a good gossip, at the very least. During the Troubles period it was an excuse for deep embarrassment, banishment, a paramilitary beating, or worse. Those Protestants and Catholics who married and stuck it out either slunk away into some quiet corner of Northern Ireland, trying to ignore the ongoing conflict while hoping the neighbours wouldn't ask too many questions, or left the place altogether, never to return.

The marriage of my own parents, John Chambers (Protestant) and Sally McBride (Catholic), fell apart in the late 1960s as Belfast burned in the early days of the Troubles. The ferocity of hatred between the city's two warring communities scorched many people desperately trying to find sanctuary in a country heading towards all-out civil war. As we'll see, my parents' marriage was among these early casualties. Their lives, and the lives of their four children, would change for ever and were shaped by the sectarian madness that tore Belfast and all of Northern Ireland apart and brought us all to the brink of an abyss that threatened and ruined our daily lives.

This isn't a book about the day-to-day events of the Troubles. There are plenty of excellent histories available detailing t.. period in all its gory glory, and from all viewpoints. If

A BELFА̀d reading one of these, or
need deep context, I'd ↱ now and as a tourist you won't
even visiting Belfast. Anywhere on this earth. As we say,
find a warmer we are the friendliest in the world – just
Northern Irish other.
not towards e ɭove history, I'm not a historian and I don't
Although book to be a dry run through of the events of
intend th book to be a dry run through of the events of
1969 ɾwards. As a child I learned the stories and legends of
the ʀattle of Boyne and the Siege of Derry at my grandfather's
and father's knees, becoming immersed in the Loyalist culture
that would shape and dominate my whole existence.

I just happened to be there at the time – an ordinary kid
in an extraordinary situation made even more complicated
by the secret of my dual heritage. This is simply the story
of a boy trying to grow up, survive, thrive, have fun and
discover himself against a backdrop of events that might
best be described as 'explosive', captivating and shocking
the world for thirty long years. I've written this book
because even I find my own story hard to believe sometimes,
and only when I see it on the shelves will I truly know that
it happened. In addition, it's a story I would like my own
children and grandchildren to read. I want them to live in
peace, harmony and understanding in a multicultural world
where everyone tolerates and respects each other. I suppose
I've always been a dreamer . . .

When they read my book, which I hope they will, they
might understand what it is to grow up in conflict, hatred
and intolerance, and work towards a better future for
themselves and others. When I was twenty, twenty-one, I

knew that if I didn't leave Northern Ireland soon, I would end up either in prison or dead, or on the dole for the rest of my life. This was the brutal reality I was faced with. My own personal journey through life and the Troubles had led me to a crossroads in my life and I made the monumental choice to leave Belfast and all those I loved behind and start a new life in London.

I would hate to think my son, daughter or nephews and nieces back in Belfast would ever have to make the same drastic judgement about their own situation.

My Loyalist heart and soul respects and loves all mankind, and providing the God you worship or the political system you follow is peaceful and respectful to all others then I don't have a problem with you and wish you a happy future. Just because I am proud of my Loyalist culture and traditions doesn't make me a hater or a bigot; it just means I am happy with the status quo in Northern Ireland and wish to maintain and celebrate the union with the UK and honour our Queen.

As a child growing up in Loyalist Belfast during the worst years of the Troubles, I hated Catholics with a passion and I could never forgive them for what I saw as their passive support of the IRA and other Republican terrorist groups. However, unlike many of my peers around me, I was never comfortable with the killing of non-combatants, regardless of political or religious background, and I mourned the death of innocent Catholics as much as innocent Protestants. In my childhood, I looked up to the Loyalist warlords and those who served them and when they killed an IRA member I celebrated with those around me. As I grew older and wise my views changed. I no longer based my opinions and hatred on religion, but on politics and the humanity shown to others.

I'm a peace-loving Loyalist and therefore want everlasting peace in Northern Ireland. We do exist, despite perceptions from some quarters, but our voices are rarely heard, drowned out by the actions of the few, and certainly nowhere near as frequently as our Republican neighbours who are very much 'on message' with their own take on events. I hope this book goes some way to redressing that balance, and that whatever 'side' you might be on (or on no side at all) you will enjoy it, and that it will make you stop and think.

Finally, the story you are about to read is my own personal journey through the Troubles and my perception of growing up in Loyalist Belfast. In no way am I speaking for the wider Loyalist community or Protestant people and the views expressed here are my own. For reasons of security, some names have been changed.

John Chambers
England, April 2020

PROLOGUE

As a child, I loved the housing estate of Glencairn. To my mind it was paradise. Cut into the hillside, and with unbeatable views of the city on one side and the Divis Mountain on the other, it was like arriving in heaven after the hell of living among the urban sectarian flashpoints of West Belfast. Here were trees, lush green fields, sparkling clear rivers and streams that rushed down from the mountainside and were filled with fish. Us kids spent long hot summers splashing about in the 'Spoon', a natural cavernous feature of the landscape filled with water, and feasted on wild berries, strawberries and nuts that grew along the banks of the river.

Here were our close family and friends, housed in the damp flats and maisonettes that had been hurriedly built to house those Protestants 'put out' of their homes in the city by avenging Catholics. They too were being burnt from their homes but back then my young Loyalist heart felt no sympathy for them; in my opinion they supported the IRA and had started the 'war'.

Up in Glencairn we felt safe and free. As long as we all obeyed the rules, of course.

These rules were not the laws of the land. They were not enforced by police, army or government officials. They were not set down in any written form, but we all knew what they were and who had made them. And even as small children, we knew that a heavy price would be extracted for those foolish enough to break the rules. A heavy price, and sometimes a very public price too.

Our two-bedroom maisonette was situated at the bottom of a small grassy hill facing St Andrew's Church and the local shopping complex, which consisted of a Chinese chippy, the VG general store, a laundrette, a newsagent's, a wine lodge and the local Ulster Defence Association – UDA – drinking club called 'Grouchos'. In fact, we could roll down it almost to our back door – a game my younger brother David and I played frequently. In the winter when the hill was covered in snow, we would make sledges out of old bits of wood and spend hours and hours going up and down the hill, never feeling the cold. Dad would have a go at us for all the mud and grass we trailed into the flat but his was a good-natured telling-off. The truth was that he was pleased to see us all happy and carefree again after the trauma of the previous few years, and the sudden and final disappearance of my mum.

One late spring afternoon I was rolling towards our back door, Dad's beloved Alsatian dog Shep (my best friend and constant companion) in hot pursuit. Dad called him Shep after the Elvis song and he was able to knock our letterbox with his nose when he wanted to come indoors. The grass had recently been cut and was damp, meaning that it stuck to every part of my clothing. I came to a halt just short of our back wall, the sweet smell of cut grass filling my nostrils, before standing up to brush it all off my jumper. As I did, I noticed my cousin, Wee Sam, running up towards our house from the direction of the main road.

'John! Davy! C'mon, hurry up! There's summin' going on down the shops!'

Wee Sam was red in the face and could hardly get his words out. 'It must be good,' I said, 'cos you look like you're about to die.'

'Not me,' he replied, 'but there's a woman down there looks likely to. C'mon, we gotta see this!'

He turned tail and without thought we ran after him. As anyone who's ever grown up on a housing estate will know, if there's a commotion taking place word gets around like lightning. In Loyalist Glencairn there was always something going on and it was violent as often as not. As we ran, it seemed that half of the estate was also making its way to the shops from every direction. 'This must be big,' I thought as I ran, my wee brother trying to keep up with me. On this estate, as in every area of Belfast afflicted by the Troubles, very few people turned away from danger. The natural sense of curiosity found in spades among Northern Irish people was too strong for that.

In the few minutes it took us to run from our house, a large crowd had already gathered outside the shops. A gang of 'hard men', who we all knew to be paramilitary enforcers, seemed to be at the centre of the action. Local women stood on the fringes of the crowd, shouting, swearing and spitting.

'Fuckin' Fenian-loving bitch!'

'Youse deserve to die, ye fuckin' Taig-loving hoor!' ('Taig' is an offensive slang term for a Catholic).

I pushed in to get a better look. At the heart of the crowd was a young woman, struggling against the grip of the men holding her. Her cheap, fashionable clothes were torn and her eyes were wild and staring, like an animal's before slaughter. She screamed for them to take their hands off her, spitting at her accusers and lashing out with her feet. It was no use. One of the bigger guys pulled her hands behind her back and dragged her against a concrete lamppost. Someone passed him a length of rope and with a few expert strokes he'd lashed the young woman against the post by her hands, quickly followed by her feet. She reminded me of a squaw captured by cowboys in the Westerns I loved to watch and then re-enact using local kids in games that could last for days.

Except this wasn't a game. This was justice Glencairn style – all perfectly normal to me and my peers and we took it in our stride. Although she was still squealing like a pig, the resistance seemed to have gone out of the woman. Smelling blood, the crowd pushed forwards and the woman's head hung low in shame and embarrassment. One of the men grabbed a hank of her long hair and wrenched her head upwards, forcing her to look him right in the eye.

'You,' he said slowly, 'have been caught going with a Taig, so you have! Do you deny it?'

Now I recognised the woman. She was a girl off the estate. I had seen her walking down Forthriver Road on her way to meet her mini-skirted mates. They'd pile into a black taxi and head into town for a bit of drinking and dancing. I guess it was on one of these nights out that she'd met the Catholic boy – the 'Taig' – who was at the centre of the allegations. Good job he wasn't here now, because he might already be lying in a pool of blood, a bullet through his head.

The woman shook her head. 'Fuck you,' she said defiantly. 'Fuck youse all.'

'Grab her hair!' shouted a female voice from the crowd. 'Cut off the fuckin' lot!'

The enforcer produced a large pair of scissors from his pocket. Slowly, deliberately, he tightened his grip on her hair before hacking savagely at the clump below his fist. Amid cheers he threw it at her feet before continuing his rough barbering skills. Within minutes he'd finished and now the woman looked like a cancer victim. Blood oozed from the indiscriminate cuts he'd made on her head and as it ran down her face it intermingled with her tears and snot. She was not a pretty sight.

'Step back!' demanded one of the enforcers. The crowd parted and someone came forward with an open tin of bright red paint. Knowing what was to come, and not wanting to be physically contaminated with the woman's shame, the crowd moved even further back.

The UDA man poured the contents of the tin all over the woman's head, allowing it to run the entire length of her body, right down to her platform boots. She looked like she'd been drowned in blood. Then a pillow was passed up, and with ham-hands the enforcer tore a big hole in the cotton, exposing the contents – feathers, hundreds and thousands of them.

'G'wan,' said a voice, 'give her the full fuckin' works.'

Without further ado the man poured the white feathers all over the woman, head to toe. They clung to the paint, giving the impression of a slaughtered goose hanging off the telegraph pole.

'That will teach ye not to go with filthy Taigs,' said the enforcer. 'Any more of this and youse'll get a beating then a bullet, so you will. Understand?'

Through the paint and the feathers came a small nod of the head.

'Good,' said the man. 'And just so ye don't forget, here's a wee something we made for you earlier.'

To laughter and jeers, the man produced a cardboard sign which he placed around the woman's neck. In the same red paint used to humiliate her, someone had written 'Fenian Lover' across the middle of the cardboard.

'Leave her there for half an hour,' commanded the man to a subordinate, 'then cut her down.' The crowd dispersed, a few women spitting on the victim as they left.

'Jesus,' said Wee Sam, wide-eyed. 'Did you see that? Looked like she'd been shot in the head and the feathers were her brain running down her face. Fuckin' amazing.'

'Course I saw it,' I said. 'I was right at the front, wasn't I? The bitch deserved it. Imagine going with Taigs, the dirty hoor.'

'Let's wait round the shops till they chop her down,' said Sam. 'See where she goes.'

We'd been playing one of our eternal games of Cowboys and Indians recently and we'd got into the idea of tracking people down stealthily. So we waited until another paramilitary cut the woman's rope and watched as she slumped to the ground.

'I think she's pissed herself,' said Sam.

'Ssh,' I replied, 'she'll hear us. Wait while she gets up.'

We watched the woman slowly pick herself up from the pavement. She wiped her eyes and looked around. The area outside the shops was now completely deserted as though nothing had happened. An angry mob had been replaced by an eerie silence.

As she stumbled off, we nudged each other. 'Look,' I said. 'Look what's happening. She's leaving a trail!'

She was too, a trail of blood-red boot prints. We gave her twenty or so yards' start, then in single file began to follow her, sidling up against walls and lamp-posts like the gang of Cherokees we imagined we were. We must have gone a good quarter-mile when she turned into a pathway leading up to a small, shabby flat. We saw her fumbling in her pocket for a key, noticing the relief on her face as she found it still there. The lock turned and she went inside without a backwards glance.

'That's it,' said Sam, 'fun's over. Let's go home.'

'Wait,' I said. I watched as the woman put on a light, looked in a mirror then drew the curtains tightly. Some part of me, the part that wasn't screaming 'Fenian bitch!' with all the others, suddenly felt hugely sorry for her. She only looked about seventeen or eighteen – not much older than my sister Margaret. What had she done wrong, other than meet a nice boy she liked? Did she deserve such brutal treatment? After this I never saw her around the estate again. She'd probably fled for her life, never to return. And who could blame her?

Something inside of me knew I'd witnessed a terrible thing, yet I knew I couldn't even begin to think like this. It was against the rules; the same unwritten rules and code of conduct that this young woman had disobeyed. Fear of the paramilitaries created a culture of silence and where we lived this was a survival strategy we all lived by. We were all products of this violent environment and we had been desensitised to events that no child should ever have to witness.

I shuddered, pulled my thin jacket close around me and with the others, headed for the safety of home.

Even now, more than forty years later, whenever I smell the sweet aroma of cut grass I am transported back to that dusky spring evening in the early seventies and the woman's brutal punishment, and I can hardly believe the madness of my childhood in Glencairn.

CHAPTER 1

There are ghosts of the past all over Belfast. Spectres that slip unseen past gable-ended houses painted with murals and linger in the so-called 'interface' zones, where Protestant and Catholic neighbourhoods collide, often violently. They lurk in the damp, overgrown back alleys of terraced streets where the bodies of both the innocent and the guilty were dumped, and flit and flicker in and around the huge bonfires lit across the city on 11 July ahead of Orangeman's Day – the holiest of holy days for Loyalists.

Such shadows are to be seen in those parts of Belfast that witnessed the first stirrings of the Troubles in the late 1960s. Catholics and Protestants alike fled these narrow streets of little houses for safer territory as their homes blazed, the result of sectarian arson. At the time it was the biggest population displacement since the Second World War. Slum clearances and the subsequent building of new houses have altered these areas almost beyond recognition, yet when I'm ever in the neighbourhood around Grosvenor Road I feel the hairs rise on the back of my neck and the ghosts of the past whisper in my ear.

In my mind's eye I see John and Sally – married with four kids, but barely out of their teens themselves – sick with fear about the increasing sectarian violence developing all around them. I imagine listening in as they discuss their situation. She's Catholic and he's Protestant. Neither of their respective families has been keen on this marriage, to say the least. The stigma of marrying someone from the 'other side' has tarnished the reputation of both families, and neighbours are whispering and sniggering behind closed doors. The houses in Little Distillery Street, where they live, are being attacked nightly. Riots are breaking out on every street corner. Belfast is burning, and in the darkness, the heat, the smoke, the noise, in the chaos and confusion, no one seems to know who friend or foe is. Lifelong neighbours are being driven from homes they've lived their whole lives in, while friendships that have lasted for decades and generations are shattered and forgotten as Belfast descends into a sectarian hell that will last three decades and cost countless lives on all sides.

I watch as John and Sally huddle in their tiny kitchen, their kids crying with fear upstairs. What will they do? Where will they go? And will any neighbourhood accept them for who they are?

The shadows are long, but indistinct. For reasons that will become clear, I have little knowledge of how or why my parents got together. All of us siblings – myself, Margaret, Jean and David – have heard stories, rumours and snatches of gossip.

But up to now, no one knows the true story. So here's what we do know: Sally McBride came from a strongly nationalist/ Republican family originating from the Falls Road, the heart of Catholic West Belfast. When my parents met, Mum was living with her father in McDonnell Street, which was near where my dad and my grandparents' family lived at the time. John Chambers shared his name with both his father and grandfather (I'm the fourth John Chambers) and came from a strongly unionist/Loyalist family originating in Sandy Row and Shankill, both Loyalist enclaves of Belfast. In the late 1950s and early 1960s Protestants and Catholics could just about live cheek by jowl, but this wasn't to last.

From an early age, my dad was in the Orange Order. This wasn't unusual – in fact, the Order provided a clear focus point for Protestants of all descriptions to celebrate their traditions and feel a sense of 'togetherness'. It's arguable that the Order acted as a kind of employment agency, ensuring that only Protestants worked in Belfast's big industries, particularly shipbuilding, causing resentment among Catholics who felt shut out. Perhaps the Order helped to find my dad a job in one of the local factories, because we think he was working in such a place when he first clapped eyes on the pretty, dark-haired girl who'd always walk the same way to her place of work.

Dad was a good-looking guy, with a big dimple and an Elvis quiff that paid tribute to the singer he loved. He had personality, charisma, and I dare say enough cheek to smile at Sally McBride as she passed by. She was slim, with a stylish hairdo and a twinkle in her eye. If she smiled back, maybe he asked her name and where she lived. Now, in Belfast, obtaining these two pieces of information is crucial because it will determine whether that person is Catholic or Protestant. At the height of the Troubles the answer you gave could be the difference between life or death but for the moment – here, in the late 1950s – it simply determines the background of the person you're talking to, and whether you wish to proceed on that basis.

So John asks Sally what her name is and where she lives, and she answers that it's 'Sally McBride' and that she lives in McDonnell Street. It's just around the corner from Little Distillery Street, where John's family live, but already he knows it's predominantly Catholic. Belfast people have a keen sense of geography – again, such knowledge has often been a matter of life and death.

Sally asks John who he is and where he's from, and he tells her. Now she knows he's a Protestant and immediately she wonders what her family will say. John is also thinking about this. People go about their daily business as peacefully as possible, but introducing a member of the opposing religion into the home is not done, not in these working-class areas of Belfast.

Still, he engages her in conversation as they walk along the street and when she turns towards home John asks Sally if he can walk her to her door. Warily, she agrees, looking round to see if any of her friends and neighbours have caught her in the act of talking to this young guy. This is a city that thrives on gossip, and in the tight-knit streets around the Falls word will quickly spread that 'wee Sally's courtin' a young fella'.

At the door of her house he asks if he can see her again. She thinks about it for a moment, then agrees. So what if he's a Protestant? Maybe if she gets to know him better, her daddy will like him too. John is thinking the same thing, but is pleased that he can walk out with her again soon.

And they do. The relationship goes from strength to strength and John and Sally fall in love. Their respective families find out and neither side is happy, so John and Sally marry in February 1961 without any fuss and decide to move to England. They arrive in London, where John gets a job working for London Underground as a ticket inspector and Sally gives birth to her first child, Margaret, in 1962. They remain in London for a while, but perhaps the pressure of dealing with a baby gets to Sally and she realises she needs close family around her. So they move back to Belfast, where Jean is born (1964) followed by me (1966) and David (1968). We are baptised in the Roman Catholic faith and two of us are initially given Catholic first names. In time these will be changed to more Protestant ones.

We are all now living in Little Distillery Street, close to the Falls Road, and by the time of my birth the area is beginning to feel the sectarian tension that will eventually lead to riots, the burning of houses, death, displacement and the arrival of the British Army for 'Operation Banner'. This was meant to calm the immediate tension; tragically it became the longest campaign in British military history. In 1966, Catholics are demanding their rights as citizens and the newly formed Civil Rights Movement (CRM) is demanding to be heard. Protestants feel angry and scared that their way of life may be destroyed forever by the resurgent Catholics. Added to this is the fear that Republican gunmen are becoming strong again, and infiltrating the CRM. This makes the Protestants nervous and suspicious of the CRM.

This uneasy situation holds for a while but by the time David is born the spark has been ignited. In August 1969, Belfast is in flames and my parents are moving from house to house, trying to find shelter and safety. The army arrives to break up the fighting, and local kids (including my sister Margaret) befriend the young, nervous soldiers who seem shocked at the levels of viciousness and hatred to be seen on British streets.

Today, I stand where Little Distillery Street used to be and hear the echoes of rioting, the whup-whup-whup of helicopters overhead and remember the acrid smell of the burning houses. I recall being three years old, and cowering under the sheets in the bedroom at night, trying not to cry as I listen to the roars of the mob, the flashes of petrol bombs crashing on to the cobblestones and the thud of rubber bullets being fired into an angry crowd. The four of us share a bed and we huddle together like frightened rabbits against the terror and mayhem going on in the street below. Even today, when I hear a car backfire I jump ten feet in the air, a relic of the trauma of hearing gunfire and not knowing where it was coming from, or when it would end.

And then, for reasons we can only speculate about, Mum leaves Belfast for London, taking Margaret and me with her. This would be around 1969. We think she rented a flat in Stockwell, perhaps through contacts she'd made. I don't remember any of this, just a vague shadow of a memory of a dark-haired woman giving me something to eat. It's sad to say, but I cannot picture the woman's face, though I assume it is my mother. Did she leave because she was terrified of what might happen to us? It's a possibility, because we know that she came back to Belfast soon after arriving in London and then took Jean and David, leaving Margaret and me with our father. Had she met someone else and was scared that her life might be in danger in Belfast for reasons other than her religion and the nature of her marriage? There are some in the family who feel this may be the case but again, we do not know for sure.

My feeling is that for whatever reason she had some kind of nervous breakdown that led her to flee Belfast in a panic. She came back for Jean and David, certainly, but why she left Margaret and me with our dad is a mystery. It seems that on her next scheduled return to Belfast Margaret and I were taken by our dad to Belfast Docks, where her boat from Liverpool was due to arrive. He waited and waited, but she didn't walk down the gangplank. Eventually, the ship's staff took pity on him and allowed him to search the vessel for his wife and two of his children. They weren't there.

I guess that by this stage my dad had had enough of Sally's to-ing and fro-ing. He was a real family man, always putting the needs of his children first, and wouldn't have been able to stand the thought of us being split up. He was one of several brothers and he must have known that he might need their support for what he had planned. Obviously, Sally wasn't coming back to Belfast, but by hook or by crook he would have all his children together in one place. There was only one thing for it and at some stage, probably in the early part of 1970, my father and a couple of his brothers made the journey to London, where they visited Sally McBride and returned home with two frightened, bewildered children, leaving their mother behind. Whether they gave Sally the option to come with them is, yet again, speculation. If they did, she must've refused because she stayed in England for the rest of her life. Whatever it was that drove her away and led her to abandon four young children must have been very powerful indeed. Mum simply disappeared from this point onwards and we just got on with being the wholly Protestant Chambers family.

It's the case that much of what I've written above is based on speculation, rumour, guesswork and fact. It's hard to know exactly where the precise truth lies in all of this, but as we know truth can very often be subjective, depending on whose version you're hearing. What we can all agree on, if nothing else, is that extreme pressure (external, internal or both) caused the breakdown of a mixed marriage in the sectarian cauldron of 1960s Belfast and that all of us – Mum, Dad and four children – were its casualties.

As I've mentioned, neither John or Sally's respective families were very happy about their marriage and to add to their troubles there was the little difficulty about my leg. When I was eighteen months old it was discovered that I had osteomyelitis in my right leg. This is an infection of the bone and if it's caught quickly it can be treated with antibiotics. Unfortunately, it wasn't spotted in time and the infection caused permanent damage, leading to long spells in hospital and multiple operations to try to contain the damage. My leg was saved, but to this day I walk with a limp and use a stick.

As a result, I spent more time in the Royal Victoria and Musgrave Park hospitals than I did at home. I was in and out all the time, and it must have been during one of my 'out' periods that we were taken to London. In hindsight, spending time in hospital was probably to my advantage because at least those stays kept me away from the trouble spots around our neighbourhood and shielded me from the breakdown of my parents' marriage. At the time, though, these places were big, impersonal and frightening places to be. The hospitals I was in tended to be located in Catholic areas, and so the majority of their patients were Catholic – I was very much outnumbered. The hospital wards seemed dark and foreboding, and the appearance of the matron at night, hearing her footsteps echo down the corridors as she walked towards the children's ward, plus nuns gliding about the place like grey ghosts, really spooked me. I missed home and my family terribly and would cry myself to sleep after the nurses had visited the children's ward to tuck us in and tell us to be quiet now it was bedtime.

To make matters worse, I was confined to bed, unable to walk due to the large plaster casts on both my legs. The days seemed endless and I looked forward to the brief appearances of my family who were only allowed to come during strict visiting hours. Although money was always tight, Dad brought little gifts and magazines up to the hospital and sometimes he would take me to the tuck shop and buy sweets and Lucozade in the old-style bottles with the yellow film around them. I always had a bottle or two beside my bed. Once my family was gone, that was it – I was alone again, with no idea when I might leave hospital to be reunited with my nearest and dearest.

At first, this was very hard for me to cope with but as time went on, I adapted to the situation. Although I had extreme difficulty walking, at some stage I was given a small four-wheeled cart in which I could push myself around the ward, causing as much mayhem and mischief as I could muster as I whizzed around the place.

I seem to remember – or perhaps I've been told – that at first my whole family would come to visit, then each parent separately, with their own extended families, then just my dad, his mum and whoever of my siblings. This might be consistent with the stories of my parents' marriage breakdown and Mum's sudden disappearance. In any case, my strongest memory of that time is of a student nurse whose surname was Brown. These were the days when hospital staff were 'Nurse So-and-So' or 'Doctor-Somebody' – the idea of calling medical people by their first names was a long way into the future. So Nurse Brown came into my life and I immediately fell in love with her. She had short brown hair and the face and temperament of an angel. In my eyes she was beautiful, and I recall her boyfriend coming to pick her up one evening. I became very jealous and sulked for a few days afterwards.

I decided that if my own mother was no longer coming to visit, Nurse Brown would have to be my foster mum. My face would light up when she arrived on duty and crumble when she finished her shift.

One day she appeared in the ward in her 'civilian' clothing. I was surprised because she'd already told me that today was her day off.

'Surprise!' she shouted as she arrived at my bedside.

'Why are you here?' I asked, beaming.

'To see you, silly,' she replied. 'I'm taking you out of here this morning. Would you like that?'

The other kids on the ward sat up in their beds to see what was going on. Nurse Brown lifted me out of my bed and into a wheelchair. I felt like royalty as I spied all those little faces looking across the ward, wondering what treats were in store for me.

'I think I'll push you round the park today,' she said. 'I bought some bird food from up the pet shop, and we can feed the squirrels too. That sound good?'

It sounded more than good to me, who'd been stuck inside for so long. For a couple of hours we trundled around Musgrave Park, an oasis of peace and calm amid a city that was tearing itself to pieces. Nurse Brown pointed out various species of birds and persuaded a few of the cheekier squirrels to take the food directly from my outstretched hand. I didn't want the day to finish and was delighted when she offered to take me back to her student nurse accommodation for tea and sandwiches.

These little outings happened regularly and I became deeply attached to this warm, understanding human being – so much so that when I was allowed home for weekends to see my family I would scream the place down and demand to stay with my nurse friend. Whether I was her favourite, or whether she knew about the break-up of my family and had taken pity on me, I guess I'll never know. But for a few crucial years in and out of hospital she became my mainstay, and I can't thank her enough for what she did for me during those painful times.

During this period it dawned on me that my mother's non-appearance at hospital was something serious. This was a little troubling to me. I saw other mums and dads visiting their sick kids and I wondered why it was that only my dad and his side of the family were coming to see me. At first, I pretended to myself that Mum was at home but was too busy to visit. Eventually, I accepted this wasn't the case and I guess that even in my childish mind I knew the truth: that she wouldn't be coming to visit, ever, because she was no longer here. Where she'd gone, I'd no idea, and no one was telling me anything. Mum's family quickly stopped coming to visit – much later, I was told that Dad had banned them from contact with any of us, even though their poorly nephew was in the hospital. Again, like so much of my early childhood the mists of time have descended on the truth of this. If it is true, I suppose it makes sense that Dad would want a clean break from Mum's family, especially at a time when the trust between Catholics and Protestants was at rock bottom. Maybe he felt it was easier to shut them out for good and raise us solely in the Protestant tradition in a family that was close-knit, and loyal in every sense of the word.

My early years in hospital coincided with several moves in and around West Belfast. We went from place to place in the hope we wouldn't be forced to move because our home had been attacked. We tried a couple of places in Roden Street and around Selby Street but the tension in this flashpoint area was too much for Dad to bear. For the sake of his family, he needed to be embedded among his own kind in an exclusively Protestant enclave. Fortunately, a solution was just around the corner (give or take a couple of miles).

After four years in and out of hospital my osteomyelitis was given the all-clear. My poor old leg wasn't in the best of shape and I would always walk with a limp, but the disease had at least subsided. There would be many more hospital visits and operations to come but for now I was a free kid. In floods of tears I bade Nurse Brown goodbye, secretly wishing she could come home with me.

'Well,' she said brightly, 'it'd be nice to see you again, but hopefully when you're much better. Anyway, your da tells me you have a new home to go to.'

I looked at my dad, standing beside me holding the suitcase that contained a few meagre possessions.

'Do we, Daddy?' I said. 'Do we have a new house?'

'Ah, John, it was going to be a surprise,' he said, winking at Nurse Brown, 'but I think the cat's out of the bag now. We're going up to Glencairn. Ever heard of it?'

I hadn't, so Dad told me that it was a new estate up beyond the Shankill. He said that my granny and granda had already moved up there, along with a couple of uncles and their families. 'It's gonna be great,' he said. 'We'll all be together in one place, and no worries about anything.'

I smiled as he hugged me. I believed him, because I knew that he was going to make everything all right as he always did.

CHAPTER 2

Taking my hand, Dad hauled me and David up the short, steep grassy bank, with Shep, my dad's beloved Alsatian, following behind. My two sisters were already at the top, shouting and squealing in excitement. 'We've got a new house, we've got a new house!' they chorused.

The new place lay at the bottom of a small hill that overlooked Forthriver Road, the main thoroughfare in and out of Glencairn. It was bigger than the houses we'd previously lived in and for the first time we had an inside toilet and bathroom.

It wasn't huge – just a two-bedroomed maisonette – but it was ours, and no longer would we need to leave it at a moment's notice because of the threat from neighbouring Catholics or Republicans – because there were no neighbouring Catholics or Republicans, not that we knew of anyway. Glencairn was (and is) exclusively Protestant, and if there were any Catholics living up here they were keeping very, very quiet about it.

However, it wasn't the view of our house, nor that of the shops just beyond the block of single-storey flats, that was exciting us this bright spring day of 1972 (ironically, the worse year for deaths in the Troubles with almost five hundred killed). Dad signalled to a point in the distance, way beyond the Crumlin Road and right across the other side of Belfast.

'What do youse see?' he said.

'Goliath!' we shouted in unison. Even as wee kids we all knew the name of the giant yellow crane that had dominated the East Belfast skyline since 1969, towering above the Harland and Wolff shipyard. Within a couple of years Goliath would be joined by 'Samson', who would be even bigger than his twin brother. For all Belfast people these are a symbol of the city but for us Protestants they have special significance because they overlook the dockyards that made the place what it is, thanks largely to the hard work of the mainly Protestant workforce. And it was, of course, where the legendarily unsinkable *Titanic* was built and set forth on her ill-fated maiden voyage and a place in the history books. Like most Belfast folk I am very proud of the fact she was built in Belfast and when cruel people say, 'But didn't she sink?' I reply, 'She was all right when she left Belfast,' and that normally shuts them up.

'Well spotted,' said Dad. 'Now, you see this place right behind us?' Dad pointed to an old and imposing big house up the top end of a driveway in Glencairn Park. 'This is Fernhill House, and it's where Lord Carson inspected the UVF men before they went off to war.'

'To fight the Provies?' I asked. I was only six, but already the language of the Troubles had begun to filter through my vocabulary. The 'Provies' were the Provisional Irish Republican Army – the enemy currently engaged in warfare with the British Army and bombing buildings in Belfast, Londonderry and many other places, killing soldiers, police officers and innocent civilians alike, and the UVF stood for the Ulster Volunteer Force, which was better known as a Loyalist paramilitary group during the Troubles.

'Nah,' said Dad, laughing, 'not them. The UVF went off to fight the Germans in the First World War. Have you heard of the Thirty-Sixth?'

I hadn't, so Dad gave me a quick history lesson. The 36th Ulster Division were the pride of Protestant Belfast (although many Catholics fought in the First World War too) and distinguished itself on the first day of the Battle of the Somme. Dad used to quote the words of Captain Wilfred Spender, who watched as the 36th Division went over the top: 'I am not an Ulsterman but yesterday, the first of July, as I followed their amazing attack, I felt that I would rather be an Ulsterman than anything else in the world.'

Even today, I feel an enormous sense of pride when I hear those words.

I loved these kinds of stories, especially about our grandfathers and great-grandfathers who'd been so brave in the face of almost certain death. In fact, my great-uncle Robert fought and tragically died two weeks before the end of the war.

'Are the UVF still around, Da?' I asked, wide-eyed. I hoped they were, as I recalled the rioting and burning I was told was the work of Catholics out to get us.

'So they are, son,' Dad said, 'but hey, let's not talk about all that now. C'mon with me now and we'll get a pastie supper.'

I jumped up and down with delight. Pastie suppers were (and still are) my favourite. Only Northern Ireland people can appreciate the delights of this deep-fried delicacy of minced pork, onions and spuds, all coated in delicious batter, with chips on the side and a Belfast Bap (a bread roll).

As we walked from the brow of the hill down to the chippy, Dad told me a few more stories about Fernhill House. It was owned by a family called Cunningham, he said, and it had stables attached to it. In one of these was housed a racehorse called Tipperary Tim. According to legend, the horse's jockey, William Dutton was told by a friend, 'Billy boy, you'll only win if all the others fall.'

'Sure enough,' said Dad, 'yer man Dutton took the horse into the Grand National in Liverpool and all the other horses fell down. And so Tipperary Tim won the race.'

'That's amazing!' I shouted. 'Does he still live in the stables? Can we go and see him? Please, Da . . .'

In response, my dad laughed. 'You're a bit late, son,' he said. 'The race was won in 1928!'

In time, Fernhill House and the surrounding area would become my childhood playground and I'd spend hours playing in the park and exploring the empty mansion and its cavernous cellars. Years later, when the Loyalists called their ceasefire as part of the Good Friday Agreement, legendary Loyalist leader Gusty Spence and the 'Combined Loyalist Military Command' choose Fernhill House to tell the world their war was at an end and offer abject and sincere remorse to their victims.

Dad seemed much happier than he had been for a while. He was working as a porter in Belfast City Hospital and he would bring us stationery – pens, pencils, typewriter rubbers and drawing paper – which he probably swiped from offices throughout the hospital. Up here, the troubles our family had endured seemed a long way off. Granted, our maisonette, though newly built, was cold in the winter because we only had an electric fire and it wasn't what you'd call roomy, but it was much better than where we'd lived previously. At this stage I was still wearing a calliper on my right leg and was allowed to share the big double bed with Dad while everyone else was in the other bedroom. It wasn't ideal but we were happy, especially Dad. He was a committed Christian and was now attending St Andrew's Church, just across the road. We were all encouraged to attend too, and I went twice on a Sunday and to Bible study during the week, plus Beavers and the Boys' Brigade. The minister, the Reverend Walter Lewis, became a family friend. He had a short beard and moustache and wore big-framed glasses. He had a friendly and welcoming face that was always ready with a smile whenever you met him. He was kind and considerate and tried to teach us about love and forgiveness, but we often drove him to distraction as we verbalised our hatred of all things Catholic and their 'evil' religion.

Also, we had family all around us now. Granny and Granddad were here, along with Dad's brother Rab and his wife Jacky and their children, plus Uncle Jim and Aunt Maureen and their kids. Dad's sister, Anne, was just down the road. Susie Chambers, my granny, was a formidable Northern Irish woman with a large bosom who took it on herself to clothe and feed us, put us to bed, discipline us when necessary and generally play the role of a mum now that ours was gone. We all loved her beyond words. She played a big part in our lives from this point onwards because Dad was working here and there and Margaret was still too young to manage the household chores.

Like most women in Glencairn, Granny took great pride in having a clean house and well-turned-out children. She was obsessed with cleaning and there wasn't a speck of dirt to be found in her home. Every year she invested in a new settee and carpets, and when the settee arrived it would be ritually covered with dust sheets, which stayed on for the full year. Even then we weren't allowed to sit on it – we had to squat on the floor instead to watch TV. This cleaning fetish even extended to our bath time, which Granny relished. She'd fill the bath with warm water and top it up with Flash floor cleaner before dropping us in. She'd probably be arrested for that now but at the time we were the best-scrubbed kids on the estate – although never for long as we rolled about in muck and grass and were always dirty when we came in from playing. To this day, when I smell Flash powder I think of my wee Granny Chambers.

Her cooking was generally good. She made us liver and onions with mashed spuds and gravy and I loved it. Once a week she would buy a single Fray Bentos steak 'n' kidney pie and split it between the four of us. Shep got to lick the tin clean as he chased it round the kitchen floor. However, I dreaded the days she'd decide to make 'champ'. This is an Irish dish made of mashed potatoes, scallions (otherwise known as spring onions, but we've always got another name for everything in Northern Ireland), butter, milk and salt and pepper. I never liked this for some reason and when my granny used to make it I'd wait until she'd left the room and throw it in the bin or at the dog, whichever was closer, as I didn't want to hurt her feelings. Also, Dad would bring home pigs' trotters every week from a butcher's down the Shankill, and when they were cooked we had them as a Friday night treat. I have to say that the thought of eating one of those now makes me feel violently ill.

I loved my granny and granddad and was pleased they lived so close to us. But there were still nagging questions about my mum which, even as a small child, I felt weren't being answered. Not long after we arrived in Glencairn, Granny called round and Dad summoned the four of us to the living room. Once we were crowded together on the settee, Granny leaned forward from the comfort of the armchair and put on her serious voice.

'Now listen to me,' she said, 'because this is the first and last time I'll say it. Now then, your ma has gone away and I'm sorry to say she won't be coming back.'

I looked at Dad. He glanced at me and smiled briefly, but didn't speak. Obviously, he was letting Granny do the talking.

'You're not to mention her again,' she continued. 'Understood? And if anybody asks, you're to say she's died.'

'Died . . .' So Mum was dead. That's why she stopped coming to the hospital to see me. I felt numb. David started to cry but was quickly hushed into silence by Granny.

'How did she die?' asked Margaret with a hint of suspicion in her voice. She was only ten, but as sharp as a tack. 'When was it? Was there a funeral? Why didn't we go, Granny?'

Due to recent events, we all knew about death and dying,

and we'd witnessed the funerals of some of those who'd been killed. They were big events, with attendees running into the hundreds. If our mum was dead, surely she'd have had a big funeral too?

'She was killed in a crash,' Granny said finally. 'That's it. You don't need to know any more. Do they, Daddy?'

She gestured to my father, who nodded his agreement. 'That's right,' he said. 'It's all in the past now. And we're having a good time living up here, eh?'

Well, we couldn't deny that. And if Mum was dead and gone, we couldn't do anything about it. In my young mind I felt I had no choice other than to accept it. People died all the time. It was no good squealing about it. Even so, when I sneaked a glance at Margaret, I could tell by her face she wasn't completely convinced by this news. But she, like the rest of us, said nothing and for the next few years at least, we did as we were told and never mentioned her.

Now I see why. Glencairn was ultra-Loyalist and even an accident of birth – such as having a Catholic mother – would be the excuse for teasing, taunting and maybe worse. If the news got out, we'd always be known as 'the Taigs down the road' and that would do all of us, Dad and his siblings included, no favours at all. What Granny was doing – in a brutal Belfast fashion, I guess – was protecting us against our new environment. Up here we were Protestant to our boots, and all traces of the Catholic in us had to be erased.

This included re-naming the two of us who had originally started life with Catholic names. In a way, this was somewhat harder to comprehend than the news of my mother's death.

Now, two of us had to become 'different' people, and would be called by their new names both in private and public. In the early days of the name-change we would occasionally forget and shout out the old names, prompting hisses and the flapping of hands. In time, we got used to it and the new names became established, remaining to this day.

Quickly we established friendships with a squad of cousins of similar age to us, plus other kids whose families had fled from the difficulties across the city. To me, the whole estate was a playground of fields, woods and streams and I was desperate to run with the other kids as they chased across the estate, playing British versus Germans, Cowboys versus Indians and even Prods versus Taigs. But I was hampered by the ever-present reminder of the problems with my leg in the shape of an ugly iron calliper that I had to wear constantly. I looked like Tiny Tim from *A Christmas Carol*, hobbling behind everyone else knowing I'd never be able to catch up. My cousins and friends use to call me 'Hop-a-Long', which really upset me back then.

Every night Dad would carry me upstairs because I still wasn't strong enough to climb steps unaided. He was the centre of my universe and because he'd taken time off from his job to look after me, I followed him around everywhere. I was probably a nuisance and forever under his feet, but he didn't seem to mind and I could see the delight on his face whenever we attended the physiotherapy clinic and the nurses confirmed my leg was getting better. I pushed myself as hard as possible during these sessions because what I wanted above everything else was to be able to run with the kids across Glencairn, climbing trees, jumping in the stream and playing with Shep.

When I was in hospital, many of the other kids were either in wheelchairs or had difficulties walking for one reason or another, so I didn't feel different. Now, though, I was acutely aware of this ugly piece of metalwork clamped around my leg and I wanted rid of it as soon as possible. Determination to be like everyone else paid off and within a year of my discharge the calliper had gone back to the hospital and I was finally free of it. I would always walk with a limp and I'd surely never run the 100 metres for Northern Ireland, but at least now I could achieve my ambition to roam the estate and park.

Sometimes the soldiers would come up to Glencairn and spend an hour or so patrolling around. The sight of a couple of Saracen armoured cars coming up Forthriver Road wasn't the cause for alarm that it might have been if we'd grown up on the Catholic Falls Road, where local women banged bin lids on the cobbles to warn their neighbours that the Brits were on their way. Up in Glencairn, these young boys from over the water were welcomed as heroes because by now they were engaged in a full-on war with the Provies, and as such they were helping to defend us Protestants. The sound of helicopters watching over them was ever-present during these patrols.

Although they always kept one eye out for trouble, the soldiers could relax a little in Glencairn and spend a bit of time chatting to local people. We kids would swarm around them as they jumped out of the back of their vehicles, following them up the road while pleading for sweeties and any little trinkets they might have on them. Sometimes we'd be lucky, receiving a handful of Blackjacks or a spare cap badge plus a wee bit of chat about school or what was on telly that night. Other times they looked and acted like they meant business and we'd leave them to their patrol. As far as we were concerned, they were taking the war directly to the IRA, and the Loyalist people loved and respected them for that. When one was killed or injured, we would go buck mad with rage; an attack on a soldier was an attack on the Crown and we hated the IRA more than ever. We couldn't wait until we were old enough to take up arms and fight them and other Republican groups. Our daily lives were dominated by the Troubles going on around us and there was no escape as we witnessed the daily carnage that played out in the streets and communities we lived in.

There was another army on Glencairn. It didn't always dress in uniform or patrol with weapons (at least not so publicly as the British) but we all knew who was in it and why it was there. This organisation was the Ulster Defence Association, the UDA, and it had been formed in the white heat of the early Troubles to defend Loyalist areas against Republican incursions and attacks, and from intruders from rival Loyalist paramilitary groups. Very quickly it became the biggest Loyalist paramilitary force in Northern Ireland and acted as a vigilante band, policing areas such as ours. The group also collected money to fund itself, distribute loans to local people where needed, and to look after the families of Loyalist prisoners accused of paramilitary activities.

Having seen their houses burned down and their traditional communities destroyed by Republican violence (particularly the events of 'Bloody Friday', 21 July 1972, a pivotal moment in Loyalist history when the IRA exploded twenty bombs across Belfast, killing nine people, injuring one hundred and thirty others and causing chaos and devastation), Loyalist men and women across Belfast queued up to join the UDA and other Protestant paramilitary groups.

One of these recruits was my father. He was a pacifist who hated violence, and a practising Christian, but nonetheless, he as a Loyalist was sickened by Republican violence and felt under enough threat to sign up to the paramilitaries. (At this time the UDA was still a legal organisation, and would remain so until it was banned in August 1992, once the UK government could no longer ignore accusations that it was primarily engaged in terrorism.) He was by no means the only man in my family to do so and he would do his bit by helping to patrol the estate (which usually involved standing around the small row of shops and the community centre, both close to our house) while keeping an eye out for any problems. Also, he was tasked with working in the UDA drinking club that had been established. It was the smallest room behind the off-licence and was dark, dingy and full of smoke. Dad could turn his hand to most things and he took on the job of keeping the bar in good order and serving the senior UDA men and women who drank there regularly, an enthusiasm no doubt born of the nightmare they were all part of. Now that Dad was involved with the paramilitaries (in a non-violent way) there was even more reason not to mention anything about my mother, not least her religion.

Despite having no musical ability (but a passion for it), Dad took it on himself to start a marching band based on Glencairn. This was to be made up of girls and would be called the Glencairn Girls Accordion Band after the instrument they were learning. Dad found some funding, equipped the band with uniforms and instruments and recruited an accordion teacher. The younger ones started out on the triangle or the cymbals until they were ready for the accordion itself. Jean and Margaret, plus all my female cousins, were co-opted into the band and after a few months of getting to grips with the tunes, the band was ready for its first parade.

Any reader not familiar with the tradition of Northern Irish Loyalist matching bands should take now a quick leap out of the early 1970s and into the future by using Google to watch a few videos of such bands in action. Marching to music is a key part of the Protestant Loyalist tradition and culture and these marches in Belfast, Londonderry, Portadown and many other places across Ulster have been established for years.

The best-known date in the marching calendar is 12 July, which commemorates the victory of Protestant William of Orange over the Catholic King James at the Battle of the Boyne in 1690, but parades take places at many other times of the year. The marchers (typically lodges of the Orange Order, but there are others too) are accompanied by bands playing traditional tunes on flutes and drums. These bands, some of which also feature the huge, powerful Lambeg bass drum, are known as 'blood and thunder' bands as they play all the best-known Loyalist tunes. Accordion bands are seen as less militaristic and often play in old people's homes or at social events not directly connected with marching. At the front of these bands – flute or accordion – is likely to be someone twirling a baton with great skill and dexterity.

Now, obviously I couldn't join this band but I'd insist on joining my dad and the girls, including female cousins, up at the community centre for their weekly rehearsal on a Thursday night. There were forty women and girls in there of all ages and I was captivated – not just by the power of the music but also by the sheer presence of these young ladies. I had my eye on a few of them, and one accordion player in particular who stole my heart. She had classic early seventies long brown hair and eyes to match. I was head over heels in love with her but of course, at this tender age, I never told her that. Instead I would pretend to be the leader of the band and would march up and down the community centre hall, twirling an invisible baton in time to the music. My antics made the girls laugh, sometimes so much so that they messed up their music and had to start again. For this I'd be banished to a corner and made to sit quietly while they got their act together. Two or three tunes later I was off the chair and marching, singing and generally acting up. However, my excitement was nothing compared to how I felt on the Big Day itself – 12 July, when Loyalist Belfast turned out in force to celebrate the Boyne in particular and Protestant culture in general.

CHAPTER 3

For kids the world over, 1 December is the beginning of the countdown to Christmas and even for the non-religious the daily opening of the advent calendar is a little thrill of excitement each day.

I loved that time of year, of course, but I loved July equally well. The start of Northern Ireland's marching season was, for me, 'the most wonderful time of year' and as the school holidays began, I couldn't wait to get started on creating one of the huge bonfires that are lit all over Ulster on 11 July to celebrate the evening before the big parades of 'The Twelfth'.

During the Troubles and for a few years afterwards, the marching season also heralded heightened sectarian tension as predominantly Catholic communities objected to Loyalist parades marching down streets in 'their' area. For their part, Loyalists simply said they had the democratic right to march down the 'King's Highway' and were determined to do so, even if it pissed off the local people to the extent that they became as mad as hell and ready to start a riot.

Today the situation is much calmer, though there are still tensions in the flashpoints where Catholic and Protestant areas collide. Back then, I neither understood nor cared for the politics of the marching season. All I wanted to do was have fun, wave a Union flag, watch the bands and march down the Shankill Road from Glencairn to the great meeting point for marchers from all over Ulster and beyond – the hallowed ground at Edenderry, commonly known in Belfast as 'The Field'.

At the beginning of July we would start to build the bonfire that would go up in flames on the night of the Eleventh. Like Guy Fawkes Night, the bonfire was only complete when there was an effigy (an 'effie', as we'd say) placed on the top; for us this was traditionally a dummy who was dressed like the Pope. Us kids would beg, steal and borrow any wood or burnable material we could find to build up our bonfire and create the best-looking Pope. As the Eleventh approached older kids would spend all night on guard by these mountains of wood, plastic, rags and old tyres so that rival gangs of kids across the estate wouldn't sneak up and steal the lot for their own fire. These older ones would sit by small fires, drinking and having fun and I wished I could grow up quickly so I could join in and do my bit for the bonfire.

Uncle Rab and Aunty Jacky lived near us with their kids Wee Sam, Linda, Mandy and Joanne. Rab was my dad's younger brother. He was a lovable rogue; handsome with black hair and a Mediterranean complexion that gave him a passing resemblance to Elvis. He knew it, too, and was very popular among Glencairn's ladies, despite Aunty Jacky's protestations to keep his eyes to himself. Like Dad, Rab was a UDA member and could turn his hand to anything. He possessed a chainsaw, and as the Eleventh rolled around he would often give our bonfire a boost by cutting down a tree or two from the nearby woods and supplying us with the fallen timber. Whether this was legal or not is debatable, but the police had bigger things to worry about just around that time. And to be honest we never worried about what the police thought about anything – we lived by the rules of the street, not the rule of law.

When the Eleventh finally arrived we were so excited we could barely eat the breakfast Granny had made us. But she insisted we sat there until we'd finished the lot and my brother and I would stuff our mouths with food until, cheeks bulging like hamsters, we'd plead with her to let us down from the table and out to the bonfire.

When she nodded her assent, we'd be off like two men and a wee lad, racing out of the back of the house and up the grassy mound to where the bonfire was situated. Although we were far too young to climb to the top of the pyre, which could be as tall as sixty feet, to add the finishing touches we'd help to gather any last-minute material and then watch in awe as the older boys made their way up the stack so the 'effie' of the Pope could be placed on top to await his fate.

As evening approached, our friends and neighbours would leave their homes and make their way to the bonfire. Loyalist music would blast from every open window; fiercely Protestant songs like 'Build My Gallows'. And we would all join in and sing at the top of our voices.

I am a loyal Ulsterman
They say this day that I must hang
Cause I fought the IRA
And they say that I must pay
They say this day that I must hang

(Chorus) So build my gallows, build them high
That I might see before I die
The Antrim glen and the hills of County Down
And I'll see again the lights of home

Or 'Shankill to the Somme':

At the age of sixteen years he left his home in tears
His mother watched as he walked out the door
As his family bade farewell, his neighbours wished him well
From the road his dad and brother took before

And as the ship set sail for France
He gave Belfast one more glance
As the ship began to move away from the shore
He could see there on the land, the proud YCV band,
And could hear them play 'The Sash My Father wore'

(Chorus) From the Shankill Road they went
Their young lives to be spent
On the first day of July, so long ago
All the deeds that they had done
And the glory they had won
We remember as long as the bright red poppies grow

I loved all this stuff, the tales of heroism now and from the past. By this age I was nothing less than a diehard Prod, proud of my heritage and learning to hate all Catholics with passion. I didn't or couldn't differentiate between IRA and ordinary Catholics; such lines were blurred in my small Loyalist world. In this respect I was no different to any other kid on Glencairn or surrounding Loyalist areas. Loyalism and Protestantism were our culture, and hatred of the enemy – the Catholics – our war cry. We had no formal lessons in hatred; in fact, at Sunday School the Reverend Lewis would do his best to preach peace and tolerance. But we had no time for anything like that, not when Belfast was burning and we were having to defend ourselves against the marauding IRA. As far as we were concerned, this was war and I would sing our songs as loudly as any adult gathered round the bonfire, which was lit when darkness fell and burned steadily, illuminating the faces of the revellers in its warm orange glow. My Loyalist identity and culture were hardwired into my DNA and I wore it like a badge of honour.

As the evening wore on, us kids squabbled and fought over the plates of food that had been prepared by the women of the estate as their contribution to the party. As with every celebration in Northern Ireland, cans and bottles of booze were plentiful and I loved to see the adults singing louder and louder the more drunk they became. Sometimes this would spill over into violence as rivalries between people on the estate were settled with fists and boots. More often than not, though, these gatherings were peaceful if rowdy affairs, and as the flames lit up the night sky and licked up towards the top of the bonfire we'd shout our encouragement.

'Fuck the Pope, let him burn!'

'Death to all Fenians!'

'No surrender!'

'Hooray, hooray, it's a holi-holi-holiday – two popes gone and the Queen lives on, holi- holi-holiday . . .'

As we screamed and roared 'the Pope' would finally topple over, engulfed in flames, and disintegrate in front of us. We had no regrets about burning such a hated symbol of the Antichrist in Rome and leader of the hated Catholic Church, our enemy, and in fact, we took more than delight in imagining his slow, agonising death.

Once the Pope was no more it was time for bed and reluctantly we allowed ourselves to be led away by Granny.

'Ach, come on, Granny, just another five minutes!' we'd beg, trying to pull her back towards the fire.

'Not on your life, you wee hallions,' she replied. 'Them grown-ups is getting wild drunk now, and it's no place for youse two. C'mon with you now . . .'

'But Granny, please . . . Margaret and Jean can stay. Why not us?'

'Do as your granny says, boys,' Dad said. He had a can of Tennent's or Harp lager in one hand and a cigarette in the other, and as he chatted to his mates he looked like he was in for the night.

We had little choice other than to leave the party but no sooner had Granny made sure David and I were in bed than we were out of it again, looking through the window at the party in full swing. Adults and teenagers were singing and shouting, dancing around the fire, snogging each other and falling over drunk. If it hadn't been a celebration of Protestant culture, it would've resembled a scene from *The Wicker Man*.

Very often our already-cramped maisonette would be bursting at the seams with several 'Scotchies'; members of Scotland-based flute bands or Orange lodges who'd made the pilgrimage from Stranraer to Larne via the ferry in time for the Twelfth celebrations. It's very much within the Northern Irish tradition of great hospitality to give these people a billet for the night, so in the early hours of the Twelfth we'd listen for our back door opening and Dad, plus a handful of Scotchies, falling through it. Once in, the whiskey bottle would be produced and there would be laughter and more songs, followed by loud snoring.

A great banging on the door at 7 a.m. put paid to any thoughts of a lie-in. The Twelfth was here, and so was Granny, her shopping bag full of the ingredients needed to make an 'Ulster Fry' – the classic Northern Ireland breakfast that will either kill or cure and satisfy any hunger or hangover. I rushed downstairs and let her in, noticing that Glencairn was awash with Loyalist flags, red, white and blue bunting, murals and countless houses had Union Jacks and Red Hand of Ulster flags flying proudly from the front. And not just flags; even the paving stones would be painted red, white and blue. This added to the sense of excitement for me and I took this as a sign of the glorious party that was about to begin. I was in a childhood Loyalist paradise . . .

Granny made her way to the kitchen, stepping over the prone Scotchies, and emptying out the contents of her bag on to the work surface. Bacon, sausages, veg roll, eggs, potato bread and soda bread. Not baked beans – opinion is split on whether they're a true ingredient of an Ulster Fry and while Granny wasn't a fan I must admit that today I like a portion of them with my Fry whenever I'm back in Belfast, all covered in lashings of HP sauce.

As the oil heated and the bacon and sausages spat and sizzled, the delicious smells wafted into the living room and up the noses of the Scotchies who rose, bleary-eyed, from their sleeping bags. I was already up, beside myself with a combination of hunger and excitement. After the Fry, Granny washed us and made sure we were in our best clothes. Margaret and Jean were looking great in their band uniforms of tartan skirt, white shirt and blue jumper. In the bathroom, Dad was shaving, smoothing down his hair and generally looking handsome as the band's leader. I still wished I could march at the front, throwing the baton high in the air, but for now I had to make do with practising with my own baton, which I'd made from a stick and an old split tennis ball perched on the top. Some of the Scotchies let me bang their drums or play their flutes and I was having the time of my life.

Later in the morning, the rest of the band arrived outside the nearby shops, looking happy and nervous at the same time. Aware they were to be marching and playing in front of thousands of spectators, they always fitted in some last-minute practice to calm themselves down and keep their anxieties at bay. When we were finally washed, dressed and looking smart we all walked down to meet them outside the shops as they arranged themselves in parade formation.

By now the route out of Glencairn was lined by hundreds of people waving Union Jacks and Red Hand flags (the Ulster

Banner), ready to cheer the marchers on their way. The weather on the day never mattered; rain or shine, my heart would almost burst with pride as Dad took up his position and gave his young band members a last quick once-over. When he was satisfied he would give the command 'March!' The drummer and accordionists would strike up a tune, something like 'It's a long way to Tipperary', 'Scotland the Brave' or 'The Billy Boys', and off they'd go, to the cheers of the whole estate.

At this age I was too young to accompany them on the entire length of the march, but I longed for the day when my poor wee legs would carry me there. Once the band were out of Glencairn the rest of my family, wearing red, white and blue clothing and carrying an assortment of flags, would all travel down to the Lower Ormeau Road, the point at which bands from across Belfast would meet before making their way to The Field. Belfast was at a standstill as we crammed into an uncle's beaten-up old motor and inched through the backstreets to our destination, constantly getting caught behind a band or lodge making their way down the Shankill. Back then, tens of thousands of Protestants turned out for the Twelfth; not just to celebrate the culture but also as a show of defiance to those we felt were threatening our very way of life. Unsurprisingly, most Catholics stayed away from the city centre that day and although there could be trouble between the communities in the 'flashpoint' areas, the IRA knew better than to attack an Orange march on the Twelfth, because the retribution would've been brutal. For one day we seemed to rule Northern Ireland and my heart would almost burst with pride.

Once we'd arrived at our destination, we'd set up camp and

spend the day cheering on the bands and singing along with their tunes. Granny and granddad would bring folding chairs and Granny would have made a packed lunch of sandwiches and treats for us. Back then, the parade was so long it took almost two hours to pass. I remember the thrill of hearing the Glencairn Girls' Accordion Band approaching our corner and clapping and cheering wildly as they passed. Dad turned to me and winked, then saluted, and I was so proud of this man who was raising us single-handedly as well as doing some good for his community.

The biggest cheers were reserved for the 'blood and thunder' bands as they marched past in a sea of colour. I could barely wait for one of these bands to strike up 'The Sash' – the number one Orange marching tune, the words of which are carved into the hearts of every good Loyalist in Northern Ireland and beyond, including Scotland, parts of England and Canada, which had a massive Loyalist community that sent bands over to take part in the parades. Even at eight or nine, I knew it off by heart:

So sure I'm an Ulster Orangeman, from Erin's Isle I came
To see my British brethren all of honour and of fame
And to tell them of my forefathers who fought in days of yore
That I might have the right to wear the sash my father wore

(Chorus) It is old but it is beautiful and its colours they are fine
It was worn at Derry, Aughrim, Enniskillen and the Boyne
My father wore it as a youth in bygone days of yore
And on the Twelfth I love to wear the sash my father wore

When some band or other started up with that, the crowd would go wild and everyone would spontaneously begin singing at the top of their voices. I'd jump up and down, dance on the spot and wave my arms in the air. I would become so excited that I had to be restrained from running straight into the parade and banging the big bass Lambeg drum myself. By the time the parade had passed us by, I was hoarse from singing, shouting and cheering, and totally knackered. Gran would escort us home via the Shankill, where we'd join the queue out of the fish shop that stretched halfway down the street. The wait was always worth it, and at 5.30 p.m. when we were rested, fed and watered, we'd take off again and wait by the road to welcome Dad's band back from Edenderry. He and the girls must have been exhausted from the march to The Field and back but as they turned into Forthriver Road they'd give their all with one last tune. As they arrived back at the shops, they were cheered like returning heroes from a battle. Before they broke up, they would strike up the national anthem and we would all stand and salute our glorious Queen. Back then, and even today, Loyalist clubs and pubs throughout Belfast and Northern Ireland always end the night with 'God Save The Queen' and if you don't stand up and pay respect you're likely to get a good slap or even a beating. We Loyalists take our loyalty to Queen and Country very seriously indeed.

Looking back, I guess it's the siege mentality ingrained in so many Loyalists that makes the Twelfth such a passionate, intense and emotional day. Sure, it's a lot of fun too, and as I got older my cousin Wee Sam and I joined the junior Orange Order. As members of the lodge we were allowed to march behind the band, holding on to the strings at the bottom of the huge banners that were carried. I've never felt so proud to be a Northern Irish Protestant because I believed I was doing my bit to uphold our traditions in the face of hatred, violence and death.

The parades have been the object of fierce controversy over the decades and, at the various Drumcree stand-offs in the 1990s, the cause of violence too. Despite all this, they've continued and as time has gone on the opposition to them has reduced to just one or two angry scenes around the flashpoint areas where Catholic and Protestant neighbourhoods co-exist. At the time of writing this, the Twelfth is now promoted as 'Orangefest', a kind of touchy-feely family/tourist fun day out of music, marching, food and drink. Some of the old guard, like me, will smile wryly at such new-fangled marketing but if it means the parades can continue without too much fuss, I'm all for it.

I never wanted the Twelfth to end. The parties around Glencairn went on all night and as we drifted to sleep we could hear the songs and the laughter and the roars and the drunkenness, and smell the still-smouldering bonfire from the Eleventh. The biggest day in the Loyalist calendar was over and I could only count down the days until it all happened again. My dreams were punctuated by the domineering thud of the Lambeg drum and the notion that I was at the front of the parade, the best band leader in the whole world. And when I woke up I knew I was in for another traditional Chambers family treat . . .

CHAPTER 4

A mid all the excitement generated by the coming of the Twelfth and the actual day itself the Chambers family, like many Protestant families across the North, needed to find time to pack its bags for the annual holiday, which traditionally began on 13 July.

In the early 1970s there was no thought of getting on a plane to Torremolinos or Benidorm. Even if we could've afforded it (which we couldn't) the idea of leaving beautiful Northern Ireland for somewhere foreign would've seemed ridiculous.

Some of the more adventurous types went to Scotland or Blackpool. In fact, half the families from Shankill and surrounding areas seem to love Blackpool and went there annually. We weren't in that category. For the Chambers clan – aunties, uncles, grandparents, cousins, friends and a few dogs – our summer Shangri-La was a place called Walkers Caravan Park in Millisle, a seaside village on the Ards Peninsula in County Down. We also stayed at the Ballyferris caravan park, a couple of miles north of Millisle and located just by the beach.

Millisle isn't more than twenty miles from Belfast, but for me it could've been on another planet altogether. It was a world away from the tension and the violence that surrounded us at all times in Belfast. Millisle was a peaceful and largely Protestant town that welcomed rowdy visitors from Belfast like us and saw to it that we had a good break – God knows, they must've known that we needed it.

Ballyferris caravan park was full of Belfast Protestants from the Shankill and surrounding areas and for us it was a home from home. We recognised neighbours and friends sunning themselves (if they were lucky – this is Northern Ireland after all) or spending time on the beach or in the local pubs. My granny and others of her generation thought nothing of sending postcards from Millisle to friends and family back in Belfast, even though it was just a few miles from our home.

However, getting to Millisle from Belfast was a challenge. Cars that were in decent enough condition to do the distance were in short supply and besides, we didn't have one of our own. So on the morning of the thirteenth around ten adults could be seen shepherding more than a dozen kids and Shep the dog, plus bags and belongings, to the bus stop that would take us into town. From there, we'd walk over to the Oxford Street Ulster Bus station in crocodile fashion, shoving each other off the pavements and fooling around until a well-aimed clip from Granny and a bellowed 'Stop yer messin'!' brought us back into line. Then we would get on the blue-and-white Ulster Bus and noisily take over the whole thing for the journey.

When we arrived it must've seemed that our entire family had monopolised the park. We were greeted by other caravanners like long-lost relatives and all their kids would team up with us to form a huge and semi-feral pack, intent on mischief and fun. Once we'd unpacked and settled in, all our caravans side by side, our destination was the big patch of grass at the centre of the site. For two weeks this was our own personal football stadium and although I wasn't much of a player (nor a fan, to be honest) I loved it when the teams were sorted out and I was picked to play on the same side as Dad. Like every other kid there, I told myself I was George Best, Manchester United's star player and a proud son of Belfast. The matches would go on for hours, or until the adults got fed up and headed for the site bar and a welcome pint of Harp lager or a vodka and brown lemonade.

Wee Sam and I were obsessed with the beach just below the site. It was full of rockpools and perfect for crab fishing. With David and cousin Pickle in tow, we'd spend ages lifting dozens of them from their pools, placing them into buckets and bringing them back up to the caravan park. Pickle, known as Steven to his parents, was a younger cousin and was so named after an incident on a train to the coast. We were all off fishing for the day on the brand-new train, and somehow Steven managed to spill a jar full of pickled onions all over the seat – and became 'Pickle' for ever after.

Back at the caravan park we'd tip the crabs out of the buckets and race them against each other. The winning 'trainers' would receive sweets or packets of crisps. Occasionally, we fished for mackerel and cooked these on the barbecue. Once when we were out in a little boat fishing for mackerel a huge fin suddenly appeared in the water and to our horror we recognised the huge shape of a shark silently shadowing us. To be fair, it was a huge plankton-munching basking shark, but nonetheless it frightened the life out of us as *Jaws* had recently been on in the cinema and we thought we were going to be eaten alive. We also went collecting willicks (the Belfast word for winkles, available right along the coast) and cockles and cooked these ourselves.

On another occasion, Wee Sam and I decided to fish in the more remote rockpools to find crabs not already harvested by the other kids. We scrambled across the rocks until we were almost at the sea's edge, casting out our lines baited with feathers or scraps of bacon rind to see if we could capture a really big crab.

As is common all over the island of Ireland, a warm and sunny day can turn into a wet and miserable one within minutes. As we were absorbed in our fishing, taking not a scrap of notice of the time, dark clouds had gathered on the horizon and a breeze was getting up. Then it started to rain.

The shower made us look up and only then did we notice what we should've seen half an hour previously. The tide had come right in and we were completely surrounded by rising sea water.

'Ah shit!' said Wee Sam, a note of panic in his voice. 'Jesus, we're trapped, we're gonna drown. What're we gonna do now?'

I stared at the water pooling all around me. The shore now looked miles off and I knew I'd never be able to swim that distance, not with my wonky leg.

'Start shouting!' I yelled. 'HELP! Help, SOS!'

Wee Sam joined in and we roared at the top of our lungs. I could feel my breath becoming shorter as panic rose in me as quickly as the tide. We were going to die – not in war-torn West Belfast but here, in our favourite place. I was almost shitting myself in fear and I started to cry. Then I started to pray; surely God wouldn't let us die here . . . just say a shark gets us?

Just then, we heard muffled shouts from the beach. A guy walking his dog along the strand had spotted us and was waving frantically to us. We waved back, and then we could see other people gathering at the shore. We recognised Wee Sam's mum and dad, along with a couple of other relatives. Among all the shouting and screaming we could just about make out one voice above all the others.

'Stay where ye are!' a man's voice hollered. 'Stay where y' are and the lifeboat will collect ye!'

I couldn't believe we were being told to stay still while the water lapped around our knees but I was in no position to argue. Just then, a moving dot appeared on the horizon and within minutes an orange and blue boat came speeding towards us. It was the RNLI rescue boat and now, a man dressed in yellow plastic overalls was shouting at us to move towards the edge of the rocks. We obeyed, and with strong sailor's hands the guy lifted us both aboard.

'Youse two are the luckiest we'ans in the world,' said the skipper as the boat pulled away from the sharp rocks and headed into open water. 'Another twenty minutes and that would've been the death of youse.'

We stared at him wide-eyed. We'd now completely forgotten

about the crabbing mission and instead were the stars in our own self-created drama. I felt like a pirate riding on the deep blue ocean and imagined we were heading into the sunset and more buccaneering adventures.

'Look,' I said to Wee Sam as the boat pulled in by the beach. Waiting to greet us was a crowd of onlookers, including almost all of our family. Like royalty, we waved and smiled to those gathered, expecting to receive a heroes' welcome. Far from it: the minute we stepped on to that beach we were grabbed and given various clips around the ear from Dad, Uncle Rab, Granny and whoever else could take a hand to us. Even Shep looked disappointed with me.

'Youse pair of stupid wee eejits!' roared Granny. 'You coulda died out there, and ruined the holiday. Youse should be locked up for the rest of the week, so you should!'

We were shocked. We thought they'd be glad to see us alive. We'd no idea how much panic we'd caused on the beach, but despite all the verbal and physical punishments we didn't let the adults' reaction get to us. We were famous and no one was going to spoil that. The rest of the holiday was spent bragging and boasting to the other kids how we'd been snatched from certain death, and how they'd never dare do what we did. Funnily enough, not one of these other kids even tried . . .

In the evening the whole clan plus friends would head back to the beach, laden with food and drink, for a picnic or barbecue. Expert bonfire-builders by nature, we'd collect driftwood from the shore and pile it into a quickly dug firepit. Once lit, the baked potatoes wrapped in tin foil would go on, followed by sausages on sticks and mackerel if we'd managed to catch any. Nine times out of ten we burned these but who cared? We were having so much fun singing and listening to scary stories about ghosts and banshees that we didn't even think about our stomachs. I'd fall asleep on my dad's knee to wake the following morning to the smell of Granny's Ulster Fry taking shape on the hob.

The funfair at Millisle was always a highlight of our time away. In terms of size it was hardly Blackpool Pleasure Beach, but to us it was a mecca. Sometimes we'd walk the two miles there from Ballyferris along the strand and as it came into view Wee Sam, Pickle, David and I would race over the sand dunes in a bid to get there first. We wanted to go on everything, all at once, and Dad always had to calm us down by reminding us that we had hours there. For me, the best part was the dodgem cars and I drove like a suicide pilot as I crashed into everyone. Dad spent time trying to win us presents from the stall and when we'd all got something we knew he'd exhausted his money and it was time to go. Again, we'd hit the beach for a picnic while Dad and his brothers visited Millisle's various pubs, talking to people they knew from Glencairn, the Shankill and beyond.

I never wanted these holidays to end and I was in despair when the final day eventually arrived. I hated packing my scruffy little suitcase with the clothes I knew I wouldn't see much of until the same time the following year. I pressed my T-shirt to my face and inhaled the mixture of sun cream, sea water and fried breakfasts. It was a smell I wanted to remember forever. Then, as the hours ticked down to departure, I'd take a walk along the beach, hoping that our bus or train would break down. I'd even consider hiding until everyone had left, then I could find an empty caravan and live in it undetected. We often hid in the old bomb shelter by the side of the caravan park, hoping not to be discovered.

Such plans came to nothing, of course, and soon we were trudging to the station, our only possessions being a case of dirty clothes and wonderful memories. As the bus pulled away towards Belfast I'd shed a few silent tears as I said goodbye to Ballyferris and the funfair at Millisle until next year, consoling myself with the thought it would only be 364 days until I was here again.

It didn't take long to adjust to life back in Glencairn. After a day or so wishing I was still down on the beach I was soon into the swing of playing down by the river, in Fernhill House, which was derelict at the time, or in the fields. Even the inevitable crawl back to school wasn't so bad because I loved my primary, Fernhill. History was my favourite subject, followed by English. By this time I was starting to take an interest in God – the Protestant version, of course – and as well as praying very hard in school assembly (my personal prayers were for the IRA to be defeated, and all Catholics assigned to hell with the Antichrist in Rome) I also attended Sunday School and eventually became a member of the Boys' Brigade.

The singing of hymns in assembly became the focus for our growing sectarian attitudes towards Catholics. As I headed towards my tenth birthday my views about the 'Fenians' were definitely hardening. Now I see how intolerant I was, but back then everything seemed to be dominated by the conflict going on all around us and it engulfed every aspect of our daily lives.

To us it was simply black and white: they hated us, we hated them and never the twain should meet. The daily news seemed a never-ending nightmare of IRA murder and slaughter, while Loyalist anger and outrage fed the hatred and paranoia between our two warring tribes.

Kids growing up in wars tend to be marked for life by the experience, and in Northern Ireland Catholic and Protestant kids who lived close to the violence were no exception. When the hymn 'Sing Hosanna' was sung at school, a gaggle of us would quietly mutter an alternative version that someone had heard somewhere, and had passed on to the rest of us:

Give me bullets in my gun, keep it firing
Give me bullets in my gun I pray
Give me bullets in my gun and we'll shoot them everyone
The members of the IRA
Sing Hosanna, Sing Hosanna, etc

If the headmaster, Mr Wilson, heard us singing this version he would throw us a hard look but wouldn't stop the service. He was a timid man and possibly didn't want to stir up any problems between him and the local paramilitaries who were now acting as a vigilante force across the estate. There were also dark rumours he was a Catholic, or had Catholic blood of some description. No wonder he looked so nervous . . .

To hear such words come out of the mouths of young children now would rightly be shocking, but they were simply a reflection of the times and the place I lived in. I've no doubt that kids on the Falls Road probably sang something similar, except they'd replace 'IRA' with 'UDA'. All of us, Catholic and Protestant, were caught up in the terrible events that were happening in Belfast and beyond. We weren't ordinary kids who could play together in the same street without considering what religion we belonged to, as children in England or Wales could. In Northern Ireland we were all part of one tribe or the other, and we had no business in each other's lives.

In 1974, when I was eight, the Ulster Workers' Council called a strike in protest about a power-sharing agreement proposed by the British and Irish governments. Loyalists saw this as a complete sell-out to the IRA and, after a series of national strikes and bombings, managed to bring down the Northern Ireland Assembly before it had even really got going. You could almost taste the anger on Glencairn and the Shankill as the paramilitaries came out of the shadows, parading in uniform while carrying weapons. People started panic-buying after a few days and shops ran out of bread, milk and other essentials that weren't being delivered due to the strike. We were bracing ourselves for all out civil war. There were bombings, shootings and intimidation, and I remember standing on the hill above our house while watching plumes of smoke rise into the air as bombs exploded in Belfast city centre. The whole skyline seemed to be on fire and it reminded me of the hell Reverend Lewis was always banging on about in church. We really thought we would be invaded by Republicans and Free Staters (Northern Ireland slang for Southern Irish people) and that our lives would change forever. From then on I hated Catholics with a passion for their passive support of the IRA and other Republican terrorists, and would celebrate if I heard that an IRA man had been killed by the army or one of ours.

Trouble came very close to home on many occasions. I recall a neighbour, a member of the Royal Ulster Constabulary (RUC), who discovered an IRA bomb under his car one morning as he prepared to go to work. We were all evacuated to the local community centre and forbidden from going to school. That itself was exciting enough, but this was on another scale: the guy in question lived a few doors down from us. Every morning he would drive his kids to school and we would walk past his car. It was lucky that he checked the vehicle before getting in that morning or he and his kids, and anyone else passing by, could have been killed. This reinforced our hatred of the IRA and showed their total disregard for the lives of innocent people, including children.

And yet, try as I might, I couldn't bring myself to celebrate the deaths of innocent Catholics. Even as a wee boy I knew there was something deeply wrong about such killings. It frightened me that you could be walking along the street, minding your own business, and next you could be dead, the victim of a gun or a bomb. Somehow, that seemed against the 'rules'. When a Republican or Loyalist member was killed I viewed this as a by-product of the ongoing war and I understood that if you live by the sword then there's a chance you will die by the sword, and that was perfectly acceptable in my world.

As I lay in bed, listening to the 'thud' of explosions across the city I imagined how I'd feel if my sisters or brother, or any of my cousins, were killed by armed men. And I knew instinctively that there were other kids in this city – kids with different surnames to mine, kids who attended other churches, yet kids nonetheless – who felt the same way.

So I continued praying; praying that the IRA would be defeated, but also that no one I knew – or no more innocent people – would be killed as a result. At church, Reverend Lewis always preached peace and at Sunday School afterwards he would tolerate no talk of 'Taigs', 'Fenians' or whatever. As the pastor on a Loyalist estate, he walked a very fine line indeed but he approached everything from a deeply Christian perspective and was respected by the whole community as a result. 'We're all the same in God's eyes, John,' he'd say to me. 'We're all God's children.' While I considered that God was a Loyalist, his words stuck with me.

My growing interest in Christianity didn't seem to prevent me becoming, at times, a 'wee little shit'. Granny and Aunty Jacky were in the habit of sending me and David down to the local shop for the 'messages', i.e., that day's shopping for our tea. At first, we took the list, loaded up the basket and paid for everything religiously. After a while, however, we noticed that the shopkeeper wasn't always paying attention to us the way he maybe should've done. It seemed easy to slip a chocolate bar or a small packet of sweets into a jeans pocket, smiling all the while at the oblivious shopkeeper. From there, we graduated to bigger and better stuff, though once we were away and looking at our haul, we'd wonder how to open a tin of baked beans without having to go back to lift a tin opener. The shopkeeper himself was a member of the church and a devotee of the Reverend Lewis, and none of us kids really liked him. We would collect all the empty bottles from Grouchos, line them up against the shop wall and throw stones at them, which pissed him off mightily.

Inevitably, there was payback for this thievery. One day, in my haste to get out of the shop with my swag, a packet of sausages fell out of the folds of my jumper and slithered slowly and shamelessly on to the shop floor. The shopkeeper looked at me and David, then quickly moved towards the door to block any sign of escape. There were other customers in the shop and one of these was dispatched to find the Reverend Lewis. He arrived, and frowned deeply when he recognised the pair of sobbing shoplifters in front of him.

'I find this hard to believe of you, John Chambers,' he said. 'Have you listened to anything I've said at Sunday School?'

Miserably, I nodded. 'I know it's wrong to steal, Reverend Lewis,' I sniffed.

'Then why did you do it, might I ask?'

I couldn't say, 'because it's easy'. I couldn't admit to the fact that I enjoyed the thrill of it.

'It's cos we're hungry, Reverend Lewis. We've no food in the house.'

For a second, Reverend Lewis looked at us pityingly. Then his eyes narrowed. 'So you're saying your grandmother is not feeding you?' he said.

'No, she's not,' I said. As soon as the words were out of my mouth I regretted them, because I knew what would come next.

'In that case,' said Reverend Lewis, 'I think we'll all take a walk up the road to your granny's and see what's going on.' I felt like a condemned man walking to the gas chamber. It was the longest journey of my life.

Predictably, Granny was mortified when she was questioned about our behaviour. Reverend Lewis had barely put a foot out of her door when the thrashing started. We were thumped all round her living room as Granny pursued us with the energy of someone half her age. That was the last time we stole from the local shop, but it certainly wasn't the last time I got into trouble.

Then there was the fighting. I wasn't a naturally violent child and I'd probably missed my graduation from the school of hard knocks due to being in hospital so much, but despite problems with my leg I could look after myself when necessary. On Glencairn there were always enemies from elsewhere in the estate to cause problems; you had to learn to fight and stand up for yourself otherwise your life could be hell. I once clobbered someone outside church who'd been picking on our David and again, Reverend Lewis was called to intervene. Another time, Wee Sam accidentally knocked into a boy nicknamed Jimbo at school. He was a good fighter and didn't take kindly to Wee Sam's clumsiness. There was a scuffle and at some stage Wee Sam managed to catch Jimbo a blow to the face. He was not happy, to put it mildly, and Wee Sam was warned this wasn't the end of the matter. There would be a re-match after school and within seconds every pupil knew what would happen as soon as the bell went.

I was excited by the fixture and took on the role of Wee Sam's manager, informing his opponent that our Sam was more than happy to have a fair dig in the park after school was out. Sam was silent and seemed unenthusiastic, which I somehow took to be a sign of strength. A poor assumption on my part, because when the hordes of kids arrived at the park as soon as 3.15 p.m. arrived Wee Sam was nowhere to be seen. Jimbo was psyching himself up to do his worst and I was beginning to run out of excuses for my cousin, who showed no sign of turning up.

Now they were here the crowd expected something. Then someone shouted, 'If yer Sam isn't here, maybe you could fight Jimbo, Chambers, so you could?'

I could have thumped the fool who suggested this, a skinny little runt who loved to stir things up but would run a mile if you said boo to him.

'Fight! Fight! Fight!' rang out from the crowd and with a heavy heart I realised there was to be no escape.

I hadn't anticipated this unfortunate turn of events, but the crowd drew nearer and I knew I couldn't escape without shaming myself forever in their eyes. They wanted blood, and they didn't care whose it was. Suddenly, I felt a blow to my face like a rock had been hurled against it, followed by a gut-wrenching punch to the stomach. All Jimbo's pent-up energy was now directed solely at me. I was down on the ground as Jimbo knocked lumps out of me, cheered on by the bloodthirsty, enthusiastic crowd. The initial shock paralysed me for a few seconds but quickly recovering my composure I started to fight back. I ducked and dived and generally avoided the worst of Jimbo's rage. He was a dirty fighter, pulling my hair, nipping my neck, pushing his fingers in my eyes and squeezing the hell out of my balls. This made me very mad indeed and soon I was getting the upper hand as I pinned him down and pummelled him, banging his head on the ground.

The pair of us were quickly spent and some amateur referee in the crowd declared a draw. Jimbo and I were happy with that; we'd both given as good as we'd got without losing face. Jimbo was still one of the school's best fighters and hard men and my reputation went up considerably. My new-found respect won me a few friends, including Jimbo himself.

As for Wee Sam, the jammy git, it transpired that our teacher Miss Curry had got wind of the fight and had detained Sam in detention as a means of avoiding it. Sam was delighted: his reputation was intact and he walked home unbloodied.

CHAPTER 5

Today, when I see news reports from war zones across the world I tend not to concentrate on what the journalist is saying or what the armed men behind them are doing. I don't look at the battered buildings, the broken-down cars, the shattered landscape. Instead, I watch the children. I notice their expressions as they play in the rubble, aware of and yet almost indifferent to the violence all around them. This is their 'normal', just as the killing zone of West Belfast in the 1970s was mine.

Right across Northern Ireland, especially in the paramilitary-dominated ghettos of Belfast and Londonderry, kids like us played around burned-out buildings, torched cars, teased soldiers, threw stones at police vehicles and generally ran feral across a wild, broken country. By the age of ten I'd grown used to seeing news reports filled with death, violence and division, but unlike other kids in mainland UK watching the same reports, I got up in the morning to go to school and stepped out of my front door into this very same landscape – like walking on to the set of a war film, day after day.

By this age I'd heard shots ring out and seen the injuries caused by bullets and beatings. But nothing could've prepared me for the scene outside Glencairn's community centre on Forthriver Road on an overcast morning in October 1976. Before heading to school I polished off my cornflakes and, kicking and protesting as ever, had my face wiped by Granny, who spat on a handkerchief and assaulted my grubby mush with it. 'Come here, ye dirty wee hallion!' she shouted as she grabbed me for the unwanted daily routine. Struggle over, I let myself out of the front door and walked the few doors to Uncle Rab's to call for Wee Sam.

He too had succumbed to the humiliating last-minute face scrub from Aunty Jacky and as we trudged down his garden path and on to the main road through the estate we muttered darkly about our so-called elders and betters.

We'd only walked a few yards when up ahead we noticed a gathering of green and grey Land Rovers and Saracen armoured cars, which we nicknamed 'Pigs'. That meant only one thing: that the RUC and the army were out in force. To the side stood a small knot of onlookers, mostly women on their way to school, the wee ones holding their hands. This group had turned away from the scene and were speaking together. As we approached, we heard murmurs from the women and the occasional shaking of a scarfed head.

'Fuckin' hell,' said Wee Sam, wide-eyed, 'somebody musta gotten kilt up there. Look at all the peelers around.'

A knot of fear tightened in my stomach as we approached

the scene. Despite being on supposedly 'safe' Loyalist territory, grim-faced soldiers gripped their SLRs tightly while uniformed police from the RUC spoke into radios and plain-clothes detectives huddled in a group. Judging by the mood hanging over the community centre on this cold, grey morning, we were about to see something unprecedented.

Maybe we should've walked on by. But we were just wee boys. Filled with childish curiosity we rubbernecked all the time. 'C'mon,' said Sam, grabbing me by the sleeve of my snorkel jacket, 'let's see what's going on!'

We ducked past the group of clucking housewives and right up to a tall soldier in full battledress. 'Hey mister, what's happenin'?' I asked. 'Is somebody dead?'

The soldier looked down on us, not unkindly. We weren't his enemy. Maybe he viewed similar-aged boys from the Catholic areas of Ardoyne and Andersonstown in a different way, but up here we were the good guys. Supposedly.

'If I were you two I'd bugger off to school pronto,' he said, in a northern English voice. 'There's nowt to look at here.'

He was wrong. There was something to look at, lying just a couple of yards from where he stood. Behind the soldier's back, down the grassy bank at the back of the community centre – UDA-controlled, of course, and a social gathering point for those in the estate – we saw a pair of shoe-clad feet sticking out at angles from beneath a brown woollen blanket. This covered the undisputable shape of a body, and surrounding it was thick, red, jellified blood. Pints of the stuff that had spread across the grass on which the body lay, creating a semi-frozen scene of complete horror.

'Jesus!' I said, stepping back a couple of paces from the soldier. 'What the fuck happened here?'

'Never you mind,' he said. 'Kids your age shouldn't be seeing things like this. And watch your language, lad.'

I ignored him and looked again. By now, a typical Belfast morning drizzle had begun to fall, covering the blanket in a fine mist. I craned my neck, and could just about see a tuft of dark, bloodstained hair sticking out of the top. Even at this age I knew that a single bullet, or even a couple of them, couldn't have created such a mess. Rooted to the spot, I hadn't noticed that Wee Sam was no longer by my side. I turned to see him talking animatedly to a boy of about our age standing beside his mum and went over. Wee Sam grabbed my sleeve, pulling me into the conversation.

'Jimmy's ma says it's the Butchers who's done him,' he whispered, pointing to the body. 'They carved him up wi' knives and all that. Just cos he's a Catholic.'

I couldn't believe it. I knew Provies killed Loyalists, and we killed them. That's how it was. In my mind that was all fair. We were under siege, and at war. But to have murdered this man just because he was a Catholic? And to have used knives on him, literally carving him up like a piece of meat? I knew something about this was terribly, terribly wrong and I wondered why God in all his wisdom would let such things happen. Was this the point when I started to lose faith in a Saviour who seemed to ignore the suffering of mortal men?

For weeks previously we'd heard whispers across Glencairn about a gang called the 'Butchers', or the 'Shankill Butchers'. We knew they were Loyalist UVF paramilitaries, but seemingly nothing like the uncles, cousins and friends who aligned themselves to the UDA or UVF, collecting for prisoners and running shebeens, illegal drinking clubs that brought in funds. Those we knew to be UDA members, hardened as they were to whatever was going on across Belfast, seemed to be talking about this particular set of murders with a mixture of awe and horror.

As time went on, it became clear that the 'Butchers' killings had little connection with everyday Loyalism and more to do with the psychopathic condition of the gang's members. It appeared they were using a black taxi to pick up their victims – innocent people on their way home – before kidnapping and murdering them. But they were also killing Protestants too; people who'd fallen foul of their notorious leader, Lenny Murphy. In short, they enjoyed killing for killing's sake, and in mid-1970s Northern Ireland the opportunity to destroy lives at random, for any scrap of a reason, was unprecedented and easy. Life was cheap and victims would be forgotten about by the next day as another victim took their place.

The politics of Loyalist feuding was way over my head back then, but like everyone else I came to regard the Butchers as nothing short of bogeymen. They invaded my dreams and seemed to be pursuing me during my waking hours. On late summer nights and into the dark nights of autumn, a group of us would gather at the bottom of the estate, playing around the woods and streams that gave this area a kind of weird beauty in the midst of all the mayhem. When darkness fell and it was time to go home, I would walk alone back up the estate, listening out in mortal fear for the distinctive sound of a wailing diesel engine climbing the hill behind me that could only be a Belfast black taxi. I was only just ten by then, but I had no reason to believe the Butchers wouldn't grab me and rip me apart with their specially sharpened knives, just for the fun of it.

These guys meant business. The body Wee Sam and I saw was the first of four that were dumped on Glencairn by the Butchers, along with others murdered in Loyalist feuds. Some months after we came upon the scene in Forthriver Road, we were playing in and around a building site in 'the Link', a new part of Glencairn still under construction. Several houses were being created and while we shouldn't have been there, nobody was stopping us from running wild around the estate and doing what we liked. We'd poked about one particular half-built house and were about to leave when I spotted what appeared to be words written on an unplastered wall.

'Gi'e us a match, Sam,' I said, 'I wanna see what's written up there.'

Sam produced a box of matches from his jeans pocket and I struck one, holding it close to the wall. The colour drained from my face as I read the words '*Help me*'. They had been written in blood. Dropping the match we legged it out of there and ran all the way home.

I told Dad, but if I expected him to be shocked I was just as surprised when his reaction was indifference. 'Just leave well alone, John,' he said, shaking his head. 'You're better off out of it.'

CHAPTER 6

Dad was beginning to look thin and weary. We'd all noticed that he'd lost quite a bit of weight recently, and that his smoker's cough had become something deeper and serious-sounding. There'd been hospital appointments and a lot of babysitting from Granny. Muttered adult conversations and strange silences when we entered the room. And Dad, in the middle of it all, trying to earn a living doing whatever came along (gardener and impromptu tuck-shop owner, which ran from our house and attracted every kid on the estate) and finding it more and more difficult to get himself off the settee of an evening to attend band practice.

Inevitably, the secret came out. Our Margaret, now thirteen, overheard Granny tearfully telling a neighbour that her boy was dying. Not only that, but Dad himself was very worried about 'what'll happen to the wee ones' when he'd gone. Margaret repeated the news to us and we spent the whole of that night and the following day clinging to each other and crying our eyes out. He was our rock, our harbour and our protection. He couldn't leave. He couldn't go anywhere without us. But Margaret was a teenager and wouldn't make this stuff up. How we found out officially I cannot remember – perhaps Margaret spoke to Granny or Granny heard us whispering and crying. Either way, we discovered that the terrible rumour was true and within days Dad was hospitalised. He would never leave.

Always a heavy smoker, Dad had contracted lung cancer, which spread throughout his body. There was no chance of recovery and I winced when I saw him in hospital because his emaciated state reminded me of a film I'd seen about Auschwitz on the TV. I cried in fear: fear of his appearance, and fear of what would happen after his death. Granny brought us to the hospital one by one to visit him and although I didn't know it, this was the last time I would see my dad alive. I remember being in the room and he lay on the bed and was so skinny that his watch had slid all the way up his arm, almost to his shoulder. I cried my heart out. Eventually, that watch found its way to me and although I still have it, I've never been able to wear it as it brings back painful memories that I have no desire to revisit.

The news came through that he'd died, and that he'd asked his family to look after us. The whole estate seemed to be in tears. Wherever we siblings went we would stop adults in their tracks, who would then look at us pityingly or start to cry. Dad was popular across Glencairn and had touched many lives, which was reflected in the numbers who attended his funeral, conducted by Reverend Lewis at St Andrew's Church. My dad's beloved Alsatian, Shep, who was my best friend, had sat underneath Dad's coffin for the three nights leading up to the funeral, whining and crying, and making the weirdest wolf-like sounds. One night I crept downstairs while everyone else was sleeping and stroked a crying Shep. Standing over my dad in his coffin I broke down and sobbed my little heart out, cursing God for letting my dad die and making my young life a misery.

On a beautiful May morning in 1976 we four kids trooped out of Granny's house dressed to the nines. I was wearing black trousers, a white shirt and my best Sunday jacket. As we walked towards the church we looked in awe at the number of people standing on the roadside. Shep followed us and stood outside the church while the service was on and followed the coffin down the road, which was heartbreaking. There must have been hundreds gathered to pay their respects, including the Glencairn Girls' Accordion Band, who formed a guard of honour before playing a couple of Dad's favourite tunes, including 'Amazing Grace'. Hearing that almost sent me over the edge. To this day, it still does and I turn the radio or TV off if it comes on. The band was renamed the John Chambers memorial band after his death and my uncles Rab and Jim took over the running of it for a few years.

As the pallbearers prepared to lower Dad's coffin into the grave, Granny ran forward and grasped the handles of the wooden casket with all her strength.

'My baby! My baby!' she wailed. 'My baby's died!'

It was horrifying and heartbreaking to see such raw, animal emotion and we all sobbed even harder.

I had shattered into pieces. There were fragments of me everywhere.

I had no real idea how close he was to death but still, seeing his body disappear underground, never to be seen again, was gut-wrenchingly shocking. As I stood by the graveside, heartbroken and beyond comforting, a voice sounded in my head. 'Where's my mammy?' it said. 'Where's my mammy, where's my mammy, where's my mammy?'

I'd not heard this voice for a good few years. Now here it was, whispering, shouting, screaming – anything to get my attention. 'She's dead!' I shouted back silently. 'Dead, dead, dead!' But something was telling me, loud and clear, that this wasn't the case. I had no idea where she was, but I felt she was somewhere out there. Perhaps I was scratching at sand; digging frantically to find a rock to grab on to as grief swirled all around me. Or maybe I was picking up something amid this fog of tears; a whispered aside and a nod in our direction. Phrases like 'their mammy *is*', as opposed to 'their mammy *was*' were overheard and passed between us. 'I never believed it anyway,' said our Margaret. 'I always thought they were lying.' After Dad's death I began to think of Mum more and realised that I was missing her.

There was another tragedy too. Shep, Dad's beloved dog, was never the same after his master's death. He went off his food and lay moaning in the corner all day long. Three weeks after the funeral, we woke one morning to find the poor dog had passed away in the night. This broke my heart all over again: not only had I lost my dad, the most important person in our universe, but now my best friend Shep, who had been on so many different adventures with me and always been at my side, was gone. The vet said he'd died of a broken heart, but at least he was back at his master's side.

Margaret, Jean, David and I clung together, physically and metaphorically, after the funeral. Granny was wrung-out with grief. She visited Dad's grave every single Sunday, winter, autumn, spring and summer come rain, hail or sunshine and would spend hours tending it, just being with a son she never got over losing. And she did not forget his dying words. She moved in with us for a while, during which time our future was discussed and our fate sealed. We would very much liked to have lived with each other but Margaret was only thirteen. It was unfair to make her a mother at such a young age. The perimeter of Dad's wish that we must be kept together would have to be stretched a little further than he might've liked.

Then we were told. No, we wouldn't be living together but we would be staying with relatives across Glencairn. And given that all of these people were within a few hundred yards of our family home, it wasn't like we were emigrating to Australia.

My new billet would be with my Uncle Rab and Aunty Jacky – but not yet. Uncle Rab had been playing the rascal once too often and was currently spending a short time at Her Majesty's pleasure. With four of her own, Aunty Jacky really didn't need the burden of raising another kid single-handedly, so after a family conference it was decided that I would go to a couple on the estate who I'll not name in full. Let's call them Alistair and Betty.

Alistair had a rigid, upright manner that went hand-in-hand with his background in the military. Betty, his wife, was nice enough but completely subservient to her husband. They did not have kids and their home was as neat as a pin. Not really a place for a snotty, ten-year-old kid drowning in grief who needed loving, not an endless list of jobs.

I'm not sure how long I lasted at Alistair and Betty's. A couple of weeks? Maybe longer? It certainly felt that way and I was relieved when Uncle Rab returned and I was able to take up my place in their family. They embraced me in ways I needed them to – physically and emotionally and showed me love and kindness. Aunty Jacky was a strikingly beautiful woman, a blonde with a lovely open face and a kind and generous nature. I recall my first night there, and just before bed all us kids lining up to give her a goodnight kiss. I'd never known anything like that before and I was embarrassed, but Aunty Jacky beckoned me over. I took my place in the line and her goodnight kiss filled me with hope that I may be happy again, soothing my soul a little and for every night thereafter.

Uncle Rab was looking for work, and always coming up with mad and often illegal money-making schemes. He declared himself available for painting and decorating at a reasonable rate. His popularity soon earned him work and Wee Sam and I would go with him at weekends, cleaning up any mess and making endless cups of tea. If he was feeling generous, Uncle Rab would sit back for twenty minutes and chain-smoke while he watched us paint a skirting board or a small bit of wall. For some reason our efforts amused him hugely and we were always pleased with the odd 50p or quid he'd give us after the job was done.

But this was the mid-seventies and there wasn't a lot of money to be had, especially on estates like ours. It was barely ten years old but already it felt rough and run-down. There was a shabbiness around it that reflected the times. Like the country itself, the estate's beauty appeared to fade into the background, while a new face full of hate, anger and horror took its place.

Once we loved playing among the trees but now we were chopping them down like crazy on the orders of Uncle Rab, who had diversified into the supply of firewood. He went into Glencairn Park with his chainsaw and wheelbarrow, Wee Sam and I in tow. Uncle Rab let rip on the first tree he considered was out of sight of the road. When it crashed to the ground, Wee Sam and I shouted 'Timber!' Then Uncle Rab chopped it up into logs and got us to wheel them back to his house. We made trip after trip until all the wood was safely stashed. Then we bagged it up and the following day began to sell it around the estate, doing a roaring trade.

Our success meant we needed more wood and, oblivious to the laws we were breaking, we simply chopped it down. Business was good enough that I could save up for a coveted Raleigh Chopper bike, which was the talk of Glencairn when it arrived. Sadly, somehow the local forestry authority got wind of what we were doing and one day they ambushed us in the woods. The head forestry fella read the riot act to Rab and told him how seriously they took our offence. Now, Uncle Rab could more than handle himself and in any other situation these eejits from the council wouldn't have lasted five seconds. This time, however, he meekly accepted everything they were saying while apologising for all of us.

He finished by promising not to do it again, which annoyed us because from that second we were unemployed.

'Why did you say that, Da?' asked Wee Sam, aggrieved. 'Now we've no money again.'

'Shut your hole,' replied Rab. 'D'you think I wanna bring the peelers up here for the sake of a few bits o'wood?'

Uncle Rab explained that if he attracted the attention of the law his licence would be revoked and he'd be returned to prison. Neither of us wanted that to happen, so reluctantly we put up with the situation and hoped we'd be earning again soon.

Uncle Rab's resourcefulness meant we didn't have long to wait. Like my dad, Uncle Rab was a UDA member and it was required of him that he help to raise money for Loyalist prisoners and their families. This was common among paramilitary organisations of all shades and different groups had their own ways of doing it. The UDA did it through sweepstake cards, asking their members to sell them to family and friends. Rab felt obliged to say 'yes' to the possession of the cards but had no intention of selling them himself. That's where Wee Sam and I came in. He gave us twenty-five pounds' worth of cards and told us that if we sold them we'd get two pounds each. It was a deal, so we split up and headed to separate ends of Glencairn.

At the first door I knocked, a woman answered in her nightdress and with a fag hanging from her mouth. With barely a 'Hello there', I went straight into my pitch, which I'd been rehearsing mentally for a few days. Without pausing for breath I told her that if she picked two winning numbers between one and fifty, she'd be twenty-five pounds better off. It was just twenty pence a ticket and most people bought a strip of five

'Who's it for?' snapped the woman, not unreasonably.

I smiled my most angelic smile. 'For the poor prisoners, missus,' I said. 'To help their poor, hungry children and lonely families.'

The woman's harsh, smoke-ravaged expression softened. 'Ach, you shoulda said sooner,' she smiled. 'God love you, out on a cold day for the prisoners. Sure, give us two strips.'

I couldn't believe how easy it had been. Maybe I'd had a lucky first experience but maybe I was a natural because within the hour I'd sold the lot. Meanwhile, Wee Sam was still to get off the mark. After this we went out a couple more times but Wee Sam showed ever-decreasing enthusiasm and finally I took over the whole operation. It wasn't always easy – I'd get the door banged in my face or told to fuck off. I didn't care. I apologised for disturbing them and went on my way towards the next sale. It wasn't quite as lucrative as the firewood game, but my pounds were mounting up and I looked forward to the time I could buy a digital watch or an Action Man.

But even as I seemed to be settling down and coming to terms with losing Dad while enjoying living with Uncle Rab and Aunty Jacky, there were fresh storm clouds on the horizon. The adults downstairs were talking again. Whiskey loosened their tongues and I would listen as they talked. The walls of Glencairn's houses were thin and I could make out much of what they were saying. They were talking about my mother.

Immediately I tuned in. It wasn't an argument as such, just an exchange of views. It wouldn't be right for the we'ans to meet their mammy's family, said one voice. Another wondered where that mammy was now, and was she still a practising Catholic?

'Aye, a Taig,' said a male voice.

71

'OK,' said a female, 'no need for that. After all, it's their mother we're talking about.'

My mother? A Catholic? A dirty Taig? A clammy feeling crept up my spine and I felt sick. It couldn't be right. Surely I'd heard wrong. But no. They were still talking about her, describing her as 'one of the other lot'.

'Ach, we'll never see her in Belfast again,' said one voice. 'She's away, and the we'ans are Protestants now. That's all there is to it. Let sleeping dogs lie.'

Perhaps the speaker had also nodded towards the ceiling because after that they spoke only in hushed whispers.

But I'd heard and it rocked my world. I now knew my mother was a Catholic, and I felt revulsion at the very thought of having 'their' blood. How could I ever tell anyone I was part-Catholic? Of course I couldn't tell anyone, ever. I'd seen what happened to people who'd associated with Catholics. I'd also seen what happened to Catholics who'd been brought up to the estate. If the Butchers knew I was part-Catholic, I thought, I'd be dragged from my bed and carved up by knives. I tried to swallow, but couldn't. My throat felt tight and my heart was racing.

My mother was a Catholic. A dirty Taig. A filthy Fenian.

A Republican, out to kill every Loyalist and take over Northern Ireland. The enemy, now and forever.

And the other thing I now knew about my Catholic mother was that she could still be alive. That knowledge scared me to death. I couldn't discuss it with anyone, because talk like that was dangerous. For the sake of everyone, I would have to bottle up and hide away the truth.

CHAPTER 7

Even the river beside the park ran thick with blood. Or at least that's what we thought when we went to play in it one day and found it running a sticky, sickly bright red. We had been playing up at Robin's Well, an old well by a derelict cottage at the top of a winding road that ran all the way up the mountains behind the park, and had cut through the fields so we could follow the river downstream when suddenly the river turned red . . .

'Jesus,' said Wee Sam, appalled. 'Wonder what happened?'

'There must be bodies up the river,' Pickle announced finally. 'I wonder if it's the Butchers again?'

'Let's go look.'

We wandered up the river. The water was still flowing a steady red, but there were no signs of any bloodied victims. Even so, I turned away and walked back towards Uncle Rab and Aunty Jacky's. Even the word 'blood' appalled me, especially now that I knew I had 'Catholic blood'. I felt unclean, tainted, impure.

As discoloured as the once-clear river now flowing past us; a bloody, muddy mess of a thing.

Aunty Jacky could shed no light on the dramatic change to the colour of the water. 'I'd keep away from there, boys,' she said. 'You never know what's been tipped in it.'

She said no more, but I think I understood. Since that first gruesome day in 1976, several more victims of the Shankill Butchers had been dumped up in Glencairn, their battered bodies slashed with knives. Even for the standards of the time these murders were particularly vicious and sectarian and hung like a dark cloud over all of Belfast, especially in Catholic areas. Even some Protestants accidentally became victims of a psychopathic gang bent on killing innocent Catholics. Each time another body was found in Glencairn I felt revulsion and fear – not just because the Butchers were bogeyman who haunted all our dreams, but because they might now somehow find out about me, my brother and sisters, and come to kill us all because of who we were.

The idea of this frightened me so much that I knew I had to tell someone I truly trusted. In private, I mentioned to Margaret, now fifteen, that I knew we were part-Catholic.

'We are, aren't we?' I said. 'Our mammy was a Catholic. I heard them talking. It's true, right?'

Wide-eyed, Margaret nodded back. 'I knew,' she said. 'I've always known. So I asked my granny and she said it was right, and that none of youse should know. John, you have to promise on Daddy's grave that you'll never tell anyone. It's really dangerous. Do you understand? Do you promise?'

I nodded. I was only eleven or twelve but I knew full well

what it meant to be the 'wrong' religion in this city. Also, I didn't want to tell anyone because I was in total denial. I was a Protestant, and proud of it. I didn't want to be anything else, especially through no fault of my own.

'What was Daddy thinking?' I asked Margaret. 'Why did he go wi' one of them? A Catholic.' I spat out the word in disgust.

Margaret shrugged her shoulders. 'Granny won't say,' she said. 'None of them will. And maybe that's for the best, John. You just have to forget about it. Forget about her. We're all Protestant now and that's what matters. Weren't you rechristened into the Protestant church at St Andrews?'

Of course. Now it made sense. David and I had been taken there one Sunday a few years previously, without explanation, and stood feeling sheepish and embarrassed as Reverend Lewis bent our heads over the font and splashed us with water while saying a prayer. I'd wondered why this had happened. Now I understood.

Margaret was streetwise and smart, and had her head screwed on. She wanted her own home. And when she got it, she said, she'd try to look after us all. I clung on to that idea, hoping that one day we'd all be together again under the same roof.

'I know summin' else too,' I said. 'Me ma's still alive, so she is.'

'How do you know that?' demanded Margaret.

'I don't. Not for sure. But I just think she is. '

Margaret looked at me. 'Who's to say?' she said finally. 'Maybe she is, maybe she isn't. And if she is, she's not doing much to look after us, is she?'

I had a feeling Margaret knew a bit more than she was letting on. But she was my oldest sister and she wouldn't put up with my line of questioning for too long. 'Like I said before, John,' she said, tight-lipped, 'some things are best forgotten about. Stop asking questions, or you'll get us all into trouble.'

Unfortunately, I wasn't one to forget easily. The pain of losing my dad came back to me in my dreams, night after night. I would hear him gently call my name and after a lengthy search around the house I'd hear that he was in the attic. Climbing the steps, I'd notice a hand coming down and helping me the rest of the way up. In the loft, I'd see that Dad had a camp bed, a gas stove and a kettle. He was hiding out up here, and I smiled with relief that he wasn't dead at all. In the dream, he'd always talk to me for a while, then ask me not to tell anyone where he was. The dream always ended with me crying and pleading for Dad to come down.

'John, John,' he'd say, 'don't cry, wee man. Everything'll be all right. You'll see.'

I'd wake up out of the dream, crying for real. 'What the fuck's the matter with you?' Wee Sam would say. Constantly woken up by my talking, shouting or crying in my sleep, he'd be pissed off with me, I could always tell. We were getting a bit older and were arguing and scrapping more frequently. In truth, we had become as close as brothers, but like brothers our rivalry had deepened. And I had this same dream for about three years after Dad's death and it always left me feeling sad and utterly depressed.

A few days later, we headed back to the river to see if it had cleared up and to our astonishment, we discovered that the blood-red had now become bruise-purple.

'What's feckin' up with this water?' said Wee Sam. 'What's goin' on with it?'

'I think it's magic,' I said. I'd just read *The Lion, the Witch and the Wardrobe* and now I believed in magic. 'It's like there's a rainbow in it. It's the Rainbow River.'

'You're a feckin' eejit,' observed Wee Sam, and with that we were scuffling and tussling on the riverbank, each trying to shove the other into the mysterious water. The day after we were back. Now it was blue. On subsequent days it was yellow, then green, then back to red. I was right. There was magic in this river and no amount of Wee Sam's taunting would tell me otherwise.

Aunty Jacky was so fed up with our bickering that she eventually ordered us out of the house and into the front garden.

'Right, I'm done wi' youse two!' she shouted. 'You're doing my head in. It's about time you sorted this out once and for all like men. Into the garden. We're going to have a boxing match.' Wee Sam and I had been members of the boxing club up in Highfield and we knew some basic boxing moves due to our training there.

As ever, word spread like wildfire that the Chambers cousins were going to battle it out. Within minutes, dozens of scruffy kids just like us were gathered at the front gate and some adults drifted over with beer in their hands and fags hanging from their mouths, eager for the show to start. It was a beautiful sunny day and the good folk of Glencairn loved nothing more than a good fair dig.

Like Muhammad Ali and Joe Frazier we stripped off our shirts and squared up to each other. Wee Sam was the better fighter, for sure, but everyone knew that I didn't go under easily.

After a few moments prowling around each other Wee Sam lashed out, connected a blow to my cheek and suddenly we were in the thick of it, digging the hell out of each other. While our audience screamed and shouted, roaring their enthusiasm and howling for blood, some of the adults were placing bets on who would win. Sam and I were thrashing it out on the grass, kicking, punching, strangling and biting, fighting Glencairn style, when we became aware of a sudden silence and a pair of black-trousered legs standing over us.

'Sweet Jesus, what are you doing? Stop that now!' shouted a commanding voice. 'Don't you think there's enough fighting in this country without you two carrying on?'

Panting and dishevelled, we stopped battling and stared up. Reverend Lewis looked down on us from upon high. 'Get up, the pair of you,' he said. 'This is no way to sort your troubles out.'

We lifted ourselves from the grass in a state of shame. Reverend Lewis told the crowd to go home. Respectfully, they obeyed his order.

'You two are cousins,' he said, turning to us. 'How did you get into this mess?'

'My ma told us to sort it out in the ring,' replied Sam, 'and so we did.'

On cue, Aunty Jacky reappeared at the front door looking shame-faced. Reverend Lewis walked up the path and had a quiet word with her, gesturing over his shoulder towards us a couple of times. Then he walked back the way he came, shaking his head in disappointment.

'There will be no more fighting between you two,' he said.

'If you want to go to heaven one day, you'll behave yourselves. God sees everything. Understood?'

We nodded and the Reverend walked off towards St Andrew's Church. I wondered how he always seemed to know when there was trouble brewing. Maybe God told him, I thought, and that night I prayed extra hard that God would forgive me and that I'd earn a place in heaven with Dad and Shep. Before I went to sleep I always knelt at the foot of the bed and asked God to help the poor and unfortunate, and stop the killing of innocent people in Northern Ireland, but most of all that He reunite us as a family once again. Deep down, I knew my prayer would never be answered but still I kept trying, in case miracles did really happen.

And as for the 'Rainbow River' . . . well, the colour change in the water wasn't 'magic', dead bodies or even divine intervention after all. A few months after we witnessed the spectacle, we discovered that a clothing factory somewhere upstream from Glencairn had been illegally tipping its waste materials into the river, which included vast quantities of fabric dye. We were a bit deflated by this mundane explanation but forever after our wee stream was always called the Rainbow River.

In September 1977, I started my time at Cairnmartin secondary school, a state school that served the communities of Glencairn, Woodvale, Ballygomartin and the upper end of the Shankill. The famous footballer Norman Whiteside (aka the Shankill skinhead) was at the school before going to play for Manchester United, and Wayne McCullough, former world champion boxer, was also a former pupil. As were many future Loyalist leaders, paramilitary members and killers . . .

It was a huge place, packed full of local kids and very well equipped. It even had its own swimming pool and language lab, courtesy of government money that was being pumped into Northern Ireland at that time in a bid to calm down the violence. There was still plenty of this inside school (and beyond its boundaries, of course) but having a pool went some way at least to cooling off tensions between the hundreds of kids who crammed through its doors every day.

I'd missed a fair bit of primary school going in and out of hospital and although I loved history and English, a school like Cairnmartin was more a test of survival than a passport to a glittering career. Most kids would just do their time then get a job in the local area, get married, have kids and go straight, while others would sign on to the dole and either waste their lives away or fall into the hands of the paramilitaries. Many of the teachers had no interest in teaching us, trying their best to get through the day until the bell rang and they could escape the madhouse. Miss Walters, the English teacher who all the boys fancied, and Miss Kelly, the drama teacher, were my favourites and always seemed to care more than the others. Mr Wilson, the maths teacher, had a massive lump growing out of the side of his face and was a right bastard. The RE teacher, who we nicknamed 'Jesus Joe', couldn't hide his hatred of us and during his class he would hand out books and told us to copy sections while he sat at the front, reading his Bible and occasionally yelling at us. To come out of school with more than a couple of O levels in an area like ours was bordering on genius.

A couple of significant things happened in the early years at Cairnmartin. The first was that someone – and I've forgotten who – brought in a seven-inch single by an English band I'd never heard of, called The Jam. Even before I'd listened to their music, I knew that this was a band for me. Lean and sharp-suited, the three members stared moodily at the camera while leaning against a wall that sported a spray-paint version of their logo. Immediately this appealed to me – the graffiti, the urban setting, the mean-looking guys in their shades and black ties. Perhaps they looked at bit like the paramilitaries who occasionally paraded on Glencairn. Maybe it was the graffiti – I was so used to seeing 'UDA' and 'UVF' sprayed up everywhere that 'The Jam' was a welcome change.

But when I heard the music, it spoke to me and my life changed forever. 'The Modern World', 'Down In The Tube Station at Midnight', 'Strange Town' and especially 'Going Underground' – three-minute explosions of urban paranoia and anger that fitted exactly with the time and place I was living through. If you lived in Belfast in the late 1970s and you couldn't understand what The Jam were trying to tell you, in my twelve-year-old opinion there was something wrong with you. And I still feel this way.

I caught The Jam on *Top Of The Pops* and I was hooked even deeper. Naturally, I loved the British flags and the red, white and blue target logos atheir colour association with us, the Loyalists. But it wasn't just that. The Jam were speaking my language; even more so than Stiff Little Fingers and The Undertones, homegrown punk bands from Northern Ireland. For me, SLF were too preachy about the Troubles (especially now they were living in London) and The Undertones sang too much about being in love. The Jam struck a course somewhere in between and pulled off masterstroke after musical masterstroke. I longed for the days that I could have a proper green army parka, a pair of black-and-white bowling shoes and a scooter. For the minute, I was stuck with hand-me-down shirts and flared trousers and a cheap snorkel jacket, complete with fake-fur hood lining. I would have to park the shiny silver Vespa of my dreams firmly in the future, when I would become a full-blown Mod.

The second thing about school was meeting Billy Smyth. Taller than me – and a bit fatter, maybe – he was a cheery kid with an open, honest face and we hit it off from the moment we met. We were in the same classes and we'd noticed each other doodling the same things on our exercise books – the 'Jam' logo and the 'Walt Jabsco' ska-man figure used by English two-tone band The Specials, plus various arrows, targets and Union Jacks. We realised we were into the same things and quickly we became best friends and, forty years later, we still are.

Billy was from the Woodvale area, which we in Glencairn considered 'posh'. It wasn't, of course, but the houses were nicer than ours and some people – including Billy's parents – *actually owned their own homes*! Hard to believe when so many others, including ourselves, were council tenants, and I guess this is where the 'posh' tag came from. In return, the people of Woodvale looked down on us roughnecks and, at first, Billy's parents were worried that he'd got a mate from the wrong end of West Belfast. When they met me – wee, thin, with a wonky leg but with manners enough – I think they changed their minds and they grew to love me.

From the off, Billy and I were competitive. We were always scrapping, play-fighting, messing and trying to impress the girls. They'd order us to sketch something in return for a kiss and Billy and I would scribble away furiously to prove who was the best artist. We'd also wind up our teachers something terrible and even at this stage we were probably being written off as no-hopers by those in charge. For now, though, we were having fun – and boy, did I need some fun at that stage of my life, because my domestic circumstances certainly weren't yielding many laughs.

As I entered my secondary school years, I was happy in Uncle Rab and Aunty Jacky's house. Despite the occasional flare-up, Wee Sam and I got along well enough. I remember us lying in our beds at night, singing all the songs from the movie *Grease* at the top of our voices and being yelled at by Uncle Rab and Aunty Jacky. Sadly, though, there were problems in Rab and Jacky's marriage. As I've mentioned, Uncle Rab was popular all over Glencairn and beyond, and his good looks got him noticed. His charm and wit landed him in various buckets of hot water and at night I'd hear him and Aunty Jacky arguing fiercely downstairs. There were late-night drinking sessions starring Uncle Rab and his buddies, and the sounds of drunken adults getting seriously out of hand. One night, the roars of a particularly heavy drinking bout so disturbed the family budgie that it started shrieking in its cage. Its cries of protest were quickly silenced by one of the drinkers, who lifted the bird from its cage, took it upstairs and pulled off its head at our bedroom door. There was blood all over the place and the guy who killed the bird got a hiding from Uncle

Rab and Uncle Jim that he'd never forget. There was violence everywhere – even the local bird population wasn't safe. The next day was a Sunday and when Aunty Jacky served the roast chicken dinner we all thought it was the budgie and refused to eat the meat.

One thing led to another and it was decided I needed to move out. Despite all the arguments and general instability, I was reluctant to go – I was very happy with them and being at their house took my mind off Dad's death – particularly when I found out where I was headed – back to Alistair and Betty's. Alistair was uptight, harsh, strict and nasty. Betty was nice enough, but in no position to argue with Alistair. He was the master, and was determined that I would be his servant.

Alistair was militaristic in his approach. When I arrived at their home, it was as if I'd joined the army as a raw recruit. The list of rules was back with a vengeance.

'You will wipe your feet when you come in, each and every time,' said Alistair, ten minutes after I'd arrived with my meagre bag of clothes. 'Then you will remove your shoes at the door, and you will keep them clean and polished. I will show you how this is done. You'll keep your feet off the sofa and you will eat your dinner at the table. You will do your homework promptly, by five o'clock, and you will be in by seven o'clock. No later. You will show respect at all times to Betty and me, and you will . . .'

On and on he droned. There were rules and regulations for everything, it seemed. I tried to tune him out but Alistair could talk the leg off a chair and after the book of rules he moved on to the list of chores.

'Chores?' I said, suddenly waking up. 'What kind o' chores?'

He looked at me in astonishment, as if I'd slapped him in the face. As far as I was concerned, chores were done by grannies, aunties and sisters. Fellas like me didn't get involved in what we saw as 'woman's work'; this was Belfast in the seventies. after all. But Alistair obviously had other ideas. He wasn't working, but he liked the idea of getting the credit for keeping the house as neat as a pin for when Betty came in from her job in the town.

'You will hoover and wash the dishes daily. Three times a week you will mop the kitchen floor and once a week you will clean my car. You will leave no mess or clutter of any kind lying on the floor. Your bedroom will remain tidy at all times . . .'

And so on. I couldn't believe what I was hearing. Why had I been put with these people? Alistair's standards were through the roof and he expected everyone else to have the same approach to life, even grubby twelve-year-old heartbroken orphans like me. Perhaps he thought that a serious dose of discipline at this stage in my life would 'cure' me of any temptation to go down the wrong path later on. If so, I could understand his reasoning. It was easy – all too easy – for kids like me to be tempted down the paramilitary route as a distraction from poverty and despair. On the other hand, he might just have been a complete feckin' control freak nutcase who also had the nerve to suggest that I call him 'Dad'. This disgusted me beyond words and my look of contempt told him exactly what I thought of this idea. Needless to say, I never did.

Alistair's bullying nature would soon be put to the test. Maybe I didn't take him seriously enough because a couple of days after I'd moved in, I finished my dinner and put the plate in the sink before rushing out to play with my mates in the square close by Alistair and Betty's house. I'd hardly got out the door when a hand grabbed me by the shirt collar and dragged me back inside.

'What's goin' on?' I yelled. 'What the feck are you doin'? That hurts, so it does!'

Alistair yanked me round to face him. His expression was one of contempt. He shoved me against the wall and loomed over me, spitting in my face as he yelled. 'Where do you think you're going?'

'Out to play,' I said. 'I done my homework and all.'

'What didn't you do?' he said menacingly.

I had to think. Kids like me just ran out to play, looking forward to the game and not reflecting on what we had or had not just done.

'Dunno,' I said finally.

'Then let me show you,' he said with disgust, and he dragged me into the kitchen, shoving my head towards the sink.

'You never, ever, go out without washing up your dishes,' he shouted. 'Do you hear me? And you never, ever, go out without asking my permission. Understood?'

I nodded. He loosened his grip on me and told me to stand where I was. Then he removed his belt. 'You need a hard lesson, boy,' he snarled. 'You'll thank me for this one day.'

He shoved me over and began thrashing me on the arse with the thick belt. I was so shocked that for a few seconds I didn't make a sound. Then I started squealing and roaring, which seemed to make him hit me even harder.

'Stop your crying!' he shouted, 'and take it like a man.' After a dozen or so blows he stopped and, panting, pushed me against the sink. He had a weird expression on his face, like he'd really enjoyed what he'd just done.

'Any more from you, you little shit, and you'll get double that. Now get upstairs and out of my sight. And don't come down again until breakfast tomorrow. Seven o'clock sharp!'

I crawled off upstairs to my tiny bedroom, snivelling and sniffing. I'd had a few clips from Dad when he was alive, and the odd backhander from Uncle Rab. That was normal in our world and it never really bothered me because it was nothing on the scale that had just been dished out to me. I lay on the bed, sobbing my heart out, and thought about Dad, and how he wouldn't have stood for any of this. On a few occasions that I'd pissed off some neighbour or other and they'd come to our house to complain, Dad had told them to 'get ta feck' and they'd quickly moved away. I knew if my dad was alive he'd have killed the bastard for the way he was treating me.

And I thought about Mum, allowing all the grief and shame that surrounded her disappearance to pull me down into an ocean of misery. I couldn't understand why Betty would stand by and watch this monster abuse me when all I needed was love and affection. At that moment I wished Alistair was dead, and I swore that when I was older I would join the paramilitaries, get an Armalite of my own and finish the fucker off. Even at this age, I knew that such a course of action was not at all beyond the realms of possibility in West Belfast.

CHAPTER 8

Maybe the intense pain had sent me into a state of shock, because I seemed to be looking down on myself as I lay on the wooden floor of the school gym, sprawled out and completely unable to move. A gang of swearing, shouting schoolboys had gathered around me, staring at the bone sticking out of my right leg. The PE teacher, Mr McCrosson, shoved a path through them then knelt down beside me. His reaction didn't fill me with much comfort, to be fair.

'Fuckin' hell,' he muttered, prompting a few adolescent whoops and sniggers, 'that's a wild terrible injury. Stay there, Chambers, while I call for an ambulance.'

I didn't bother to say that I wasn't going anywhere. I wouldn't be getting up and carrying on as though nothing had happened any minute soon. What I wanted to say was that I shouldn't have been playing basketball, or doing bloody PE of any sort. The school had been warned about my bad leg but every week, almost without fail, I'd been ordered into my school sports kit and forced to take part. Up to this point I hadn't minded so much. In fact, I always thought a bit of PE might help strengthen my leg. But some games I couldn't take part in and if I refused the PE teacher would make me sit in the changing room and write lines. So I played when I shouldn't have been to avoid doing lines.

This was about as bad a fracture as it could be and the pain was indescribable. We'd been playing basketball in the gym and I'd not done much – just a sudden turn to my right as I jumped for the ball, a guy called Pip beside me – when one of the bones in my right femur decided the time was right to snap and tear right through my skin. Due to my childhood bone disease, my leg was weak and I could never bend it fully. My wailing coincided with that of the ambulance as it made its way to the Royal Victoria Hospital, just off the Falls Road – the epicentre of nationalist Catholic Belfast. Even as I screamed and cried, the thought that Catholic doctors and nurses might soon be poking and prodding me crept into my mind, adding insult to injury. The inbuilt sectarian bitterness that came from growing up on an estate like Glencairn, plus the knowledge that I was 'tainted' with Catholic blood, was never far from the surface, even in extreme moments like this. I knew no differently.

The Royal Victoria Hospital has a well-earned international reputation for specialist treatment of bomb and bullet-related injuries, and while mine wasn't caused by either of these, it was serious enough to warrant a full-on treatment plan. This would require a whole six months in hospital, in traction and with little else to do other than read comics and watch TV.

Personally, I was over the moon. I couldn't go to school (and missed out large chunks of my education) and I'd be away from Alistair and Betty's house for what seemed like a lifetime. I was delighted by that, because things had grown a whole lot worse in the few months I'd been there. The only good thing about this time was Betty's cooking – I have to say, she did make unbelievably tasty meals.

Alistair treated me like a slave and although I complained about his brutality to my family, there was very little anyone could do. We'd been farmed out all over the place and there was no room to squeeze me in anywhere else. It was either Alistair and Betty's house or a children's home. After a couple of particularly nasty hidings, Uncle Rab went down to Alistair's and physically threatened him. He may even have punched him, but whatever the threat level it only ever seemed to be temporary and within a week or two he was back to his old barrack-room behaviour, criticising everything I did or didn't do and taking off his belt when he felt it necessary. I remember one Boxing Day. It was snowing heavy and Glencairn was like the Antarctic; we'd run out of milk and he ordered me to go to the shop to get another couple of pints. Because Glencairn was up on a hillside we'd usually get a good, deep covering of snow; great for us kids to mess about on in the holidays, but not so good if you wanted to travel any distance.

'Ach, come on,' I said, when he demanded that I leave the house, 'the Spar is shut. It's Boxing Day. Where'm I gonna get milk from now?'

Alistair gave me a nasty smile. 'Go down the Shankill,' he said. 'You'll find a shop open there. Move it.'

Being Boxing Day, there were no taxis and Glencairn to the Shankill and back was a round trip of about four miles. Alistair had a car sitting on the driveway but he wasn't for giving me a lift. I would have to walk through the dark, the snow and the cold, and on the day after Christmas Day. Aged twelve. We both stood for a while in silence, me wondering whether to defy him and take the hit (literally) or just get on with it and keep the peace. Then he grabbed my snorkel jacket from its place in the hallway and held it out to me, the way you'd show a lead to a dog reluctant to take a walk.

'The sooner you go, the sooner you'll be back,' he said. So I set off, and every step of the way I cursed Alistair and Betty, prayed to my dad in heaven to ask God to put an end to the life of misery I was leading, and silently shouted at my mum for a) deserting us and b) being a Catholic, which had obviously cursed me. And then I cursed God for putting me through this hell.

'You've been ages,' sneered Alistair when I finally arrived home, wet, bedraggled, freezing and scared shitless after a walk through a darkened and eerily quiet Belfast. All sorts of stuff happened to people on these streets – we heard about it every day, and it was commonplace to hear about Prods killing random Taigs, and Taigs blowing up innocent Prods. Being just twelve years old didn't necessarily protect you from any of that.

'Can I have a cup of tea, please?' I said. 'I'm freezing.'

'No, you can't,' he said. 'We'll need this milk for a few days . . . unless you fancy another walk down the road tomorrow?'

And with that, the bastard sent me to bed. No wonder that I saw six long months in hospital as a strange kind of holiday and wished I could stay there until Margaret was married and took me to live with her.

That elation quickly wore off as reality sank in. There would be no playing out for me, no messing with Billy and friends at school, no hanging out around Glencairn with Wee Sam, Pickle or David. In hospital, I was a prisoner of my own weakness and at Royal Victoria I was aware of being surrounded by Catholics, kids as well as staff.

To be honest, I see now that I had something of a nervous breakdown in there. Night after night I cried myself to sleep. My leg didn't appear to be healing, despite several operations, and I was always in pain. I missed my family desperately, especially my dad and Shep. The whole domestic situation with Alistair and Betty, and Alistair's brutality, was sinking in and I felt depressed and helpless. And then, of course, there was the issue of my mother – who she was and where she was. At the age of twelve or thirteen, you often don't realise how difficult your life is, or can be, and I'd tried my very best to keep up appearances. But in hospital, away from family and friends, and in what I considered to be 'hostile' territory I couldn't keep up the pretence any longer. I recall howling like a wounded animal for a whole day as the doctors and nurses tried everything to calm me down. I wished that I were dead, and could be with Dad and Shep in heaven.

Quite soon I was moved to Musgrave Park Hospital, where I had spent much time as a young child enjoying the company of Nurse Brown. In a way, it was a home away from home. The other kids on the children's ward gradually began to acknowledge and speak to me. At first I was wary of them until I realised they were just kids, and that it didn't matter whether they were Catholic or Protestant. In fact, the longer I remained there the more I became intrigued by the Catholic kids. I was surprised and a wee bit disappointed to find that they didn't have horns or run around shouting praises to the Pope or were smelly. In fact, they were a lot more like me than I'd ever expected, or been told.

I became close to a Catholic girl called Fiona. She was suffering from leukaemia and had had a leg amputated. She'd lost all her hair and had to wear a comical-looking wig, which she hated and sometimes threw under the bed to howls of laughter from me and others. Despite all this, she was a cheery soul, always laughing, joking and teasing. We would talk for hours; sometimes it was about the differences between Protestants and Catholics, but more often than not it was about music, TV shows, films – the usual kids' stuff. She loved ABBA, and if they came on the radio she'd sing her head off, encouraging us all to join in. Despite my Jam fixation, I added my wonderful vocals to the likes of 'Waterloo' and 'Dancing Queen'. We played board games, did jigsaws and crossword puzzles together; anything to relieve the boredom of a long stay in hospital. Gradually, I realised that Fiona was becoming a friend. It didn't matter that she was a Catholic and I just ignored this fact. She was a lovely girl enduring a serious illness with good humour and courage. As the weeks passed, I could see that she was becoming more unwell; despite this, she still took the time to talk to me and always cheered me up.

After undergoing yet another operation on my leg, I returned to the ward in a state of semi-consciousness. I was in traction apparatus that was built around my bed. The pulley system held my leg up in the air and was very uncomfortable. As the mists cleared and I became aware of my surroundings I noticed that Fiona's bed was empty. When the ward sister came by to check on me, I asked her where my friend was.

'John, I've got something really upsetting and sad to tell you,' she said, taking my hand. 'I'm afraid that Fiona has been taken to intensive care. She's very, very poorly. I don't know if you say your prayers, John, but if you do, please say a wee one for her.'

Of course I said my prayers and although I couldn't get down on my knees like I would do at home, I screwed my eyes up tight and added Fiona's name to the list of people I regularly prayed for. Sadly, this time God wasn't listening and when I was told, a few days later, that Fiona wouldn't be coming back I cried myself to sleep. Again.

'God works in mysterious ways,' said Reverend Lewis when I told him the bad news. He always said this, and I was beginning not to believe him. Our friendly neighbourhood vicar came to visit me regularly and although I appreciated his visits I felt mortified when he would insist on kneeling at the foot of my bed as we prayed together. I could see the other kids sniggering and smirking at the other end of the ward and I wished the ground would swallow me up.

Six months went by and the leg that I thought would never get better finally healed. Eventually I was free to go, but while I was pleased to get out of hospital I dreaded what awaited me back on Glencairn. There was still no space for me anywhere other than Alistair and Betty's, and if I thought

Alistair may have mellowed while I was in hospital, I'd be wrong. By now, Betty was expecting a baby and as the nest was being prepared I was made to feel like the cuckoo who had very much overstayed his welcome. There was no let-up in Alistair's treatment of me, and within hours of my return I was back to cleaning, vacuuming, polishing, scrubbing floors, fetching the 'messages' (the word we use in Northern Ireland for groceries – don't ask me why) and being the general dogsbody. And I was still using crutches.

By this time, my sister Margaret knew what was going on and although only sixteen herself, would challenge Alistair about his behaviour.

'He's a lazy little arse,' she was told, 'and I'm keeping him busy because otherwise he'll just go around creating trouble. Is that what you want?'

The truth was that I didn't need to 'create' any trouble. There was enough of this going on all around us. Northern Ireland was heading into the days of the Republican hunger strikes in the Maze prison and the tension across Belfast was ratcheted up to boiling point. Every death brought angry people on to the streets and as the protests became louder, so the daily bombings and shootings increased. Riots were happening all over the place and the killing of soldiers and police officers prompted widespread anger among the Loyalist community. Northern Ireland felt ready to explode and with every passing day and death I hated the IRA more and more.

In the midst of all this anarchy, discipline on Glencairn was maintained by the UDA and they could be very harsh policemen indeed. Teenage boys who got up to no good were particular targets. Right across the estate, young boys who'd fallen foul of the paramilitaries for various reasons were threatened, beaten or non-fatally shot as a punishment. The latter was known as 'kneecapping'; very often it applied to the knees, but the paramilitaries extended it to other parts of the body, including calves, thighs and arms. We all knew boys who'd been kneecapped for something or other and we lived in fear of the knock on the door and the message to meet such-and-suchabody up at the UDA-run Community Centre immediately. When this happened, the terrified boy would scuttle up to the appointment where he'd be told of his fate. A beating was bad, but a kneecapping was much worse and could end in permanent disability. One afternoon I was passing a block of derelict flats with my brother David when we heard a couple of shots from inside the building, followed by terrible screaming. We ran inside to find a teenage boy lying on the floor, his face a mask of agony, and blood pouring from both knees. Those who'd dispensed the rough justice had disappeared in a flash, and the kid's screams were punctuated by the sound of an ambulance siren wailing up towards Glencairn. The paramilitaries doled out the most savage punishments possible to those who'd upset them, but they almost always had the courtesy to phone for an ambulance minutes beforehand and tell the operator what was about to occur. The boy was a known 'hood', a young troublemaker, and I felt he'd got what he deserved.

Some boys took kneecappings in their stride, so to speak, and would ask the shooter (who was invariably known to them, Glencairn being such a tight-knit community) for permission to change out of their best jeans and into an old pair before the shot was delivered, or if they were going on holiday to postpone the punishment until they'd returned.

So it was difficult for Margaret to argue against Alistair's insistence that his methods would keep me out of trouble, even though I knew the bastard was a bully who enjoyed tormenting me. The best I could hope for was that now she was going with a fella called Richard she might get married soon, and she'd always promised me that if she got a house of her own I would be allowed to live there. In the meantime, I just had to sweat it out with the pair of them and wait until I could escape.

Matters came to a head one winter's day a few months after I came out of hospital. Betty had gone in to have her baby and, as usual, I was keeping house and catering to Alistair's every whim. It was that bleak time just after New Year when all the partying is over and done and all you've got to look forward to are the dark days at the tail end of winter. Alistair was rabbiting on, demanding that I do this, do that, cook this, clean that. On and on, until I could stand no more. Compared to this, I'd rather be in a children's home, or dead. Or anywhere else at all. I knew that at some stage he'd be heading into town to see Betty and the new baby. Once he'd left, so would I.

'And mind you don't forget to polish the table and chairs,' was Alistair's parting shot as he closed the front door.

'Fat chance, mate,' I thought.

I waited until I heard Alistair's car make its way down the road before dashing upstairs to get ready. It was a freezing cold late afternoon and I stuffed a couple of extra jumpers into my school bag, just in case. I never had much money – a couple of quid here and there, borrowed from Margaret or Granny if they were feeling generous. I also had a bit left over from Christmas that I hadn't spent. It was enough to get me where I wanted to go.

I grabbed my bag and coat and slammed the front door hard, hoping never to have to see this place again. I trudged along the icy pavements to the phone box by the shops. There was no guarantee that it wasn't banjaxed, so I said a wee prayer to God and this time He listened. Looking around to make sure the coast was clear, I slipped into the box and dialled the number of the local taxi firm, Alpha Cabs. There was no way I was walking down into the town on a winter's day ever again.

When he arrived, the driver attempted to make some conversation but I was non-committal. I said I was meeting someone at the main bus station in Oxford Street.

'So youse'll need a ride back, then?' he asked.

'Ach. Probably not . . . we might look round the shops for a bit.'

'Up to you,' he said, 'but don't hang around down there too long, will ye? It's not a place for kids after dark.'

In those days, Belfast wasn't a place for anyone after dark. Fear and death stalked the streets. You got lost, or you met the wrong person, or you were just plain unlucky. Either way, you could wind up dead. I had no intention of lingering around the city centre for long.

We arrived at the bus station. 'Take care, wee man,' said the driver as he took my fare money. He drove off and now I was alone. I walked up and down the stands, looking for the destination I wanted, casting my mind back five or six years to the last time I'd felt truly happy. I conjured up images of warm summer days, the smell of sea air, the feeling of the sun on my skin. Fish 'n' chips on the beach, and my dad and his brothers swilling pints of Harp while we kids threw sand at each other, laughing and squealing. Better times: the days before Dad died, the days when we were a family bonded by love and laughter, even though our mother was gone. I wanted to go back to those days.

'Is this the bus to Ballyferris?' I asked the middle-aged driver who was enjoying a cigarette while he waited for someone to board his bus.

'Why,' he said, laughing, 'are ye goin' on yer holidays? Not much sun there today . . .'

'I'm just going there,' I said.

'Well then, get on,' he said. 'The last stop is Millisle. That near enough for ye?'

I nodded. Millisle was just fine. Better, in fact. After a ten-minute wait the driver extinguished yet another cigarette in the ashtray by his seat and reversed the bus out of the station. This was it. I was leaving home, never to return. I stared out of the window into the heart of darkness that was Belfast and was pleased to see it disappear. I would miss my sisters and brother, but they could always come to visit. And I knew they would, because they felt the same way as me.

An hour or so later, we'd arrived. I must've nodded off because the driver came down the length of the vehicle and gave me a gentle shove.

'Hi you,' he said. 'C'mon on and wake up. We're here. Millisle. It's where you wanted, right?'

I rubbed my eyes. The driver smelled of diesel and fags. 'It's grand,' I muttered, picking up my bag and moving off down the aisle. I could sense him watching me as I stepped off the bus and into the darkness, limping away as quickly as I could before he started asking awkward questions.

Now I was here, I wasn't sure what to do. Out of season, the village was empty, deserted and silent. I hadn't expected a sudden shift in the seasons but now, in winter, Millisle seemed strange and unwelcoming, just as in summer it was friendly and bustling. Instinctively, I headed for the funfair, the place I was always at my happiest during our family holidays. The gates were locked, and greasy tarpaulin covers lay over the dodgem cars that were all covered in snow. I rattled the gates a couple of times, somehow expecting them to open for me so that I could enter the magic kingdom. They didn't, so without even thinking I hauled myself over the six-foot fence and collapsed in a heap on the other side.

I wandered round the deserted funfair. I don't know what I was looking for – a comforting memory, perhaps, or a friendly ghost from the past. But only silence was here to welcome me. I'd expected to be warmed and protected by this place. Now, all it held were reminders of happier times past, never to return.

I was very cold. I pulled my jacket around me but it was hopeless on this freezing winter's night by the sea. I lifted the corner of a tarpaulin covering a dodgem car and climbed in, curling up like a hibernating animal on the plastic seat. I pulled the tarpaulin sheet back over myself and hoped that I would fall asleep quickly. Maybe, just maybe, it would all be all right in the morning.

As I discovered very quickly, the cold was too intense for sleep. I pictured Dad's face, watching with pleasure as I rammed a dodgem car into everything that moved, shouting and screaming with childhood delight. I felt him put a protective arm around my shoulder as he led me back towards the caravan park, the summer sun setting in the distance. And I knew that I would never see or feel his physical presence again. I started to cry, and for a whole hour, shivering under the tarpaulin, I howled my eyes out, raging against the unfairness of losing Dad, of not knowing where my mum was, of having to live with a bully, of having to exist in a country that was tearing itself apart and a God who didn't seem to care for me.

I cried till I was all cried out. By now, my fingers were sore and numb with cold and I couldn't feel my toes. If I stayed here, I'd be lucky to last the night. Wearily, I lifted up the sheet and uncurled myself out of the dodgem car. Then I climbed the fence out of the funfair and stood on the pavement for a while, wondering what to do.

Finally, I realised that if I went to the police and told them I'd run away, they'd probably send me to a children's home. And if that meant not having to go back to Alistair and Betty's, fair enough – I'd prefer that. I'd coped with months in hospital; I could probably look after myself within the confines of a home, no matter who else was in there. I went to a public phone box and called the police, telling myself that one day, when I was older, I would beat the fuck out of Alistair and I'd also try to find my mum. She wasn't dead, I was convinced of that. And if she was alive, somehow she could be found. That meant I had something to live for.

The cops came and took me to the nearest police station. The peeler manning the security gate at the station looked surprised to see a bedraggled boy coming in.

'Bejesus, what are you doing out on a night like this?' he said. 'You look half dead . . .'

'I've run away,' I said. 'I hate where I'm living. I want to go into a kids' home. Can you help me?'

Then I started crying.

'All right son,' said the cop, 'catch yerself on and calm down. Now, what's happened?'

I told the cop about losing my dad and Shep, and all the hassle I was having at home. He listened patiently as I sobbed out the sorry tale.

'Not a lot I can do, son,' he said when I'd finished. 'There's no crime being committed and you're only a wee boy so you're gonna have to go home. Tell you what, though – the chippy over the road is still open. Do youse want a pastie supper before I drive ye back to Belfast?'

I was, and always have been, a sucker for a pastie supper and I was bloody starving by this stage. 'All right,' I said, smiling. 'Thanks.'

'No problem,' said the policeman. 'And when we get you home I'll go in and have a word with this fella. Give him a warning, like. How about that?'

It was a deal and full of the delights of a pastie supper I sat in the back of the unmarked police car, nice and warm as it travelled back to the city. The last place I wanted to go was

Alistair and Betty's, but oddly the experience of running away had given me a bit of determination not to put up with any more shit from him, and to focus on my future. The peeler was as good as his word and explained to Alistair what had happened, before letting him know about the bullying and the beatings. From the safety of the car I could see the officer giving Alistair a good talking-to. Then he summoned me out with a wave of his hand and ushered me to the front door, where an embarrassed and angry Alistair stood waiting.

'So there'll be no more trouble here now, right?' The officer looked at Alistair until he nodded his assent. 'Good. Then I'll say goodnight.'

As soon as he was away around the corner Alistair dragged me into the kitchen and gave me a hiding. In the middle of the beating Uncle Rab arrived and pulled him off me. Strangely, I wasn't bothered by Alistair's violence. I sensed that things would change now, and that he wouldn't be very keen on the police or social services turning up to his door regularly. From then on, Alistair eased off with his bullying and blustering and it was only a matter of months before Margaret announced she was getting married. Finally, I would be able to escape this house and be back among my real family again, who loved and cared for me unconditionally.

CHAPTER 9

I was ticking off the days until Margaret and Richard's wedding. My liberation from the stress of living with Alistair and Betty couldn't come soon enough. Mags and Rick were planning to buy a house and were looking at a terraced property in Ottawa Street in the Woodvale area, which is at the top of the Shankill. The house was in a Loyalist enclave and most people there owned their own homes. However, it was just around the corner from the Catholic and ultra-nationalist Ardoyne area. Despite 'peace walls' and barriers, at the time this was arguably one of the most tense and dangerous boundaries between Protestants and Catholics in the whole of Belfast.

I didn't care. I just wanted away from Alistair and Betty's and I thought that a move from Glencairn might do me good too. I was growing up quickly but was still very conflicted between my Loyalist instincts and the knowledge that my Catholic mother could be still alive somewhere. I prayed to God constantly to give me an answer but given that He seemed to be very quiet on the subject I could only conclude that He was working in mysterious ways.

My behaviour at the time highlighted the inner conflicts I was feeling. At night, I still knelt at the end of my bed and said my prayers, like a good Christian boy. By day, though, I was beginning to slide off the rails and into trouble. It started with a bit of petty pilfering here and there, which left me feeling guilty – but it didn't seem to stop my light fingers examining the shelves of various shops to see what I could walk away with. Then there was the glue . . .

In the early 1980s, sniffing solvents was a cheap and easy way of getting high and leaving your surroundings behind for a while. It was the craic, especially among kids like us who needed very little excuse for wanting to escape the terrifying environment of unceasing violence that swirled around us. At the time the BBC series *The Young Ones* was drawing in thousands of young viewers with its mad antics. My entire school seemed to be watching this show, addicted to its anarchic humour that reflected our own lives.

Around school, word spread very quickly that a jar of Timebond, Evo-Stik or UHU, plus a carrier bag, were all you needed to have a weird yet entertaining experience. I've always had an addictive personality and was the sort of kid who would try anything for a laugh. I persuaded Billy that having a go with the glue would be a great idea and, having nicked the necessary equipment from Woolworths in the town, we were ready to take our first trip.

I enjoyed it from the very start. I liked being out of my head, even for a short time, and I loved the feeling of escapism that glue gave me. Although I was still wary of Alistair's methods of discipline, I also knew that I had one foot out of his door and by the time of Margaret's wedding to Richard, I was fifteen and had pretty much stopped giving a fuck what Alistair and Betty felt. When the date was set I literally jumped for joy around my bedroom. Alistair came pounding up the stairs, screaming at me to stop in case I woke the baby.

'What the hell do you think you're doing!' he yelled, inches from my face. 'Stop that at once!'

In response, I just smiled.

'And you can take that stupid grin off your face,' he said.

'Why should I?' I replied. 'I'm out of here in a few weeks and I can't bloody wait. So go fuck yourself!'

'If it were up to me, I'd hoof you out now,' he said, slamming my bedroom door.

The day of Margaret's wedding came soon enough, and we all went up to Paisley Park, a big Loyalist club in Highfield, for the reception, following the service at St Andrew's on Glencairn. As with all good Northern Irish events – weddings, funerals, baptisms and birthdays – it was a very drunken affair, for the adults anyway. I took great delight in seeing Alistair get so scunnered that he threw up all over the place. Control gave structure to his miserable little life, and seeing him lose it was a joy to behold. David and I were pageboys and we paraded proudly down the aisle behind our sister in our matching outfits. I looked angelic that day, but behind the smiles there was the usual sadness that Dad wasn't around to celebrate such an important moment in his family's life. Still, Granda did a great job of giving Margaret away, apart from the fact he was a bit deaf at the time, and when Reverend Lewis asked if anyone present objected to the marriage, Granda said 'I do', to sniggers all around the room.

A few months later, Margaret made good the promise she'd made years ago and I moved into Ottawa Street with the newlyweds. God bless them, they were very tolerant, especially Rick. Mags had told him about her secret Catholic side and although he was shocked it didn't put him off marrying her. After all, we came from good Protestant stock on Dad's side of the family and were Loyalist through and through. Rick also dealt well with the fact that a young teenage boy would soon be joining them in their first home. They weren't much older than kids themselves, but family was family and Margaret was determined to fulfil her role as this family's rock and anchor, despite having a ready-made teenage nightmare under their roof.

Down in the Woodvale/Ardoyne boundary, rioting was a daily occurrence. Catholic and Protestant kids who in any other circumstances would be out playing football together were spending their spare time hurling bricks, bottles and petrol bombs at each other before running as hard as hell away from the army and the police. For us, it was pure entertainment and also for the older paramilitaries on both sides of the divide. They would encourage us teenagers to go out and cause trouble, thereby diverting police and army attention away from their own activities. 'Go and kick up a bloody racket, boys,' they'd say, handing us a milk crate full of petrol bombs. In time, I learned how to make these myself and enjoyed hurling these over at the Catholic lads, then seeing them running from the flames.

Inevitably, trouble caught up with me. I'd started seeing a girl from Snugville Street off the Shankill, and although nothing serious was going on, we enjoyed regular snogging sessions in the local park. One night, after a prolonged session, the girl realised she was going to be late home. I offered to take her on a short cut, which, unfortunately, went right through the boundary and of course, there was a riot going on at the very moment we passed through it. Petrol bombs were flying everywhere and one of my mates scored an own goal when the one he'd just hurled struck me on the arm. Within seconds the flames spread right up my sleeve and I flailed around like a dervish trying to extinguish the fire. Far from trying to help me, my mates were in stitches laughing.

'Quick!' shouted the guy who'd thrown the device, 'get some more petrol! Chambers is going out!' Unsurprisingly, the humour in Belfast at that time was as black as black can be.

The stupid thing was that we were just kids getting caught up and dragged into violence and political manoeuvring. We'd come home from school, do a bit of homework (well, some of us would) and go out for an hour's rioting before someone shouted that it was time for tea. Catholic and Protestant kids would immediately down tools and run home to their dinner tables before venturing out an hour later, ready to fight again. It was like something from The Jam's 'Eton Rifles':

> 'What a catalyst you turned out to be/Loaded the guns then you run off home for your tea/Left me standing like a guilty schoolboy' . . .'

We were all just pawns in a bigger game and one day our turn would come to play paramilitaries properly. No wonder I loved that band so much . . . they spoke the truth and provided the soundtrack to my teenage life.

Meanwhile, our glue-sniffing was getting out of hand. One day we were high as kites when we were caught by the police. Billy and I were in a derelict house in the Woodvale, inhaling deeply into our plastic bags, when we heard a disembodied voice speaking as though it was from the depths of hell.

'Don't move!' it shouted, 'Or we'll shoot!'

We looked up to see the barrels of two rifles pointing at us, and behind the guns a pair of riot-helmeted RUC.

'Don't shoot,' I pleaded, trying desperately to get my head together, 'please don't shoot . . . '

'Get up off the floor,' said one of the officers, 'and raise your hands.'

Perhaps they thought we were preparing petrol bombs or hiding weapons. Anyway, we did as we were told and as soon as they recognised a pair of buck eejits with sores around their mouths and clutching plastic bags they lowered their guns.

One of them asked where we lived. I told the guy and unfortunately for me, it was just around the corner. The officers took me home and delivered me into the arms of Margaret, who gave me the almightiest bollocking once they'd gone. I deserved everything I got but sadly it didn't put me off the solvents, or running riot against the local Catholics whenever I got the chance. Billy and I were mad into the glue at this stage, so much so that a tin of Evo-Stik actually saved my life, or at least saved me from a serious injury. We were sniffing up in Glencairn, by the river and away from prying eyes, when we began squabbling over something trivial. This quickly escalated into a fight – nothing unusual about that, because we were always scrapping and it was never serious. This time, though, Billy produced the knife he always carried and tried to stab me. Luckily, he only managed to hit the tin of glue in my pocket, puncturing the metal and causing the solvent to leak all down my trousers. After it had happened he ran one way and I ran the other.

I only noticed this once I'd come down and for a while I couldn't work out what had happened. Had I fallen somehow? Then I really thought about it, and had a flashback of Billy approaching me with the blade. The following day he called at Margaret's, sheepishly asking her if I was all right.

'Sure he is,' she said. 'He's in his bed. Go on up and wake him up.'

Gingerly, Billy knocked the door and came in. I'd just woken up. His face was a picture.

'Are ye OK, Chambers?' he said.

'Aye. Why shouldn't I be?'

'It's just that . . . you know . . . the knife and all.'

Now I remembered. 'Ah yeah, no worries,' I said, 'I always knew you had shite aim.' Then I pulled out the tin of glue and showed him the hole he'd made. The look of relief on his face was a picture and we both had a laugh about it all. The Jam's 'Thick as Thieves' always reminds me of my friendship with Billy:

Times were so tough, but not as tough as they are now
We were so close and nothing came between us and the world

No personal situations
Thick as thieves us, we'd stick together for all time
And we meant it but it turns out just for a while
We stole the friendship that bound us together . . .

Incidents like this were not unusual in the brutal streets of Loyalist West Belfast, and as I neared the end of school they were increasing in frequency. Margaret and Richard must've known that within me were the makings of a 'hood' – a teenage tearaway who would cause as much trouble as possible before he was either kneecapped by the paramilitaries or taken into their ranks. This was a common route kids like me followed back then. Margaret did her best with me, getting me a job at the local VG store on the Woodvale Road. The owner was a friend of snooker star Alex 'Hurricane' Higgins and he often came into the shop. I managed to get his autograph just after he won the world title.

Oddly, it was around this time that my Christianity deepened. I'd become bored with what I saw as the bland services that went on at St Andrews and was looking for something more powerful. I was also sick of Reverend Lewis's stock answer for everything – 'God moves in mysterious ways' – and I wanted more from my religion. Perhaps I wanted to maintain my connection with Dad through a deeper relationship with God. Whatever the reason, I started to attend a Pentecostal church on the Shankill Road – one of these places where people spoke in tongues and waved their arms frantically in the air as they received the Holy Spirit. There were mad sessions of praying and faith healing (although these never seemed to work) and the music was more upbeat and fun to sing. It was a scream, literally, and I really enjoyed it for a time.

I was working at the VG with another member of this congregation, who I knew as 'brother George'. He was younger than me and clearly had what we might politely describe as 'learning difficulties'. When the shop was quiet, he and I would sneak into the storeroom, get down on our knees, pray and praise the Lord. I would lead these prayers, thinking that perhaps I had the makings of a minister or a pastor. One day, the shift manager Lexi walked in on us as we sang our praises to the heavens.

'What the fuck are youse two eejits doing?' he said, after a shocked pause.

Shamefaced, we got up off our knees, brushed ourselves down and went back to work. Praying was one of the more innocent pastimes you could indulge along the Shankill but I must admit that it did look a bit strange. Even so, I kept going with the Pentecostal services and prayer meetings alongside the rioting and glue-sniffing and shoplifting. There would be huge gatherings that I'd attend in the Ulster Hall and I remember being moved to tears by the gospel singing of a black woman who was over from England. I stared at her in astonishment – black people were a real rarity in Belfast back then. There were only two I knew, one from Shankill and the other in Glencairn. Looking back, it's hard to explain or reconcile these two aspects of my personality – my Christianity and my recklessness – except to say that these were very mad times indeed, and they provoked some very peculiar responses.

Certainly, I needed something to focus on. I was heading for a big fat zero in terms of school exams, mainly because I often didn't show up for lessons, spending hours by the glens and swimming in the Spoon in the summer. I was about to turn sixteen and already I felt like I'd been written off. I was one of the many kids that the education system in Belfast completely failed. For the majority growing up where I did, there were very few options. Just surviving the madness all around me was my main priority. The idea of going on to do A levels then study at university was laughable, I didn't know anybody in my family or circle of friends who fell into that category and at this time that was normal where I lived. And the teachers themselves appeared not to give a shit. They were probably only too glad to see us walk down the school drive for the very last time. Some of the teachers were afraid and in awe of their pupils as they were the offspring of Loyalist leaders, and many of my contemporaries would go on to take up arms and fight the IRA. Laughing and joking, we ritually set our school ties on fire and headed to the shop to buy tins of beer and cider.

The only two things that school gave me were a love of books and reading, and – when I turned eighteen – financial compensation for forcing me to do PE at the time I broke my weak leg. That shouldn't have happened and Granny Chambers was on to the local authority like a ton of bricks. As part of the claim I was taken to see Professor Adair, a specialist at one of the Belfast hospitals. Before we went in, Granny demanded that I exaggerate my limp so my compensation would be guaranteed. I did as I was told but I'm sure it didn't fool the specialist. In any case, my leg was bad enough without needing to act. My right leg has never been as strong as my left leg, plus there is a lot of muscle wastage and scars. I've never been able to bend it fully and this was made worse after my school leg break. So we were delighted when the news came that I would receive the money – eight grand – on my eighteenth birthday. I had plans to share it with my sisters, brother and grandparents, but something deep down told me this might not go according to plan.

Now that I was sixteen, I could qualify for a council flat of my own, and after a bit of string-pulling here and there with legendary Shankill housing officer Fenton Butler I was allocated a maisonette back up in Glencairn. Margaret and Richard probably sighed with relief when I finally threw my bits and pieces in my old kitbag and headed off up to the estate once again. By this time they were starting a family of their own and I guess the last thing they needed was a troublesome teen under their roof. Still, while I was there they were brilliant with me and I can never repay the kindness and love they showed me during those difficult times.

At the time I was a scruffy wee sod, still in Alistair's hand-me-downs and whatever I could occasionally afford, which wasn't much. It was the early 1980s, but my dress sense was firmly in the late 1970s and our Margaret could see this was a bit embarrassing for a teenager who wanted to look cool.

'You spend so much time listening to The Jam and The Who,' she said one day. 'Why don't you just become a Mod?'

I wasn't convinced. I loved the music, and by now I was into Secret Affair, The Chords, The Lambrettas, The Selecter,

Madness, The Specials. I'd fallen for it all, but I wasn't sure about going the whole hog and dressing like the bands I admired, probably because I could never afford to be like Paul Weller, in his top-dollar Fred Perry and Lonsdale gear, and didn't want to show myself up by looking like a cut-price version. But Margaret had other ideas.

'I'm gonna take you down the town next Saturday,' she said, 'and get you some of those wee loafers and a Mod haircut. How about that?'

Well, I could hardly refuse my big sister and when the weekend arrived she came good on her promise. By now I was aware there was a collection of Mods hanging about Belfast centre, posing on their scooters outside the City Hall, and I longed to join them. At that time I was hanging out with Mods from Ballysillan and the Shankill and breaking out of those circles would take a while. Even so, a pair of loafers and a Welleresque haircut was a good start. Richard fell into heaps of laughter when I returned home after the makeover – he was always teasing the hell out of me, like I was his kid brother – but despite that I was really pleased with how I looked. I turned this way and that in the mirror, checking out my new hair and promising myself that as soon as I laid hands on that compensation money, a shiny silver Vespa would be mine. I would be the best-dressed Mod in Glencairn.

Back on Glencairn, I started to spend more time with a few mates, including a girl called Lizzy. She was well known on the estate for being a tough cookie and she'd never back down from a fight. Lizzy was a rebellious soul who didn't care what people thought of her, which is maybe why she breached all the rules of the estate by going with a Catholic boy called Sean, who came from the Short Strand area of the city. Her relatives did not approve at all, but Lizzy persisted and eventually she and Sean had a baby together. As ever, the sectarian difficulties involved eventually broke up the relationship, but Lizzy and Sean stayed friendly for the sake of the child.

Sometimes, Billy and I would go up to Lizzy's flat after a session on the glue and we'd sit round drinking cans of lager and talking rubbish. The four of us – me, Billy, Lizzy and Sean – were there one damp early autumn night when we were shaken out of our stupor by a huge commotion outside.

'Open up! C'mon!' shouted a male voice. 'Open up now, before we break down the fuckin' door!'

'Who the fuck's that?' said Sean, looking up slowly. 'Are youse expecting anyone?' His words were slurred but underneath them I could detect a note of panic.

'Dunno,' said Lizzy. 'Who cares? Just ignore 'em, they'll go away.'

Far from disappearing, the banging grew louder. Muffled shouts could be heard from beyond the cheap, battered wooden door.

'They're gonna wake the we'an up,' said Sean. Their little son was sleeping soundly upstairs.

'I think they're gonna hoof the door in,' I said.

Now we were alert. Judging by the insistency of the knock it was clear this was no ordinary visit. Only soldiers, cops or paramilitaries hammered on doors in that way, and it was unlikely to be the first two. Sean's face was white with fear – as well it should've been. There was only one reason left for a late-night visit. Catholics who ventured on to Glencairn ran the risk of a severe beating from Loyalist paramilitaries. Or worse.

'Are you gonna open it, Lizzy?' he said nervously.

'It's either that or they're gonna kick the fuckin' thing in,' she replied.

Sean threw a panicked glance around the room. 'Should I run out the kitchen window?' he said.

'The boys'll be round the back already, so they will,' she said.

I'd already guessed that. Unwanted visitors always covered all bases, rarely letting their victims escape scot-free. In a word, we were fucked.

Sean looked over at his terrified ex. The local UDA commander had already posted written warnings to anyone, male or female, consorting with Catholics – 'the enemy'. We all knew what happened when you broke the rules. Sean had repeatedly ignored pleas from Lizzy not to visit and would turn up, late at night, drunk or high, or both. He was running a terrible risk, but although they'd split they'd remained on reasonably good terms and he wanted to see his son.

'All right,' he said, getting up slowly, 'I'll see who it is . . .'

Glue-sniffing was how we met Sean in the first place. Of course, kids from across the Protestant/Catholic divide were at it, and ironically such bad habits actually helped to break down barriers. Lizzy had some friends on an estate close to the town and they were glue-sniffing down there. Eventually they invited me and Billy to meet up with them. We were nervous, as the estate was predominately Catholic, but Lizzy had said we needn't worry.

'They're just into sniffing and having the craic,' she'd said. 'There's nothing else going on with them.'

We were just sixteen-year-olds keen to break out of the bleak reality of Glencairn and see other parts of our city. Besides, these boys were sniffers like us, so at least we'd have something in common.

We found we got on with Sean and his mates rather better than we could've expected. In my head, it was still taboo to associate with Catholics, and I was meant to hate them with all my heart, but Sean was an all right guy.

So we spent hours hanging about down there and I found Sean to be not that different from me, although we never strayed on to conversations about religion or politics – the twin taboo subjects for everyone in Northern Ireland at that time.

We didn't tell anyone else around Glencairn where we were going; it wouldn't have gone down well at all. Eventually, Lizzy and Sean found a place to live, with their new baby, in Manor Street. This was close to the notorious Crumlin Road jail, and a Catholic area. The street itself was divided: one end Catholic, the other end Protestant.

The relationship was very volatile, reflecting the times in Belfast then. Their lives were chaotic. One time, Sean took me and Billy out and we broke into a sports shop, stealing a load of sports equipment and other bits and pieces that we planned to sell and raise some funds for glue and beer. We stashed this in Sean's place along Manor Street and thought we'd got clean away with it – that is, until the police turned up about an hour after we'd arrived home. We heard later that an undercover army surveillance team was keeping watch on a noted 'Provie' in a house nearby and, seeing us bringing home our loot, had immediately called the cops. We were lucky to get off with a warning.

A small damp terraced house in the middle of a conflict zone was hardly the place to raise a child and so Lizzy eventually came back to Glencairn, where a council flat was provided for her. Despite the warnings, Sean's visits to the estate continued and soon the UDA found out. Lizzy received a personal message that spelled out, in no uncertain terms, that there would be trouble if Sean was seen around the estate again. You'd have thought that a paramilitary threat would've been enough to put anyone off visiting enemy territory, but it didn't seem to stop Sean – hence the knock at the door.

He opened it, and on the step stood a group of five lads, no older than about eighteen or nineteen. A hard-faced boy with an evil-looking scar running down his cheek was at the front of the group, announcing himself as the boss. We knew who he was, of course: Macky, the unofficial leader of the younger UDA members across the estate, and he had close contact with more senior commanders.

'Hi, Sean,' he said. 'We heard you were here . . . again. We want a word.'

Pushing Sean back through the hall, the gang entered the maisonette and slammed the door shut.

'Ach, come on fellas,' Lizzy protested, 'he's only after seein' the we'an. He's making no trouble. Let him off, and I'll promise he won't come back again.'

'I'm sorry, Lizzy,' Macky said, looking guilty, 'but you can't say you wasn't warned. We're gonna give him a bit of a kicking, like it or not. Maybe you should go in the kitchen.'

We did as we were told. We shut the door and sat at the rickety kitchen table and, silently, listened to Sean getting the hiding of his life. Luckily for him, they'd come with no weapons: no baseball bats, sticks, knuckledusters or nunchakus. No firearms, either. Yet it could easily have come to that had the senior UDA men wished it.

Even so, the sound of fists and boots connecting with flesh was nauseating. Sean seemed to be pinging off every badly constructed wall. I hoped he wouldn't try to resist, because if he did it would be much worse for him. We could hear sectarian insults raining upon him as heavily as the blows he was taking.

'Fuckin' Taig!'

'Bog-trotter bastard!'

'Fenian cunt!'

After fifteen long minutes the violence stopped. The kitchen door opened and Macky's head popped round it. 'We're done,' he said. 'Sorry about the mess, Lizzy. And sorry about Sean. You know, he's probably the best thing that ever happened to you . . .'

We stood open-mouthed. Did Macky just say that? Yes he did, and meant it too. But such was the state of Northern Ireland that any personal feelings had to be put aside in pursuit of the war. It was a brutal country, with no room for empathy of any sort, and Catholics were our mortal enemies.

The attackers left and we watched out of the kitchen window as a battered Sean fled down the hill, across a field and out of the estate, his yellow puffa jacket now streaked red with his own blood.

'I guess that's the end of him,' said Lizzy. 'Hopefully he's not dumb enough to come back again.'

'Hope not,' I replied. 'Because next time he's a dead man, for sure.'

It was just another night on a bleak Belfast estate. Beatings were nothing new; I'd heard and seen enough of them already to last me a lifetime. Most people hated the thought of it – though there were plenty of psychopaths in both camps who relished violence for violence's sake – but it was just part of everyday existence, along with everything else. We endured, not enjoyed, the situation.

CHAPTER 10

M id-November 1982: I sat bolt up in bed, jerked out of a deep sleep by the fusillade of cracks that had just sounded a few yards from where I was staying in Glencairn. We were used to hearing gunshots, of course, but they'd only ever come from the various boundaries between the Shankill and Falls roads, unless it was a local punishment shooting.

Instinct told me not to look out of the bedroom window immediately. The gunman, or gunmen, might still be around and take a pot-shot at you for being nosey. You might also get fingered as a witness, leading to unwelcome visits from the RUC or army. The worst thing would be to be known as a 'tout', or an informer, which would put you in severe danger of a beating or of death at the hands of the paramilitaries.

Within thirty seconds of the shots I heard the squeal of tyres as a getaway vehicle left the estate at high speed. Now it was safe to look. I ran to the window and peered round the edge of my thin curtains. Already, people were leaving their homes and running towards a white Rover car that had stopped at the back of some homes on Forthriver Road, a couple of streets across from my flat. Its engine was running and the car's headlights were on. Even at fifty yards I could see that its windows were shattered and bullets had torn through the bodywork. Instinctively, I knew that in the car were the bloodied remains of some poor individual targeted for whatever reason – a Catholic, a Protestant, a policeman or a soldier, or just an innocent civilian caught up in the kind of inter-paramilitary feuds that happened all the time around here.

Without hesitation I threw on a T-shirt, jeans and a coat, and ran out of the back door to join the rest of the mob now milling around the car. Incidents like this always provoked a ghoulish fascination among those living close by, myself included, and like the others I'd never think twice about getting a closer look. It was just part and parcel of the horrific obsession with terrorism, death and destruction that was a living nightmare for everyone in Northern Ireland, particularly those of us trapped in the estates around Belfast and Londonderry.

As I got nearer the car, I could see the form of a dark-haired figure slumped half-in, half-out of the driver's door. He (I assumed it was a 'he', but at that moment it was hard to tell) was covered in blood, which was pouring from his body on to the pavement. The distant wail of sirens coming our way heralded the fact that someone had called the emergency services. Within minutes they would surround the place, forcing us all back behind the barriers as they carried out their investigations before removing body and vehicle.

For now, though, we were free to get up as close as we liked.

I'd seen bodies before but nothing ever prepares you for the sight of a freshly murdered man shot to death by high-velocity weapons. His head hung low and the blood that was flowing from his nose and mouth made him look like he was weeping thick red tears. I recognised a couple of leading UDA men who were milling around the Rover. They looked extremely serious as they muttered among themselves. Here and there, a bystander would come up to the men, have a word, take a look at the body and walk away. There seemed to be no anger, no outrage – the atmosphere was weirdly calm, in a way you wouldn't expect from something that had all the hallmarks of a Provie 'hit'. I knew one of the younger lads now engaged in conversation with a paramilitary and when he'd finished I sidled over to him and led him to a quiet spot out of earshot of anyone else.

'What's goin' on?' I said. 'Who's the dead man? Why's everyone acting so normal?'

The lad looked around to see if anyone was listening to us. 'Promise to shut yer hole,' he said, 'and I'll tell ye . . .'

I nodded, and he leant his mouth toward my right ear. 'It's Murphy,' he said. 'You know . . . the Butcher?'

My eyes widened and I turned around to look at the dead man in the car. The black curly hair, the slight frame, the flashy gold necklace. It was him, all right. I'd seen him many times around the Shankill and Glencairn . . . Lenny Murphy, the leader of the notorious Shankill Butchers, who'd kidnapped and tortured both Catholics and Protestants and regularly dumped the bodies by our house and the community centre. The gang that invaded my nightmares as a young boy and were forever only spoken of in whispers. We all knew that Murphy had been released from jail earlier in the year. The paramilitary bosses expected him to be a good boy from then on, but rumour had it that he'd resumed his campaign of torture and death. Now he was the victim and there was a long list of people who wanted him dead, Republican and Loyalists.

'What the f—? How the fuck did . . .?'

Again, my pal leant in close to my ear. 'The Provies done him,' he said.

'Dead on,' I said with sarcasm. 'How could they get up here and away without being spotted?'

The lad shrugged before melting away into the crowd. Clearly, he wanted to say more but didn't dare. I was amazed. Paramilitaries were constantly posted on lookout right across Glencairn. In the old days my dad had been one of those doing this job for the UDA. No one came into and left this estate without their knowledge. If the IRA had done it, they were either suicidally brave or those lookouts had, for some reason, not been required to do their job this night. I'd heard mutterings of Murphy being a 'bad animal' and bringing shame on the Loyalist paramilitaries, especially when he made the mistake of killing Protestants. For years, Glencairn had been associated with the aftermath of the Butchers' murders and although it wasn't exactly the most salubrious place in Belfast, this kind of reputation brought dishonour on us all.

As the hours went by the story began to be pieced together. Lenny Murphy's girlfriend lived on Glencairn and he regularly visited her. Glencairn being wholly Protestant, Murphy would've assumed he was safe, but clearly someone was watching his movements carefully. A day or so after the murder the IRA issued this statement:

> *'Lenny Murphy (master butcher) has been responsible for the horrific murders of over twenty innocent nationalists in the Belfast area and a number of Protestants. The IRA has been aware for some time that since his release recently from prison, Murphy was attempting to re-establish a similar murder gang to which he led in the mid-seventies and, in fact, he was responsible for a number of the recent sectarian murders in the Belfast area. The IRA takes this opportunity to restate its policy of non-sectarian attacks, while retaining its right to take unequivocal action against those who direct or motivate sectarian slaughter against the nationalist population.'*

We all knew that an IRA 'hit' like this couldn't have happened without help from the other side. No one would confirm that, of course. But neither did anyone deny it. Exactly what had gone on between Republicans and Loyalists was never fully explained, but it seemed very clear that the UDA and/or UVF had wanted rid of Murphy and hadn't wanted to do it themselves. Rumours circulated about the Loyalist and Republican paramilitaries joining forces to get rid of a mutual problem, and the rumours persist to this day.

All I could think was 'good riddance'.

Meanwhile, the authorities were hoping that us Protestant kids would find ways of meeting and collaborating with our Catholic counterparts in a far less violent way. The powers that be felt that if Us and Them worked together, we would find that we were all the same under the skin. As ever, it was a typically simplistic government approach to a very complicated problem and those of us who'd left school without any qualifications were to be the guinea pigs.

Anyone who was a teen in the early 1980s will remember the dreaded YTS – the Youth Training Scheme. If you weren't going to college and hadn't got a full-time job, you were forced to go on one of these things. They weren't much more than cheap labour in low-skilled occupations, and in Northern Ireland we had the added pleasure of being forced to work alongside the enemy in the hope that we'd all put down the bricks, bottles and bullets and become best friends forever. As if . . .

Reluctantly, I signed up for such a scheme based on the Crumlin Road, just down from the Ardoyne. I was told that Catholic boys would be attending this too, but I had no choice – it was either this or go without money. By now I'd had a few non-violent brushes with Catholics – Fiona in the hospital and Lizzy's ex-boyfriend Sean – and they hadn't turned out to be as bad as I'd been led to believe, or have horns and be smelly. True, I was still going down to the Crumlin Road/Ardoyne interface and enjoying a good riot. But this was kids' stuff, even though we young rioters from either side didn't quite realise that, little by little, we were being groomed into the clutches of the paramilitary organisations who ran most of the local youth clubs and discos.

Ironically, one of the YTS instructors was Davy Payne, a legendary leading UDA commander. By this time he'd left the UDA, the result of some feud or other, and had set himself up as a community worker advocating cooperation between Protestants and Catholics. However, his reputation as a hard man who'd allegedly tortured and killed a number of people went before him. It's hard to believe that he was put in charge of a bunch of Catholics, given his deep-rooted hatred of them, but those were the crazy times we all lived in. I used to think he was an easy target for an IRA hit squad from Ardoyne bent on revenge and I'm sure it must have crossed his mind too.

My job involved painting various places, including the Maze racecourse and a Catholic chapel up near Ardoyne. Us Prods found it weird being in there and some wrote Loyalist graffiti on the walls. Given it was wintertime, the cold and rain seeped into my bones and each day felt like eight hours of sheer misery. A bus took us, Protestants and Catholics, out to the workplace and we were all pissed off by the work and the freezing conditions. One time we drove past a group of Catholic lads standing on a street corner, who immediately began to hurl stones at the bus when we stopped at a traffic light. Maybe they'd spotted my Union Jack shirt, which I wore constantly as part of my new identity as a Mod. In any case, the Catholics on the bus took immediate offence, shouting and screaming for the lads on the corner to pack it in. We Protestants had a laugh that our Catholic colleagues were getting a wee taste of their own medicine.

We got on with the Catholics on a superficial level but deeper down there was still a huge amount of suspicion, fear and downright hatred on both sides. One of my Catholic colleagues was a lad by the name of Begley, and many years later I learned he was the brother of Thomas Begley, the IRA man who in 1993 walked into Frizzell's fish shop on the Shankill Road carrying a bomb. It exploded, killing him, a UDA member and eight members of the public, injuring dozens of others – an outrage that still causes pain on the Shankill. I knew many of those victims from Glencairn, school and the surrounding areas.

I also knew that not all these Catholic boys were bad. I knew they weren't all terrorists or at least supporters of the IRA. There were many good kids among us. Although I still didn't dare speak a word about it, the idea that I was part-Catholic wasn't as terrible to me as it once had been. I could see that all of us living in West and North Belfast, Catholics and Protestants alike, were just trying to exist amid brutal and dangerous conditions. We were all human. I realised I didn't hate Catholics – I just hated the paramilitaries who acted in their name and killed innocent Protestant and Catholic people alike. And for that reason, plus my family's UDA links, it was inevitable that I would get swept into the tide of active sectarianism. At seventeen, I was exactly the right age to be groomed, and one incident convinced me that I should lay my cards on the table and do what I saw as the right thing by Loyalism.

One night, as usual, I was in the nearby park with Billy, glue-sniffing our heads off. A gang of boys our age were hanging about nearby, some of whom were junior members of the UVF. This must have been during one of the frequent feuding periods with the UDA because the boys wandered over, making threatening gestures and accusing us of being from the rival group. Within seconds this turned to a scuffle; blows and insults were exchanged but the fight dissipated as quickly as it had started.

That wasn't the end. Billy had taken a blow to the nose and no way were we going to let that go. Discreetly, we observed the gang mooch off, the leader now with a similarly aged girl in tow. We followed them, then diverted off the path and sneaked behind a tree, waiting for him to come past. When he did, we jumped out and gave him a digging he wouldn't forget in a hurry. The girl ran off squealing as we piled into her boyfriend. Leaving him in a heap we ran off laughing. I went home, locked the door and cracked open a can of lager and a new bag of glue, pleased that I'd got one up on that little UVF piece of shite.

My triumph wasn't to last. A couple of hours later there were a series of loud bangs on the door. I tried to ignore it, reassuring myself that it was locked. But I knew that wouldn't stop them. If I didn't answer they'd kick it through.

'Don't even think o' fighting back, you wee fucker,' snarled the leader as the gang pushed their way in. They forced me back into my living room and, with fists, feet and baseball bats, gave me the hiding of my life. I knew them all, and they were good Loyalist boys just like me. I'd been to school with most of them. That didn't stop them smashing my arm and leaving me feeling that every other bone in my body was broken too. I was taken to the Royal Victoria Hospital in town, the place I'd spent so much time in during my childhood, to be fixed up by doctors who treated similar paramilitary-related injuries on a daily basis.

I was in for a few days, and during my stay I had a visit from a male relative with close connections to the UDA.

'Well, now,' he said. 'What have ye learned from this?'

'That I shouldn't pick on UVF boys?'

He laughed. 'Aye, maybe. But more than that – do you not think it's time you had some protection?'

'Huh?'

'C'mon – ye know what I'm sayin'. How long have we been asking you to join us? Now here's your moment.'

I thought about it. I wasn't interested in planting bombs or shooting anyone, that was for sure. It was almost inevitable that I'd join the UDA one day, and I had a half-romantic notion about taking the war to the IRA and fighting for my people, plus lots of my school friends had already joined the UDA or UVF. That said, the UDA weren't just paramilitaries. They ran schemes for kids like me on the estate and they genuinely looked after people. And if anyone was to ever beat the hell out of me again, they'd get it back twice as brutally.

'All right,' I said, 'consider me in.'

'Good man,' said my relative, looking pleased. The senior UDA guys would be delighted to have reeled in another one for the cause. As I mentioned, the UDA was still legal, although I had no intention of getting involved in the paramilitary side of things.

A few days later I went down to the Shankill and met a man I knew was a senior member of the Shankill UDA. He took me down to the bottom of the Shankill overlooking Peters Hill, produced a Bible, and told me he would swear me in, there and then. I suppressed a giggle, thinking this was more like the Boy

Scouts. The man saw me about to laugh and clipped me round the ear.

'I think you should take this very seriously,' he said, pointing to the Bible. 'This is not a game, so it isn't.'

Immediately I straightened up and did as I was told. With bible in one hand, I repeated the words whispered furtively to me as the man looked round for anyone coming. They went something like this:

'I, John Chambers, am a Protestant by birth, do swear to defend my comrades and my country by any and all means against Republicanism.

'I further swear that I will never divulge any information about my comrades to anyone and I am fully aware that the penalty for such an act of treason is death. I willingly take this oath on the Holy Bible witnessed by my peers.'

Within seconds I was a part of Ulster's largest paramilitary force.

'I, John Chambers, am a Protestant by birth . . .' True, I guess. Except for one small technical detail – my Catholic mother, whose name and religion I never dared speak, especially to the hard man of the UDA standing right in front of me . . .

CHAPTER 11

MOD! The very word sent a thrilling shiver up my spine. I was already wearing some of the clothing that eighties Mods were fond of – boating blazers, Fred Perry shirts, Lonsdale T-shirts, badger shoes (so-called because they were striped black and white), Union Jack T-shirts and the iconic parka – a proper one – which I got in the army surplus shop in the Shankill.

As I developed as a Mod, I started wearing sixties' style clothes and we often visited the charity shops as they always had loads of original Mod clothes for sale. Also, my taste in music evolved and I started getting into soul and Northern Soul, spending ages trying to learn to do the soul step. I remember once trying to do this while on acid at the Delta club. It wasn't my greatest moment, I have to say, and my cool image took a hit that night.

I could hardly wait for the day I turned eighteen, because that was when my compensation money would arrive and I had my eye on a Vespa scooter that would turn every head on Glencairn.

In a way, being a Mod suited my conflict of identity. My life had always been full of contradictions. I was part-Catholic, although that religion had never played a part in my life, yet I'd signed up for a Loyalist paramilitary organisation. I was a fierce Loyalist, yet a pacifist. I couldn't envisage killing anyone. If Gerry Adams himself had walked into my line of fire I couldn't have pulled the trigger. That kind of thing wasn't me at all.

Just like Jimmy, the central character in *Quadrophenia*, the best film about Mods ever made and the soundtrack to my Mod lifestyle, I was pulled in all directions. Who was 'The Real Me'? Like many youngsters, then and now, I was trying on all sorts of guises to see which would fit best, but in the heated political situation of Northern Ireland in the early 1980s you needed to decide pretty damn quick whose side you were on.

Mod gave me an identity. I loved looking cool and sharp, which did me no harm at all when it came to the girls. I found I could walk the walk and talk the talk, and I had no problem turning female heads on Glencairn and up the Shankill – anywhere pretty girls hung out. I started to spend time in the Ballysillan area, just above the Shankill, and met fellow Loyalist Mods, many of whom were also signed up to or had family in the UDA or UVF. The paramilitaries were quick to spot the growing trend and started to put on Mod nights in their clubs and shebeens. We'd turn up in our parkas, loafers, Ben Sherman shirts and Sta-Prest trousers, looking the dog's bollocks and ready to party. We went to Friday night paramilitary-run discos in the Silverstream community centre and Ballysillan leisure centre. This is where I met Sonya, my first serious girlfriend and a fellow Mod. While most of my mates and the male population fantasised about big-boobed blondes I had always been more attracted to mixed-race girls and use to fancy the Indian squaws in the old cowboy films. Sonya was mixed-race on her dad's side and I thought she was beautiful. We went out on and off for a while and moved in the same Mod circles for many years after we split up.

I sneered at the mainstream fashions of the time, like heavy metal and New Romantic groups like the Human League – although secretly I liked some of their tunes. All these soppy wee boys wearing horrible sports casual gear and desperately trying to grow moustaches. And the Catholics were even worse – Jesus, which teenager in their right mind would wear a jumper and a tweed jacket? Seemingly, lots of Catholic boys did, using Martin McGuinness as some kind of style icon.

As ever, violence was a constant companion. There were frequent running battles with skinhead gangs from Glencairn and the Shankill. They'd attend the same discos and parties as we did in the Shankill leisure centre and it would be a poor night indeed if we didn't all have a big punch-up to round it off. Among these skinheads was a tough little character called Johnny Adair. He wasn't big, but he made up for his lack of stature with a fearsome reputation as a fighter. He was in a band too, and was a leading light in the youth wing of the UDA. Years later he would become perhaps the most notorious Loyalist paramilitary of them all – but he has his own tales to tell of those times, so let's leave him to his street battles and return to music, girls and clothes.

Once there was a rumour going about for days that there would be a big battle between the Mods and skinheads taking place in Woodvale Park on the following Saturday. Everyone was talking about it and on the day me and Billy had a sniff of glue before heading up to the Woodvale Park in anticipation of the fight to come. When we got there, we couldn't see any other Mods, but there seemed to be hundreds of skinheads. When they spotted the two of us they chased us out of the park and halfway down the Shankill. I was terrified, as if they had caught us they would have beaten us to a pulp.

Then there were drugs. Despite the paramilitaries' fear and loathing of anything more mood-altering than Harp or Guinness, and despite the threat of kneecapping or worse for taking them, we young Northern Irish mods took to a whole range of uppers, downers and psychedelics with the same enthusiasm as our counterparts on the mainland. And perhaps with even more enthusiasm, because if everyday life was bad in Thatcher's England, Wales or Scotland, believe me it was five times worse in Northern Ireland. We had more to escape from than everyone else put together and if we had the chance to get out of our heads, we took it. Well, I certainly did.

Glue was my gateway into drugs and of course I'd started sniffing with my mates while at school. Timebond was my adhesive of choice, though I didn't mind Evo-Stik and would even resort to Bridgeport – used to fix punctures to bicycle tyres – if I was desperate. Us sniffers couldn't get enough of the stuff and with limited funds we'd shoplift it where we could. I was once waiting for a friend outside a builder's yard off the Shankill when I noticed a truck pull up. To my delight, I watched as the delivery driver unloaded box after box of my beloved Timebond and stacked them against a warehouse wall.

It was too good an opportunity to miss. I persuaded my cousin Pickle, who didn't sniff glue, to help me and that night we nipped down to the builder's yard and removed box after box of the stuff, which we took up to Glencairn and hid at Davey's, a friend of mine who also enjoyed a good sniff. Naturally, I got high on my own supply and went off to the local park, where I lay on the grass and watched the stars drift across the heavens in their timeless dance.

A few days of glue-bingeing and I was soon after getting hold of more solvent. I went up to Davey's to help myself to my stash and was surprised to see a queue of kids outside his house. I joined the line and when I got to the front I was amazed to see Big Barbara, Davey's ma, taking orders.

'Hi, John,' she said breezily, 'how aboutcha? How many tins are ye after?'

I couldn't believe her cheek and demanded to see Davey right away.

'What the fuck's goin' on here?' I said, when he finally came down from his bedroom.

'It's her,' he said, nodding towards his mum. 'She's been trying this stuff and has got right into it. She's been dancing in the street in her knickers, and saying all sorts of bad shite to people.'

I looked at Big Barbara. Her eyes were red and she had that glazed, hang-dog expression that goes hand-in-hand with the happy sniffer. I figured that she'd tried it, liked it and had decided to turn the rest of Glencairn on to it – at a price, of course. Cutting my losses I grabbed a few more tins of Timebond and headed off to my favourite spot to lose my mind again.

Next came marijuana. There was a suspicion cannabis, hashish – whatever you want to call it – was only for hippies, but as this particular peace-loving subculture was rarely spotted in Belfast, we Mods thought we'd have some of it for ourselves. Philip, a Mod acquaintance from Ballysillan, had a Jack Russell terrier he'd thoughtfully named 'Paul Weller' and we always found it hilarious that a couple of Belfast kids like us had 'Paul Weller' trailing behind us wherever we went. Phil also had a sister known locally as Mad Maggie, who worked in a local butcher's. I was round one afternoon when Maggie came home from her shift with a bag of off-cuts, mainly pig's trotters, that her boss had given her.

She was away on a date and ordered us to keep an eye on the trotters, which she'd put to boil on the cooker. The smell of these things was diabolical, but she was Mad Maggie and no one dared mess with her. So we did as we were told, and decided we'd get stoned in the process. We smoked joint after joint, giggling at stupid stuff in the way only stoned teenage boys can, while Paul Weller looked at us from the floor in disgust. Finally, an attack of the munchies overtook us but, as ever on Glencairn, the cupboard was bare.

There was only one thing for it. We turned off the pan, drained the trotters and scoffed the lot – meat, marrow, hair, toenails and God knows what else. Now and then we'd throw a bit to the disgruntled Paul Weller, who hid his small share behind the bin in disgust. Obviously, he was hoping to save them for later, but when he settled down for a nap we tip-toed over him and nicked the lot. Soon after Phil and I fell into our own dreamy sleep, which I'd have enjoyed immensely had I not been awakened a few minutes later by a dog trying to lick the face off me. I shook Paul Weller off, stumbled up, washed my face of slobber and put the kettle on.

Just then, Mad Maggie came in with her date. She took one look at me, then saw the two greasy plates on the kitchen table and the empty pan on the stove.

'Jesus, Chambers,' she said, 'you're looking a bit rough. Ruff-ruff . . . geddit?'

I was still in a very hazy state and had no idea what she was getting at. 'What's so feckin' funny?' I said, watching the pair of them cracking up.

'It's youse two,' said the boyfriend. 'Youse've had the dog's dinner, haven't you?'

I stared at Paul Weller, now trying to claw his way up Mad Maggie's legs, mad with hunger. My stomach turned queasily and I thought I was going to boke.

'Those have been lying about the butcher's these last two weeks,' Maggie said. 'They're only fit for himself, Paul Weller, to eat. Now youse have had them. And by the looks of it, you're gonna be looking at yer dinner again pretty soon.'

I needed no further warnings. Grabbing my parka I pushed past them and out of the front, staggering home via a series of discreet alleyways. I vowed it would be the last time I'd get stoned with Paul Weller.

Then there was acid. I knew about this stuff from my

deepening love of the Small Faces, who'd started out as a tight little Mod band in the mid-1960s and had gone all psychedelic towards the end of that decade. If it was good enough for them, I reckoned, it was good enough for me. And so, after a while spent trying to source LSD (not an easy task on Glencairn) I finally manage to obtain a few tabs and in my own crazy way, decided to take three at once during a snowstorm.

I sat in Ballysillan park and watched, fascinated, as the snowflakes drifting earthwards changed from white to a wild variety of colours. It reminded me of the Rainbow River incident a few years previously. I must have been gabbling away ten to the dozen because my mates were looking at me as though I'd gone bananas. 'Enjoy the trip,' one of them said, 'we'll see you later.'

Little did I know that this was only the beginning and I would be locked in a psychedelic world of wonder for the next ten hours. As the night wore on and the acid took hold of me, I began to get paranoid and was seeing things that couldn't possibly be real. The moon had now turned into a giant purple and blue ball of fire and was playing pinball with a million different-coloured stars. I watched in amazement as they bounced off each other and flew across the universe, to suddenly reappear right in front of my nose.

This was weird, and I was getting the sense that I wasn't enjoying it. In an effort to come down, I decided to jog round the park and see if that brought me back to reality. As I trudged through the snow and slid all over the place I gradually started to feel more in control and coming to a shed at the back of some shops I sat down to catch my breath.

Suddenly I heard the familiar driving electronic theme tune of the TV series *Doctor Who* and it seemed to fill every part of my being and soul. Right in front of me I watched gobsmacked as the Tardis materialised from thin air and the blue doors swung opened invitingly. Reality had been suspended and looking around I could see that there was no one or nothing in the universe but me and the Tardis. Taking a few steps forward I entered and the door slammed closed behind me.

I stepped up to the console and fiddling with the time rotor I spun the dials and suddenly the engine started to rev up and the Tardis vibrated violently. The display automatically spun backwards through the years – 1984, 1972, 1960, 1920, 1901, 1876, 1848 and stopped on 1841.

Nervously I pushed the door open and stepped outside – straight into a scene from Victorian England. I was in a busy London street, the sun was shining and people dressed in Victorian clothes were going about their daily business. There were horses and carts everywhere; the smell was appalling and I stood in wonder as I took in the incredible scenes before me.

Although my eyes and ears were telling me I was in Victorian England, somewhere at the back of my acid-infused consciousness I knew I couldn't really have travelled back through time – could I ? Then I panicked – how the hell was I going to get back to Ballysillan and the 1980s?

In my altered state I really did believe that I was now stuck in Victorian England. I didn't consider the sheer ridiculousness of the situation I found myself in; my only concern was getting back to the future and I started to freak out and run up and down the streets, dodging horses and begging people to help me, but they didn't seem to know I was there and this just freaked me out more.

Eventually, I came across the Tardis again and this time it opened from the top and I hurriedly climbed in and closed the door above me. Peace descended as I closed my eyes and tried to block out the nightmare I'd found myself in. I must have fallen asleep and was awoken suddenly as the Tardis started to vibrate again. Opening my eyes I braced myself for another journey through time and space.

By now, I was getting the sense that I'd taken something out of this world. There were moments of clarity when I realised I'd had far too much LSD. Then suddenly, the trip would kick in again and I'd be flying through space and time, destination unknown. Suddenly, the top door of the Tardis opened and light flooded in. To my amazement a man was staring down at me. I was also relieved to see that he was dressed in clothes that were definitely 1980s and not 1800s.

'What the fuckin' Jaysus are you doing in there?' he said. 'Are ye a tramp or somethin'? That's a wild bad place for anyone to sleep, so it is.'

I clambered out and taking in the scene I realised that my Tardis had been an industrial wheelie bin and the guy had come to drop off some rubbish. I had spent the night covered in shit and waste and smelt like a bad weekend.

Holding his nose, the guy offered me a hand and dragged me to my feet. He asked me again what I'd been doing lying in a bin all night. It was a very good question.

'I dunno,' I said, 'but it's been a fuckin' weird night all right.

I dunno how to describe it, really – so I won't. Thanks for helping me out.'

The guy looked as though he had seen a ghost. He nodded and made his way back to his van. I made off down the hill and home for a long soothing bath, during which I had a good long talk with myself about the dangers of acid. But me being me, with my addictive personality, it wasn't long before I was taking another trip, though on a far lower dose. I'd never make that mistake again.

The days ticked down until my eighteenth birthday and soon after it happened I received the long-awaited eight thousand pounds in compensation for my busted leg. Quite rightly, my sister Margaret suggested that I invest it into a property, and back in mid-eighties Belfast I could've got something pretty decent for that kind of money. She always had a good business head on her and she could see that having a house of my own would be a great investment for the future. Realistically, of course, that was never going to happen. An eighteen-year-old like me with eight grand in his back pocket doesn't think logically or sensibly about anything. There were too many clothes to buy, too many records to collect, too many drugs to take, too many girls to charm. And there was also the crowning glory: a Vespa scooter of my very own.

As soon as the cheque was cashed I went out and bought the bike I'd coveted for ages. I went to the scooter shop on the Malone Road, which had cashed in on the Mod revival and had started selling Vespas and Lambrettas. My first bike was a wee brand-new red 100cc Vespa. I added lights and mirrors, a fox tail and Mod logos to it and called it Little Eva for some reason.

I brought it back to Glencairn and decided to take it for an off-road trial around a large piece of open ground. Round and round I went, a good portion of the estate's kids watching me, when the inevitable happened – I skidded and flew off the side of the bike as it crashed to the ground. I swear you could hear the laughter from Glencairn to the Ulster Hall . . .

Then there was the time I was going to work very early one winter morning. Again, the bike skidded and I ended up in a ditch. Cold as it was, I decided to sleep there until I'd sobered up from whatever pills, potions and powders I'd been taking the night before. Another occasion, I'd been riding around town and on the way back home my scooter broke down at the top of the Falls Road. Not a place you really want to break down as a Loyalist, particularly on a scooter. I had to push the bloody thing from the Falls to the Shankill, all the while hoping that some gang or other didn't crawl out of the shadows to ask me what I was doing, where I was going and what religion I was . . .

All that said, these were the greatest days of my life and they were about to get a whole lot more interesting. At some party or other I met Jacqueline McFall, a wee Mod girl from the Shankill area. She was into photography and would take her little camera with her wherever she went. We became best of friends and she took many amazing pictures of the Mod scene around this time, including several of yours truly. By now, I'd gone down the 'psychedelic Mod' route and was rocking a look that wouldn't have disgraced Steve Marriott in 1968 – beads, eyeliner, floral shirts, the lot. I took a lot of ribbing from the traditionalists, plus many others whose paths I crossed, but I didn't care. I knew I looked the dog's bollocks and that's what counted. Also, I was beginning to branch out and away from Glencairn in ways I'd never previously imagined . . .

CHAPTER 12

Owning the scooter meant I no longer had to wait for buses or black taxis that never arrived, or risk walking through heavily Nationalist areas where my eyeliner and beads would attract very unwelcome attention. It was bad enough walking down the Shankill in all the clobber; skirting the Ardoyne or Unity flats as a Loyalist in a paisley-patterned shirt was sheer suicide.

Of course, Mod as a movement wasn't confined to us Prods. We knew that a sizeable number of Belfast Catholics were also into the clothes, the music and the drugs. I'm guessing that not many of them wore Union Jack T-shirts or had red, white and blue roundels painted on their parkas like we did, but aside from that they were just the same as us. Jacqueline's photographs show gangs of boys and girls congregating in several spots around Belfast and no one has 'Catholic' or 'Protestant' tattooed on their forehead. All we see is a gang of young kids smiling, laughing and having fun together – just as it should be when you're that age.

Mod took no notice of religion. There was no place for hatred or division among the scooter boys and girls who gathered on a Saturday afternoon by the City Hall, or drank in the Abercorn bar in Castle Lane (which, ironically, was the scene of an infamous IRA bombing in 1972 that killed two young Catholic women and injured 130 other innocent people – a particularly disgraceful act in a terrifying year). Sectarian insults and deep-rooted suspicions were put aside when Mods from both sides of the fence danced at the Delta club in Donegall Street or drank strong tea and smoked fags in the Capri Cafe in Upper Garfield Street. When Mods gathered, there was no time for this kind of talk. Hanging out, being cool and looking sharp were the only things Mods were interested in. For those moments, all the violence and oppression and misery were put aside.

I say 'put aside' because putting aside such ingrained beliefs was about as much as anyone could do in those deeply divided days. You couldn't forgive or forget, not when there was so much senseless killing happening on both sides. In my view, every outrage committed against our community had to be avenged, and if I heard about IRA men killed by the Brits or the Loyalists I celebrated as happily as I'd always done.

And yet . . . there was still the lurking knowledge that a part of my background was linked to the very community from which the IRA and its Republican offshoots came. Allied to that, I was now one of those Mods who were mixing freely with Catholic boys and girls in the city centre, dancing the night away with them and sharing cigarettes, weed, pills, whatever, in various bars and cafes. My heart was as Protestant and Loyalist as it always had been, but by now my head was telling me that under the skin, we poor sods who were stuck in the middle of a war zone were all the same. Being Belfast kids, we only needed a couple of seconds' conversation to find out where someone was from and what religion they were but when the Mods came together this didn't seem to matter. A person's religion was becoming irrelevant to me, but I still hated the IRA all right.

At first I was nervous. I'd encountered Catholics before, of course, but only when I was younger. Now I was hanging around with Catholic kids who, like me, were already associating with paramilitary groups. Involvement in the UDA, UVF, IRA, INLA (Irish National Liberation Army), etc was born of tradition. It was what you did if you came from Glencairn, Ardoyne, Shankill, Andersonstown. But when you pulled on your mohair suit – and, being newly minted I had a few of these handmade, so I claim to be the best-dressed Mod in Belfast at the time – and fired up your Vespa, your political associations were put aside. We just didn't talk about any of that stuff, and it was better that way.

The more I got to know Catholics, the less I hated them. I was no longer lumping them all into one big bunch of terrorists. The boys I was talking to as we sat astride our scooters by the City Hall, checking out each other's suits, shirts, shoes and girlfriends, had had similar experiences to me. I knew that, and so did they. But on those precious Saturday afternoons, when

151

we all felt young and vibrant and just happy to be alive, none of that mattered. We ignored the madness going on around us as best as we could and yet there was always the possibility of being caught up in a bomb or gun attack from Loyalist or Republican terrorists.

I became friendly with lots of Catholic Mods, including Bobby from the Antrim Road, who became a firm friend. I also hung out with Keith from the Westland and we spent a lot of time together. And in particular Zulu and Tom, two Mods from Ardoyne. One night they invited me up to a club they regularly frequented in their neighbourhood. Like many Loyalist and Republican clubs and bars it had a wire cage around the perimeter and doormen always on guard in case of an attack, which could happen at any time.

All my instincts told me not to go; it was in the middle of Ardoyne, the Catholic enclave bordered by Protestant West Belfast and one of the IRA's most important heartlands. For a Prod, it couldn't be any more dangerous. I imagined how ironic it would be if I was drinking in a Catholic area with Catholic friends and the UFF (Ulster Freedom Fighters) or UVF attacked the place and I was killed. My crazy side, however, ignored all that and, pilled-up and cockily confident, I fell in line behind Tom and Zulu and entered the club.

The three of us stood by the bar in our gear, chatting away ten to the dozen. After I while, I realised that a group of older men on the other side of the bar were staring at me. All the while I knew I should be winding my neck in, keeping my head down and saying very little. By now, though, I was aware I'd already said too much.

Zulu and Tom had already noticed. Tom nipped to the jakes for a pee and on the way back one of the men stopped him, looked over at me and whispered something in his ear. The smile on Tom's face froze as he received the message.

'See those wans over there,' he said as he resumed his position at the bar. 'They reckon they can tell you're a Prod.'

'Fuck, I knew it,' I said. 'They've been eyeballin' me since we walked in.'

My stomach had turned to water. There was no knowing what these hard cases would do if they took a hold of me.

'Here's what's gonna happen,' said Tom. 'You and me will slowly make our way to the back door. Zulu'll keep these fellas talking, then go to the jakes. Then he'll climb out the window. OK?'

I wasn't in a position to argue. The plan went smoothly and within minutes we were out of the door and away as fast as we could. We soon realised that mixing in the city centre on a Saturday was one thing; doing the same in our neighbourhoods was asking for big trouble, and I doubt we'd have got away so easily in Glencairn or Ballysillan.

But as usual I was up for anything and many times I ignored the risks involved, putting myself in real danger. Once I was at a party up the Antrim Rd and a gang of wee Provies came in, asking everyone what religion they were. I lied through my teeth and said I was a Catholic from Manor Street, which was half true as I had been living there at the time. Another night I met a very cute and sexy Mod girl who made a beeline for me and made it clear that if I were to come back to her flat we would have a very good time indeed. I didn't need a second invitation and soon we were in a taxi, speeding through Belfast with a nice handful of pills in my coat pocket.

She wasn't wrong, we had a lot of fun in her flat that night. By the time I'd dragged my head up from the pillow the following morning she'd gone off to work. I lurched into the kitchen, made myself a cup of good strong Nambarrie tea and helped myself to the rest of her loaf of bread. After an hour of mooching about I opened the curtains and looked out at the view. Immediately, a horrible realisation dawned. I was somewhere up in the Divis Tower, a grim but iconic high-rise building in the middle of the fiercely Republican Divis Flats. Many people had been killed, injured or kidnapped within the vicinity of this place, including Jean McConville, a Protestant woman who converted to Catholicism for the sake of her husband. She had ten kids, and her only crime was to help a wounded soldier. For that, she was taken away from her family and murdered by the IRA.

Quietly, I left the flat, gently shutting the door behind me. I made my way down a series of piss-stained stairways, avoiding the strange glances of a few women going in the opposite direction. The bleakness of this place was indescribable; the houses up on Glencairn were bad enough but this was truly a horrible, dangerous and dirty dump. With as much calm as I could muster I left the estate, not looking left, right or behind me, and walked the half-mile or so towards the city centre, where I had a much-needed Ulster Fry to celebrate yet another escape from Republican West Belfast.

Even so, my associations with Catholic boys and girls were becoming ever closer. A very young Catholic boy with a huge

Above left: Me as a chubby baby. We were living in Little Distillery Street at the time (c. 1967).

Above right and centre: Two photos of my sister, Mags. In one, she's held by my Mum (on the left) in 1963, when I was barely a twinkle in Dad's eye. The other picture shows Dad and Mags catching their breath during the Twelfth parades in Belfast, in about 1974.

Below: My siblings and I in a school photo, taken around 1973 – that's yours truly on the left.

Above: One of my lengthy hospital stays. I'm about twelve, and behind the smiles I was depressed and angry. I can't remember the girl's name now, but she was a patient like me and we sometimes visited each other from our respective wards.

Below: It's amazing how quickly I relaxed and made friends. The ties that bind are always stronger than the forces that divide us. In this photo, I'm with Cosmo and Martin, my ward mates. I felt trapped and was bed-bound for months with the frame on my leg.

Above left: Holding my niece, Charlene, on Ottawa Street, where I went to live with Mags and Rick. I was going through my Pentecostal phase at the time, and not long out of Alistair and Betty's, hence the terrible haircut and clothes. 1982.

Above right: Around the time I started getting into the Mod scene – you can see the haircut emerging. Needs some work, but still look cooler than before!

Below: Me – far right – on my precious red Vespa, Little Eva, turning heads on the estate. This was taken outside the Capri Café, where all the Mods use to hang out. I'm talking to Karen Keating, Gloria Hunniford's daughter, who died tragically young of cancer. She was making a documentary which I featured in. You can find it on YouTube if you search for 'Belfast mods'.

These awesome pictures, all taken by Jay McFall, document my teenaged mod-odyssey. I was a real face in the mod community, and just couldn't get enough of the sharp styles. I loved everything about it – still do.

Above: With Phil (left), promotor and manager of the The Score, the band I was in, and Keith (right), a mate from the Westland.

Right: At band practice. I couldn't actually play or sing – I think they wanted me because I look cool ...

Above: In those days of being young and cool, I hoped I'd 'I die before I get old', as The Who famously put it.

Right: With David Holmes, the superstar DJ. Back then he was known as 'Homer', and our paths crossed often in the mod clubs and bars of Belfast and beyond. He's done alright for himself!

© Jay McFall

Above left: Me at twenty-six. I was living in South London at the time and had just started my training in market research, which lead me into advertising, where I really thrived.

Above right: Me with Sim, my wife to be, shortly after we met in the King's Arms. I was skinny as a rake back them and fit as hell, thanks to the mad hours of raving.

Below: This picture was taken minutes after David and I got off the train to meet Mum again for the first time. It doesn't capture all the jangling emotions and nerves of what was one of the most important moments of our lives.

Left: David, Mum and I in her living room, the night we all met. Although things were never perfect, and some questions went unanswered, it's amazing how quickly and deeply our scars healed just having her back in our lives.

Above: Out with mum and her sister in law, Mary, after a bottle of wine or three. Mum and I use to get well plastered and sings Irish songs. She knew the words to the Sash, and we'd howl it out.

Below: Four siblings reunited for a cousin's wedding in the late eighties – they say the Irish do weddings and funerals best of all. I'd have to agree. . .

Above left: I was so lucky to find this beautiful woman, my soul mate. The gods were kind to me for once. And yes, I know, I'm punching well above my weight!

Above right: My beautiful family: Sim, Autumn and Jude. Jude had just broken both his wrist – thought he was superman and jumped of a roof. Painful lesson.

Below left: 'Howdy there, partner!' Playing at Wild West cowboys (and cowgirls) in Blackpool.

Below right: On holiday in Lanzarote, 2019.

The two great loves of my life – beer, and my soulmate, Sim. Not necessarily in that order. We tied the knot after ten years, and been together for twenty-six. Still going strong. Me and Sim, that is – not the beer. Cheers, folks!

passion for music was DJing down the Abercorn and we all got to know and respect this kid, who was barely out of school. His name was David Holmes and he went on to become one of the world's foremost DJs, producers and re-mixers. It's amazing to think that these early experiences in the Mod clubs and cafes inspired him to become the success story he is today.

Meanwhile, I'd gone from chatting to Catholics to actually dating them. I met a girl called Kathy who lived a couple of minutes from the Royal Victoria Hospital along the Falls Road. She was small and very pretty and from the moment we met we had great banter together. She was also a trained hairdresser and would cut my hair for nothing, which was also quite appealing. She could have been the one for me to settle down with, but I was young and had ants in my pants and didn't want to be tied down at the time. Pills and parties were my thing, not tea and nights in front of the telly. Kathy understood this and we were both in it for the craic.

I didn't think about her being Catholic. Well, not much. The issue would only arise when we wanted to visit each other's houses. From the off, Kathy was honest with her parents about the fact she was dating a Protestant and they seemed to be fine about it. We got on well and it was never spoken about, though no doubt that as parents they had their concerns. I liked them too, but I wasn't entirely comfortable spending time in the Falls Road area. Although neither of us told anyone outside of the Mod scene that we were dating someone from the 'other side', these things could become common knowledge very quickly, as I'd previously discovered.

I was always fearful when Kathy wanted to come up to

Glencairn. I made sure nobody was in the flat whenever she came and I told no one she was a Catholic. Kathy had a car (probably another attraction for me) and I remember one night the two of us driving up the Shankill towards Glencairn when we came to a sudden stop. We'd run out of petrol but luckily I knew there was a garage a few hundred yards up the road. Without thinking, I grabbed a battered metal petrol can from her boot and made my way up the road. I filled the can, paid up and strolled back to the car. I arrived to be greeted by a very white-faced Kathy, huddled in her seat so that she was almost under the driver's wheel.

'S'matter wi' you?' I said. 'I've only been a couple of minutes.'

'You fuckin' eejit!' she snapped back. 'Didn't ye think? Wee Catholic girl on her own up the Shankill?'

I hadn't thought, but when I did I felt sick to the stomach. If, for some reason, her identity had been discovered, she'd have been in deep shit. Even young women were shown no mercy if they turned out to be Taigs in the wrong neighbourhood. When we finally returned to my flat, she was still shaking with fear.

The proximity of Catholic kids sometimes brought me back to the dark place – the unspoken secret that rattled around my mind and, at low points, threatened to overwhelm me completely. These crashes would usually happen when I was coming down off whatever I'd been throwing down my neck the previous evening – booze, pills, powders. I'd sit in my flat alone and think about my family – the father I'd adored and lost so early, the mother I'd never known who was out there somewhere, but who wouldn't or couldn't get in touch with us. My sisters, bringing up families without the help of proud grandparents. And to top it all, the endless cycle of violence and misery that was part of the fabric of everyday life in Northern Ireland. *'Today, an RUC man was killed by a car bomb at his home in Portadown . . . Two masked men broke into a house in North Belfast and shot dead a Sinn Fein councillor . . . A Protestant man on his way to work in Newry last night was the victim of a sectarian shooting . . . Two children were badly injured when a bomb went off in central Londonderry. No warning was given . . .'* On and on it went: murders, bombing, riots, robberies, protests, kneecappings, torture, imprisonment. The hedonism and escapism provided by the Mod movement in Belfast was grand while it lasted, but the relentless tide of horror and misery washed it away, day after day after day.

In such low moments, I would feel so trapped that I'd consider suicide. One night, while stoned, I attempted to cut my wrists. At that time, I was down at my sister Jean's in the Woodvale. She found me and helped to patch me up with plasters and a bandage. It wasn't a serious attempt – more a cry for help than anything else – but it was enough to leave scars that can be seen to this day.

There were times that I sat in my flat up in Glencairn, filled with misery. There seemed to be nothing in my life other than getting wasted. Sure, there was the Mod thing and that made me very happy, but I couldn't be a Mod 24/7. The times I was on my own were filled with depression and anger with the world. I was angry with God too because I felt He'd let me down and handed me a very bad deal indeed.

I began to realise that the thing that would make me most

happy would be to find my mum. I loved my dad, but I couldn't bring him back, no matter how much I hoped and prayed. I had no idea where to turn, and to whom. I could hardly ask anyone around Glencairn how to go about finding my Catholic mother. Neither could I confide in my Catholic Mod friends – I was aware that some of them were involved in Republican paramilitary groups and although we never talked about that stuff, you never really trusted anyone. If you did, you might end up paying for it with your life.

In my desperation I picked up my pen and wrote a letter to 'Dear Deidre', the agony aunt on the *Sun* newspaper. I gave her an outline of the story, anonymously of course, and asked her for advice. I posted it to an address in London and promptly forgot about it. A month or so later my brother David came rushing over to my place in Glencairn clutching a copy of the daily tabloid.

'Fuckin' hell, John, you seen this? Someone's written in with our story, so they have . . .'

I read it word for word. I can't remember much about the advice she gave, but I think it was something around asking the Salvation Army or a missing persons' office.

David looked at me quizzically. 'Did you write that, did you?' he said.

'Away with ye,' I replied dismissively. 'Why would I bother doin' that? Who cares about her anyway? She abandoned us, remember?'

That was the view of my sisters, and it was one I could understand. They had no wish to find our mum because they were bitter they'd been left in such difficult circumstances.

They wished her no harm, but neither did they want to see her turn up on their doorsteps after all this time. David felt the same as me – that having our mum in our lives would make it complete – but I didn't want him to feel that I was desperate. Plus, there was the ever-present threat of someone on Glencairn finding out about the Chambers family and its dirty little shameful secret. The sort of exposure that could've seen us all turfed off the estate, or worse. In the event I did try the Salvation Army but they wanted this, that and the other bits of information and I had no idea where or how to find these. So that came to a dead end.

My work commitments were very patchy around this time. As part of the YTS scheme we were offered placements across Belfast and for some reason I ended up at the Mater Hospital along the Crumlin Road. At first, I worked in the medical records department, then in the labs. In the latter, I got to wear a doctor's white coat and I always got a sneaky buzz when I had to travel to another part of the hospital and saw people I knew from school or the Shankill and Glencairn. I always hoped they'd look at me and think, 'Jesus, how did Chambers end up qualifying as a doctor?'

Eventually I was assigned to the hospital's mortuary. It wasn't the greatest career move for me, given that I was (and still am) squeamish about blood, body fluids and all the rest. I worked alongside a guy who was a raging alcoholic, and after two weeks in that particular department I understood why. He needed regular hits of booze just to cope with all the dead bodies in various stages of dissection. On my first day, the stench in there hit me like a brick in a sock. My colleague quickly slapped some Vicks extra-strong vapour rub on to my top lip and that kind of helped – but not much.

I watched in horror as he wheeled a dead person on a trolley towards me and told me to get scrubbed up. In a daze I complied and, hiding behind him, I saw him pull the sheet back. Lying there was someone's dear old granddad, very bloated and very dead. I wanted to faint but before I could move my colleague produced a scalpel, cut through the body and started pulling out various organs. He handed them to me, telling me to put them in various bowls on the table next to the trolley. Within a few minutes he got out an electric saw, cut the top of the dead man's skull open and removed the brain. Needless to say, by this time I was in deep shock.

Looking back, it seems mad that someone of my age was even allowed in the mortuary, let alone assisting an alcoholic who barely knew what day it was. I only worked in there a few weeks, taking part in about five or six autopsies, but I hated it and couldn't get out of there fast enough. The worst aspect was the smell – it lingered for hours and hours on the clothes and at lunchtimes I couldn't face eating. I'd sit on a wall outside the hospital, almost smoking myself to death in an attempt to smell of something other than death.

Finally, I got back my old job in the medical records department. This suited me much better, though spending time in any department in this spooky old Victorian building could be very weird. In the corridors I would regularly pass Catholic priests and nuns who were visiting the sick of their parishes and think nothing of it. One day, as I was heading towards the canteen, I passed a small room and noticed an old nun sitting on the bed, absorbed in her knitting. A day or so later I passed the same room and glanced in – but there was nothing there, no bed, no furniture and no nun. I mentioned this to Muriel, a colleague of mine, and asked her why the room had been totally cleared out.

'Ach, that room's not been used for years,' she said. 'We've had no bed in it for as long as I can remember.'

'But I saw a nun in it yesterday,' I said, 'just sitting there on the bed. An old nun, doing her knitting . . .'

Muriel smiled. 'I don't know what you saw, John,' she said, 'but I can tell you that no one's used that room for many, many years. Maybe you saw a ghost, hey?'

Who knows what I saw, but after that I started to chat to Muriel more regularly. She was a nice woman and seemed to take a genuine interest in who I was and the life I was living. She seemed to understand that I was in a bit of a bad place and would buy me food to take home, including curry pies, which I loved.

There were about six or seven other YTS kids working around the hospital, mostly Catholic, and I started to chat with them and make some friends. They were different from the Ardoyne boys I'd worked with previously and they all seemed better off than me, which wasn't hard. There was Maggie, a deaf girl I got on with like a house on fire who taught me the basics of sign language. There was another guy, Eamonn, who wanted to be a priest. I found that amazing and fascinating. There was Catherine, who had severe epilepsy and had up to a dozen fits a day. I often looked after her while she was fitting, making sure she wasn't banging her head or swallowing her tongue.

And then there was Dessie, a six foot three skinny drip of a Catholic Mod with whom I clicked immediately. If anything, he was even better dressed than I was and I looked up to him. At that height, I hadn't much choice.

Muriel was also a Catholic, but that didn't bother me by now. Something about her manner allowed me to let my guard down and one afternoon, when the department was empty and quiet, I told her the story of my background.

'My God,' she said when I'd finished my sorry tale, 'that's terrible. Poor wee kids, no mammy and daddy to look after ye. C'mon – let me buy you dinner and we'll talk about it some more.'

This kind woman took me under her wing and seemed to feel very sorry for me, and for us all. She agreed to speak to a Catholic priest that she knew, in confidence, and tell him what I'd told her. If he was willing, she said, she could arrange a meeting between the two of us to discuss the situation and what I might be able to do to find my mum.

In the event, I did meet the priest. He wasn't the disciple of the Antichrist that I believed all Catholic priests to be; instead, he was an older, good-natured man and a decent person who genuinely wanted to help. I felt humbled by him, and a bit guilty that I'd just believed everything I'd ever been told about Catholics and their religious men and women. But again, I hit a brick wall. I had no idea of Mum's maiden name, or what her surname might be now, and I didn't have a clue where any of her family might be – if she had any at all. And in a city with more than a hundred thousand Catholics in it, the chances of one priest somehow knowing of a woman called Sally who married a Protestant was very slim.

So for the moment, that was that. I continued my old habit of walking round Belfast city centre, looking at various women some twenty years older than me and wondering if any of them could be her. I scanned faces for some spark of familiarity or recognition, but there was nothing. I didn't want to annoy my own family by asking any questions about our mum. As far as they were concerned, we assumed she was dead. And in a way, she was. Dead to us, certainly.

CHAPTER 13

It was inevitable that for Belfast's Mods, the city centre get-together on a Saturday afternoon would quickly lose its novelty if we didn't find a bit of variety now and then. Sometimes we'd rally out in convoy to the seaside towns of Bangor or Portrush on a bank holiday, or get to gigs or all-dayers in other parts of the province. We also mimicked the sixties Mods by having running battles with the skinheads and punks along promenades and seafronts across Northern Ireland. One year I was arrested for fighting and was fined fifty pounds. It was just like a scene from *Quadrophenia*; all the Mods and skinheads in the courtroom together. I didn't half get a buzz from being a rebel.

Hundreds of us would meet up at the City Hall and drive down the coast on our scooters. When mine was out of action I took the train and it was jam-packed with Mods of all shapes and sizes. Once again, I felt like an extra in *Quadrophenia*.

The mecca, though, was London. I'd never set foot on the mainland, never mind the capital city, and I was desperately keen to cross the water, head down south and see the bright lights for myself. I couldn't wait to set foot in Carnaby Street, home to all the cool clothing labels we coveted, or hang out in an espresso bar in Soho, waiting for Paul Weller (the singer, not the dog) or Steve Marriott to walk by. As ever, I was romanticising and I had a sneaking suspicion that I might just be twenty years too late, but none of that would stop me.

Finally, the opportunity arrived to attend a Mod all-dayer at the Ilford Palais. Not the most glamorous location, I must admit, it being stuck in the arse end of east London but it was good enough for our first trip away and we knew there would be hundreds of other Mods from all over Britain going too, so we were in good company.

About thirty of us travelled from Belfast to Liverpool by boat. Then we caught the train down to London and headed straight for Carnaby Street. It felt like a religious pilgrimage and I was hypnotised by the sheer joy of just being there and drinking in the Mod culture it had given birth to. But my excitement was to be short-lived. As we walked around the legendary area and drank in the super-cool atmosphere, suddenly we heard a massive roar and what sounded like a football stampede, then three terrified young Mods ran past us as if the devil was on their tails.

Time stood still as we waited to see what had scared them and made them take such desperate flight. Then, from a side street, about fifty skinheads appeared from nowhere, many of them wearing Chelsea and Rangers football scarves and covered in Loyalist and swastika tattoos. These psychos were obviously baying for blood – Mod blood, to be exact.

The moment they spotted us they stopped dead and some even grinned at the Mod bounty fate had delivered them. We were in some deep shit and I searched my mind frantically for a way out.

There was only a few of us together at this stage and my heart leaped into my throat as I anticipated the beating I was about to receive. But if nothing else, I was used to brutal violence and two things came to my mind at once.

The first was that I'd experienced many gang battles between Mods and skinheads in the backstreets of the Shankill and Ballysillan, and survived largely intact. But here we were vastly outnumbered, on foreign soil (so to speak), and these guys wanted to rip us apart, limb by limb, while savouring every moment of our agony and humiliation.

My second thought was about the Rangers scarves and the Loyalist/English Pride-style tattoos a good number of them were sporting. An idea started to take shape in my terrified brain. Rangers was the team of choice for much of the Protestant population of Northern Ireland and, along with Chelsea and Linfield, were inextricably woven into the core of our Loyalist culture. I hoped these baying skinheads, or some of them at least, would hold the same pride and love for Queen and country as me and I thought this might just save us.

I glanced over at the leaders in the front row as they hurled insults and threats. My heart sunk when I noticed some of them had already pulled out weapons, including blades, and were preparing to attack us. This was our last chance. My survival instinct kicked in. I took a deep breath and played my hand.

'Stay back,' I said, as calmly as I could to the boys behind me. I was aware that some of our lot were Catholics and, if anything, were probably in far more danger than I was. I stepped forward and, looking for their 'top boy', I suggested they all slow down and tell me what the problem was.

You could have heard a pin drop as the fella in question looked me up and down as though I'd just insulted his mother. I could tell he was moments away from lunging at me and all hell kicking off.

Then I heard a familiar accent calling out from the skinhead crowd.

'Are youse from Belfast?' said the voice.

There was what seemed like a lifetime's pause before I answered.

'Feckin' right,' I said, 'from the glorious Shankill Road!'

Now I was praying I'd made a good call.

'That right?' he replied. 'So who d'you know?'

I wheeled off a few names of skinheads and assorted bad boys I knew and had grown up with on the Shankill and Glencairn and this satisfied them. We were safe, for now at least. It turned out the guy who spoke, Biff, had grown up in Glencairn, now lived and worked in London and was involved with other Loyalists living in the capital. His crew were a nasty bunch and I pitied those who had the misfortune to come across them, especially if you weren't a WASP. If they had known some of the Mods present were Catholics, nothing would have stopped them kicking the shit out of me and the others and I silently thanked the gods for delivering us from evil.

With the situation defused, I told the others to look around a bit and I'd catch up with them later. I didn't want the skins chatting with them, finding out some of them were Catholic and undoing all my capital work. They insisted I joined them for a pint or two in the Shakespeare's Head pub nearby and it must have looked a bit weird: a sixties-style Mod, wearing eyeliner and a Beatles suit, drinking and laughing with a gang of psycho Nazi skinheads.

But I had spent my life growing up among Loyalist killers and paramilitaries and nothing really fazed me any more. I didn't particularly like Biff and his crew, but chatting with him over a few pints I realised there was much more to him than the stereotypical skinhead. His English girlfriend had just given birth to their first child and he was 'trying to get on the straight and narrow', whatever that meant.

After a few hours of drinking and snorting speed with Biff and the others I left them in the pub and return to the sanity of my Mod mates. I was to come across Biff and his crew later that weekend, when they and dozens of other skinheads and punks ambushed and attacked Mods coming into or out of the all-dayer in the Ilford Palais. Luckily, I was safely inside, stoned out of my mind and living the Mod dream and I didn't concern myself with the antics of those fools, though I did have a chat with Biff while grabbing some fresh air and a fag outside.

Safely back in Belfast, we started to plan other trips abroad, specifically to 'the South'. Enemy territory. Taig country.

The Badlands. In spite of my new-found friendships with Catholics, the thought of crossing the border filled me with suspicion. Going down the Falls was bad enough, but into the thick of the Republican Promised Land? I was wary all right, but it didn't stop me and Billy planning a trip to an all-dayer in Dublin with a couple of girlfriends.

The first time we went down by car and when we hit the Irish capital city we ran out of both money and petrol, right in the middle of O'Connell Street. We were sitting there, wondering what to do next, when a huge Irish fella came up to the car and started grabbing at the door handle. We were half-laughing, half-scared of what was going on. Billy wound the window down and stared at the guy.

'Fuck off, willya,' he said in his best Belfast snarl.

It seemed to be enough. The message was that you didn't mess with the boys from the North, no matter which side they were on. Muttering something, he mooched off and we were safe again. Except we still had no money and no petrol. There was only one thing for it: begging. We stood outside McDonald's, giving it the 'old soldier' and hoping a few people at least would feel sorry for these four poor kids. It worked, and soon we had just enough to get us back to Belfast.

I didn't think much of Dublin. Belfast was hardly Las Vegas, but Dublin had a real downbeat, dirty, shabby feel to it back then. I wasn't keen on the Dublin accent, probably because I was conscious of my own accent standing out like a sore thumb. We went down a couple more times and on the way back would stop at Dundalk, just close to the border with Northern Ireland. This was a real Provie hole and my paranoia level was off the scale there. I was always glad to get back to the safety of Glencairn and the Shankill.

And then there was Noddy. I'd met him and his girlfriend Maria in one of the Mod clubs in Belfast, most likely the Delta or the Abercorn. We quickly became friends and I enjoyed having a chat with them when our paths crossed. Noddy (real name Gerard Clarke) was a beautiful, gentle and wise soul. He was one of those rare people who seemed to have time for everyone and seemed genuinely interested in what you had to say. He was a top bloke and I had a lot of time for him. Maria was also a beautiful person and friendly to all.

The fact they were Catholic never entered my mind and this was testament to how far I had moved on from the entrenched prejudices of my childhood. Noddy and Maria were among a group of about thirty hardcore Mods, including Billy and me, who went anywhere for an all-dayer, party, gig or a rave-up by the seaside. Our love of the Mod culture transcended hundreds of years of sectarian conflict and suspicion and give me a hint of a better future.

In October 1986, a group of about fifty Belfast Mods, including myself, Noddy and Maria, signed up for an all-dayer in Dublin's CIE hall. We were all anticipating a great day out and couldn't wait to meet and mix with the Dublin Mods who had organised the event. We had clubbed together for an Ulster Bus to take us to the event, drop off and pick us up when it was over. Being nice kind people, we had a whip round for the bus driver and collected enough for him to have some lunch. What we didn't know at that stage was that his lunch would be a liquid one.

The all-dayer was a great success and I spent ages chatting to Noddy and Maria by the huge staircase in the lobby. When the event was over, we all made our way to the bus pick-up point and began the long, slow and boring journey home. It was a miserable autumn night and rain pelted down the windows of the bus as we left Dublin and headed for the motorway, back to sunny Belfast. After a while we'd all settled down and I remember chatting to those around me, including Noddy and Maria about the day gone and upcoming events we were looking forward to in the near future. As we came into Drogheda I noticed the rain was really bucketing down and visibility was very poor. Somewhere in the back of my mind a little voice whispered that the bus was going too fast and the driver was driving a bit erratically.

A girl called me up to the middle of the bus and I went and sat in the seat behind her by the window and chilled with her for a while. I'd had a few drinks and some pills and I was halfway between sleep and a drug-infused haze when suddenly I became aware that the bus was out of control. In horror, I watched out of the window as it drifted in and out of lane, narrowly missing fast-moving traffic coming from both ways, before skidding to the right and crashing with a huge bang into the side of something very solid, a bridge or a brick wall, that brought it to a violent, shuddering stop.

The impact of the crash threw me forward. I smashed my head on the seat in front of me and was almost knocked out by the force of it. I waited for the pain to tear through my body and in the background I could hear the sound of breaking glass, car horns and alarms going off, cars skidding and crashing. As the bus's internal lights blinked out, screaming filled the air all around me and for a moment I thought I must be dreaming or on a very bad trip.

But this was no nightmare and the horror had just begun. As I recovered from the immediate shock of what had just happened my eyes drifted around the bus. All I could see were bodies, blood, broken glass and wreckage strewn all over the place. It looked as though a bomb had gone off and I could see and smell destruction all around me. I glanced at the back of the bus and to my utter disbelief the whole of its back section had been ripped off. The seats that Noddy, Maria and others had occupied had completely disappeared.

I looked out of the gaping hole and my heart almost stopped. Bodies and debris littered the road and I could clearly see Noddy lying sickeningly still on the rain-soaked tarmac, illuminated by vehicles caught up in the accident and others who had stopped to help, or gawk in amazement at what they'd just witnessed.

As my traumatised mind tried to process all this, I staggered up and checked myself for injuries. I was relieved to find I was mostly in one piece, although my head was bleeding and I was starting to slip into shock. As I turned and looked out the window to my left, I froze in terror as I watched a car lose control, cross the lanes and crash violently at speed into the bus right below where I was sitting. I'd automatically braced myself for the impact and my whole body rocked as the shockwaves of the crash reverberated through the bus and my aching body.

From this point on everything becomes hazy, as if I'm watching events happen to someone else and I'm oddly detached from my own body and mind. I should have been panicking and fighting to get off the bus and the danger below me. That car could've blown up or engulfed me in fire at any moment. But I just sat there for what seemed like ages and although I could see everything around me and hear ambulances and fire brigade approaching, I was frozen to the spot in deep shock.

Eventually, someone guided me off the bus and I walked as if in a trance to where Noddy lay on the damp, wet ground, lifeless. As the rain drenched me, I looked down on him and, bowing my head, I said a silent prayer for Noddy, Maria and the other injured boys and girls on this bus. Then I cursed the type of god who would let such a thing happen.

After a while, ambulance crews came to check on me and the other walking wounded, patching us up where necessary. We were led to a nearby hotel, given hot, reviving drinks and interviewed by the Garda (the Irish police). To this day I cannot remember whether we stayed in the hotel overnight or how we got back to Belfast. My next memory is of lying on the sofa in my flat and being fussed over by my sisters and other family members. The *Ulster News* had carried the story about the crash and those killed and injured, and my family had spent hours not knowing if I was alive or dead. I should have called them from the hotel the night before but I was away with the fairies and it had not even entered my battered brain to let them know I was alive and well.

In the days that followed, the Belfast Mod community banded together in shock. One of our own had been killed, and others injured, and many gathered outside the City Hall in sombre groups, chatting and remembering Noddy and those injured in the crash. Maria was still in hospital fighting for her life, while many others were scarred emotionally and physically and would never fully recover from the trauma of what they had gone through.

I was numb to it all, hibernating at home and licking my wounds, and I couldn't face a world that seemed so unfair. In fact, I refused point blank to talk about the accident and months later, when many of those involved in the crash began the process of suing Ulster Bus and claiming compensation, I wanted nothing to do with it, missing the opportunity for a substantial pay-out. Looking back, I was probably suffering from post-traumatic stress disorder (PTSD) – but this was Belfast and many people suffered from that, whether they knew it or not. The response was just to get on with life, which I did, but the psychological wounds lasted for years to come.

Mods from all over the island of Ireland, north and south, travelled to the Falls Road for Noddy's funeral. Catholic and Protestant stood shoulder-to-shoulder, forming a guard of honour as we buried one of our own. Even then I felt nervous as I stood outside Noddy's house, trying not to catch the eyes of a few mourners who seemed to be staring right at me, trying to discern if I was Catholic or Protestant.

Putting my fears aside, I ignored them. This was not about religion and as I paid my respects to Noddy's friends and family I felt nothing but love and gratitude from them. I came away from that awful event wondering why we couldn't always live in peace and harmony and move on from centuries of the suspicion and mistrust that ruled and ruined our daily lives.

RIP, Noddy – you were one of the best.

CHAPTER 14

By now, I was torn. Pulled in all directions over my loyalty to my Mod friends (especially the Catholic ones) and loyalty – with a capital 'L' – to the religion and culture that had nurtured and sustained me throughout my life. Although I was careful not to broadcast it, I'd felt I had to join the UDA; scores of my friends from Ballysillan, Glencairn and surrounding some of which I was lifted for areas were also signing up. No matter that I was running around with Catholic girls and boys at the weekends, there were still sections of this community who were out to kill me and my kind, and if I had to defend myself against that by whatever means, so be it. I always said that I couldn't kill anyone and I meant it. But protecting my community and its traditions was another matter. At the time, paranoia among Protestants and Loyalists was at boiling point, and the constant threat of civil war with IRA-supporting nationalists drove countless other ordinary kids like me into the ranks of Loyalist paramilitaries although, like me, many of them remained on the fringes and never took part in the 'military' operations.

So, let's wind back the clock a year or so to a dreary day in November 1985. For most of that year, the talk around Belfast had been about the Anglo–Irish Agreement, drawn up and signed by British Prime Minister Margaret Thatcher and her Irish equivalent, Garret FitzGerald. This agreement gave the Republic of Ireland some say in Northern Irish matters in return for them dropping their claim to our country by agreeing that any change to its status could only come with the consent of a majority.

Predictably, Loyalists saw this as a complete sell-out. We relied upon the British government to support us as loyal subjects and now they were talking to the very people we saw as the enemy. We saw this as the first step on the road to a united Ireland, the situation we feared the most. The backlash was huge – strikes, resignations, anger and violence all over Northern Ireland. We were Protestants and by God would we protest about this betrayal. A week or so after the Anglo–Irish Agreement was signed a mass rally was planned for Saturday, 23 November outside the City Hall. Usually, we Mods would've gathered here at the weekend, but not this one – and certainly not any of our Catholic counterparts. It seemed that every Loyalist in Belfast and beyond had gathered in the city centre that day; more than a hundred thousand people amid a sea of red, white and blue. It was like 12 July, except with drizzle and a hell of a lot more anger.

I was there with a lot of my mates from Glencairn and the Shankill. It was an event not to be missed. We pushed and shoved our way to as near to the front of the crowd as we could get, and managed to climb up some scaffolding above H Samuel, the jeweller's shop facing the City Hall. There were dozens of us hanging off the metal poles and if the whole thing had collapsed there'd have been a terrible tragedy. But it didn't, and as we clung on we enjoyed the spectacle of the vast crowd below us as they waited for the day's speakers.

The Ulster Unionist Party leader, James Molyneaux, spoke and while he said all the right things, he wasn't a patch on the next man up – the infamous Ian Paisley. Anyone who knows anything about Northern Irish politics will remember 'the Big Man'. You either loved him or hated him, but no one could ever deny that his heart wasn't right at the centre of Loyalism. Of course, he had quite a turnaround many years later when he shared power with Martin McGuinness. But in 1985, there seemed more chance of Big Ian becoming Pope than there was of him getting all chummy with the IRA.

Anyway, this massive crowd hung on to his every word as his booming tones rang out right across Donegall Square and beyond.

'Where do the terrorists operate from?' he roared. 'From the Irish Republic! Where do the terrorists return to for sanctuary? To the Irish Republic! And yet Mrs Thatcher tells us that that Republic must have some say in our province. We say Never! Never! Never! Never!'

The crowd roared back its approval, united in one voice. We were determined that a united Ireland would not happen to us proud Protestants, and in later speeches Paisley would say that we were on 'the verge of civil war', with the possibility of hand-to-hand fighting in every street. It was scary stuff, particularly for us on the front line in Belfast and despite my non-sectarian approach to Mod-dom, I was as angry as anyone else that we were being sold down the river by Mrs Thatcher. Then, in typical Belfast style, some kid or other broke into a nearby sports shop and soon the square was filled with flying tennis and golf balls, mostly aimed at the police. It livened the mood a little, but there was no doubting the fierce anger that hung over the crowd on that grey autumn afternoon.

I knew I couldn't kill anyone, but there's no doubt that as a member of the UDA I was now among killers – or at least guys who would go on to kill. I abhorred all sectarian killings, but those were the times and people did whatever they felt was right, or whatever their consciences could handle. I knew I'd never be able to square away the killing of a Catholic as justifiable political act, and I think the UDA guys who were training me and the other young lads who'd joined around that time knew this. They didn't put pressure on me to go out and pull the trigger – I'd have been useless anyway, and for a paramilitary organisation having someone like me on the front line would've been counter-productive, to say the least.

In the meantime, I'd regularly go down the Shankill to various places, where I'd learn to map read and march in line. There were lectures on the history of the Loyalist movement and training in compass-reading techniques. They were preparing us as foot soldiers for civil war. As I've said, it was all a bit Boy Scouts or Boys' Brigade to me, but to others it was deadly serious – not a game, but a matter of life and death. These were the lads who would go on to be the 'top boys' of

Loyalist paramilitarism and in time would become infamous in Belfast and well beyond. They'd do time in the Maze prison or in 'the Crum' – the damp, dank Crumlin Road gaol that is now a major tourist attraction in Belfast. I have to confess that I was in there too – but not for any romantic notion of defending Loyalism against hordes of Republican invaders. In fact, it was for motoring offences.

I had a very reckless approach to taxing and insuring my scooter and given that I was prone to crashing or falling off it, this wasn't great behaviour. Time after time the RUC would flag me down and demand that I produce my documents at the nearest station. Of course, I never had any of these so it would be off to court, and a fine that I couldn't or wouldn't pay. This happened so frequently that eventually the magistrate demanded that I either pay the fine straight away or spend three days in Crumlin Road gaol.

Well, I didn't have much else to do that weekend, to be honest. And I didn't want to be slapped with a big fine that would be on my mind for ages. So to the surprise of the magistrate I said, 'I'll take prison, please,' and with that I was marched down the steps of the dock and through the tunnel that links the courthouse with the gaol. As I walked I thought about all the paramilitary hard men from both sides who'd been taken on this very journey, many receiving multiple life sentences for the terrible stuff they'd done. I wasn't exactly in their ranks, but a taste of the Crum would be something to tell the boys when I was finally sprung on the Monday.

Unfortunately for me, I'd overlooked two things. The first was that my time in prison coincided with a bank holiday

Monday. There wouldn't be enough screws present that day to take me through the release procedure, so I'd have to come out on the Tuesday instead. That took the wind out of my sails a wee bit. The second was my clothing. I'd arrived at court complete with sixties paisley shirt, eyeliner and a string of beads around my neck. This wasn't great gear for going to prison in and when I arrived in the prison to take the obligatory shower the screw in charge gave me a filthy look.

'Are ye seriously goin' in there looking like a fruit?' he asked. 'D'ye think that'll be fun for ye?'

I looked at myself in the cracked mirror. The guy was right. Some of the fellas in here were psychos, not exactly sympathetic to lads who looked a bit gay, as I'm sure I did. I couldn't do much about the shirt, but I scrubbed off the eyeliner and handed in the love beads for safekeeping. Then, in an act of defiance, I scratched the words 'Mods UTC' ('Up The Hoods') on the door of the shower with a pen before handing that in too. I headed into the prison and to my cell for what turned out to be a pleasant few days. Because I wasn't in for anything heinous, nobody took any notice of me. Also, I was a skinny lad with hollow legs and I enjoyed the carb-heavy prison food served up to us three times a day. I can't say I was sorry to be released but it was an experience, and I could always talk it up a bit for the benefit of my mates.

Many years later I took my young son on an organised tour of the prison, which is now a museum. I showed him the shower, and the graffiti that I'd etched on to the door. An American tourist overheard me talking to my boy about my 'time' in the Crum, and for the rest of the tour he and his

fellow visitors treated me like royalty – Republican, no do
I didn't tell them the truth . . . why let the facts get in the
of a good yarn?

As I've said, the spell in gaol was towards the end of a long
period of joyriding, shoplifting and drug-taking, some of
which I was lifted for, much of which I got away with. In
the 1980s, stealing cars and joyriding was almost a full-time
occupation for many of Northern Ireland's teenage males,
especially in the Loyalist and Republican-controlled ghettos.
There was always a danger that an untrained driver would
crash, accidentally or deliberately, into an army checkpoint
and be shot dead, and this happened on multiple occasions
during the Troubles. I wasn't confident enough to drive, but
I was a regular passenger in cars that had been stolen by my
mates in Belfast city centre and driven at high speed back up
to Glencairn, where they'd be burned out.

This was the scenario one such Saturday night, when we
jacked a car just for the hell of it. The experts could be in
there with the engine started in five seconds flat, and there
was little chance of being caught red-handed. We belted up
the Crumlin Road, not bothering ourselves with red lights or
pedestrian crossings, and celebrated reaching our home turf
with a screeching handbrake turn, perfect in every technical
sense except that it ended with a side-on smash into a nice new
Opel Ascona car parked on the other side of the road.

None of us were hurt, but as we stared at the damage we'd
inflicted on the Ascona we realised we'd committed a crime that
could see us all shivering in fear as, one by one, our kneecaps
were removed by a bullet from a Browning pistol. The car we'd

just hit belonged to a top UDA man, a guy known to all of us as a character who took no nonsense, especially from a gang of hoods. Sensibly, we bolted from the car and ran as fast as our legs could take us.

Unfortunately, Glencairn is a small place and word quickly reached the UDA as to the identity of the joyriders. The following day we all received the inevitable summons to the community centre, where the paramilitaries were waiting. To say we were shitting it is an understatement.

'Don't even fuckin' think of denying it!' screamed the enraged commander when we tried to do just that. 'If youse think you're gonna get away with this, youse are more stupid that ye look!'

With that, he pulled a pistol from his waistband. A couple of our gang started to cry. I could feel my balls disappearing into my stomach as I thought about the prospect of hobbling around the estate for the rest of my life.

'Now,' he said, brandishing the pistol in our faces, 'did ye smash my car up or didn't ye?'

Miserably, we nodded in unison. Our fate was sealed. Whatever happened to us next, we'd just have to accept. It was simply part and parcel of life in Loyalist West Belfast back then.

The commander looked us up and down, this group of shuffling, shaking, sniffling boys. Perhaps something about our pathetic appearance softened his heart. Maybe he realised that we'd not meant to do what we did, that it was an accident that only affected him personally, not the Loyalist movement as a whole.

'Here's what's going to happen,' he said, after watching us sweat for a minute or so. 'I'm going to buy a new car, and every Saturday youse are gonna come up to my house and clean it inside and out. And if it's still dirty, you'll start all over again. You got that?'

I couldn't believe what I was hearing. He was letting us off! Well, not quite, but washing a car was a whole sight easier than walking with a missing kneecap. We glanced at each other in shock, barely suppressing our smiles of relief, until the commander banged his fist on a table.

'And if I ever catch youse joyriding again,' he said in a menacingly low tone, 'there'll be no question of what will happen to you. Got that?'

We trooped out like a gang of monkeys released from a cage. And two Saturdays later we were at the commander's house armed with buckets, sponges and cleaning liquid. After we finished, his was the shiniest car on the estate.

We got off very lightly because the UDA controlled everything on Glencairn. And I should've known better, being in their ranks. They were helpful on occasions, though. One time, a guy downstairs from me had a party and got clean off his head. He came upstairs, slabbering to me about some rubbish or other. Whatever I said back to him obviously offended him because he went ahead and smashed all my windows. I didn't bother with the police – you just wouldn't – and instead had a quiet word with a couple of the senior UDA guys on the estate. A couple of days later, the slabberer knocked my door and apologised for his behaviour before fixing every one of my broken windows.

Part of our duty as young UDA members was collecting money for the organisation and keeping the local hoods in check, which was kind of ironic as I and other young members were among those hoods. During my time, my main task was actually welfare stuff, including the Loyalist Prisoner Aid, supporting the families of those inside. When I was going out with Kathy, the Catholic girl, I was supposed to take her out one night but I'd lost all my money on cards. So I went to the top UDA money lender and got a fifty-pound loan to take her out for a meal. A bit cheeky, getting the UDA to pay for a meal with a Catholic, and I'm sure if they had known I would have been in some serious trouble, but I didn't give a shit at the time. As I knew and got on with some of the top players in Glencairn I took liberties like this from time to time.

There was another occasion that a notorious party took place on the estate that seemed to be gate-crashed by just about everyone living there. A gang of hoods somehow brought a horse into the house and filled it full of drink. In a pissed-up state of fear, it managed to shit everywhere before passing out on the kitchen floor. The owner of the house went to the UDA the day after and asked for two hundred pounds for new carpets, wallpaper, etc, blaming the hoods for bringing the animal in and allowing it to 'rub its arse all over my wall'. She got it too.

By this time I'd long blown my compensation money and was on and off the dole in between a succession of catering jobs around Belfast. Cooking was something I enjoyed and was good at, in spite of my shite education. I was just about together enough to hold down a few decent-ish jobs in between the rest of my mad existence and I was lucky to pick up just enough knowledge to help me in the future. I worked for a while in Musgrave Park Hospital, which was kind of weird as I had spent so much of my childhood in there as a patient. I also worked in a few Italian restaurants and an Indian.

After years of acting the maggot, as they say in Northern Ireland, and generally being a pain in the arse, particularly to my long-suffering family, I realised that if I carried on this way I would either end up in prison, on the dole for the rest of my life, or dead. I was rapidly heading out of my teens and was running out of excuses to misbehave.

At the time the old guard of the UDA, like my Uncle Rab and others, were being pushed aside by the more militant and violent young turks. This created lots of tensions and feuds, not only between the various UDA units in and around Glencairn and the Shankill, but often with the local UVF. When the bullets started flying it didn't matter who or what you were, if you were in the wrong place at the wrong time it could end up getting you killed. I was once in the Tyndale club (a legendary Loyalist club that was like the Old West and very violent) up in Ballysillan with a large group of UDA men from Glencairn when a fight broke out. We were chased from the club and all over Ballysillan with bullets flying all over the place. It was events like these that made me decide that the life of a UDA member wasn't for me.

Very shortly after this incident, I came to the understanding that if I wanted any kind of a life out of trouble, or the Troubles, I would have to leave my home and my family. I wasn't alone. Across Northern Ireland many kids with backgrounds like mine were thinking the same thing. They'd shove any spare money they had into an old biscuit tin, saving up for the day they could get the boat over to Stranraer or Liverpool, and then on to the big cities. Or maybe they'd even have enough for a plane ticket that would take them to America, where friends and relatives who'd already escaped were waiting.

One of these escapees was my friend Jacqueline McFall, the photographer. From our first meeting via the Mod scene, Jacqueline and I had become close, and when she moved up to Glencairn we started hanging around together a lot. She was very clear about wanting out of Belfast. The photos she took of us Mods around the city were amazing, but behind all the cool clothing and polished scooters was a bunch of kids whose futures were uncertain, to say the very least. At any time, any one of us could've ended up dead, or given a terrible hiding for something we'd done or not done. We were in the wrong place at the wrong time, and those of us who wanted little or no part of the ongoing war soon realised this, and made plans to get out.

Jacqueline moved to London to start a new life and I envied her. I missed her too. She had (and still has) a down-to-earth sense of humour and looked at life through the eyes of a true artist. She was bright and had her head screwed on. In short, she was good for me and when she'd gone I felt cut adrift.

I wanted to follow her but at that point I didn't quite have the guts to pack my bag, get on the boat and do a Dick Whittington to London. It seemed a big journey, physically and metaphorically, and I was still torn between wanting to get away and the love I had for my siblings, friends and extended family across Glencairn and the Shankill.

So instead, in a kind of compromise, I went to the Isle of Man. Don't ask me why. Maybe because it didn't feel so far from Belfast as London did. Perhaps I just wanted to try out the feeling of leaving home before I really did leave home for good. In any case, I wasn't long over there. I got low-paid kitchen work in one of the hotels in Douglas and for a couple of weeks I slogged it out as the realisation dawned on me that this definitely wasn't London, or anything like it. The only memorable event about the whole fortnight was that two gay guys from Dublin kept trying to hit on me. Being from Loyalist Belfast, the gay scene wasn't exactly familiar to me – despite all my street smarts and living by the seat of my pants I could be incredibly naive sometimes – and at first I just thought these two were being friendly. As I hadn't met many people from 'down South' up to this point, they intrigued me. It was only when they insisted on me coming back to their room for more drinks that the penny dropped.

So, with my tail between my legs, I re-boarded the Belfast boat and went home. When I arrived back to the flat, the place was a ghost town. All those who dossed down there, crashing on my sofa or wherever they could lay their heads, were away camping. I was in almost complete isolation, and as I sat there, bored and fed up, I decided not to hang around for more than a couple of days. London was calling, and it was time for me to answer it.

CHAPTER 15

Jacqueline didn't sound so surprised when I phoned her and told her I was coming to London.

'At last, Chambers,' she said. 'What took ye so fuckin' long?'

'Dunno,' I said, 'faffin' about as usual. What's your place like? Can I crash on you for a wee bit?'

'Yeah, course you can. But I'll warn ye now . . . this place is a madhouse, so it is.'

'Nothing new there, then. We've come from a madhouse, Jacq.'

'Wait and see, Chambers,' she said, 'wait and see . . .'

I put the phone down, still laughing. No place on earth could be as crazy as Belfast. London might be full of nutters and psychos, but generally they weren't carrying automatic weapons. Whatever I might meet in London, it would be nothing compared to Northern Ireland. We were all being dragged into it, Catholics and Protestants, and some of us would be dragged much deeper than others. I'd had it with all that stuff. I just wanted to get away, make a new life and have some fun without constantly looking over my shoulder.

Also – and perhaps it wasn't so obvious to me at the time, but looking back I see some significance – there was the fact that my parents had spent time in England. My feelings about my mother were still strong and maybe subconsciously I felt that if I hadn't found her in Belfast, there could be a chance that she could walk past me on the streets of London. Admittedly, in a capital city of (then) 6 million people the chances of that happening were remote, to say the least, but there was no harm in wondering what might be.

Still, I wasn't entirely confident about hitting London on my own, so I arranged to go with Finn, a friend from Glencairn. Like me, he was a bit of a hood and forever in trouble with either the RUC or the UDA – or both, which wasn't a great place to be. Plus, I fancied the hell out of Finn's sister and would use the excuse of going round to his for planning meetings to eye up his lovely sibling. Predictably, she wasn't interested in me at all, so all I got was a crazy guy for a travelling companion who would no doubt get into as much trouble in London as he had done in Belfast.

We settled on a date in October 1987 as our farewell to Belfast. There was no need to book the flight; in those days you just turned up at the British Midland desk at Aldergrove Airport (now fancily re-named 'Belfast International'), bought a ticket and got on the plane. Not that I'd ever been on one before, so I was sitting in my flat that morning in a state of nervous anticipation when there was a knock at the door. I opened it, expecting Finn, to find my cousins Pickle and Karen on the step. They told me Finn had been arrested for theft, the details being that he'd broken into my auntie's house and stolen a video recorder and TV, among other items, and had been arrested while trying to sell them.

'Cheeky bastard!' I said. 'Looks like I'll be going to London on my own, then . . .'

I got the bus into the city centre then took the airport bus up to Aldergrove. All the while I stared out of the window, watching my home city disappear into the distance and wondering whether I'd be back in a few weeks or if I'd ever return at all. Soldiers and heavily armed police mixed with shoppers and families on a day out. Young and old submitted to security checks and searches taking place outside department stores. There were large concrete anti-terrorist barriers in place everywhere. Helicopters buzzed above us, police stations had been turned into fortified military bases and unseen eyes watched everything via CCTV cameras. This was our normal – about as far from normal as you could possibly get, and yet we'd lived like this for years. I hadn't known any other way of existence. Adjusting to a country without such restrictions would take some doing.

I purchased my ticket and headed for the departure lounge via the Harp bar, where I downed a few pints before boarding. I was almost shitting myself with fear as I boarded the plane and was glad to see that you could smoke if you didn't mind sitting at the back of the plane. I made a beeline for the rear seats and broke out the fags before I'd even fastened my seatbelt. Although the flight was short, I hated every second, and even today I'm not comfortable travelling this way. Still, it was either that or a trip that took the best part of two days by boat, bus or rail, so I just gritted my teeth and smoked the time away.

I landed at Heathrow and made my way by Tube up to Walthamstow, where Jacqueline was living. I'd been to London before, of course, but now I was looking at it through the eyes of someone who would be living there. And even on the Tube, the differences between London and Belfast were amazing. Sure, people travelling in the carriages weren't exactly warm and friendly. Most sat with newspapers up to their faces, or plugged into their Walkmans. There was a bit of tension in the air, not helped when a couple of drunken posh blokes got on at Kensington and started shouting about this and that.

They didn't bother me, because what tension there was had nothing on an average early evening in Belfast. People here were from all corners of the globe and they could come and go as they pleased with little fear of attack, death by car bomb or random sectarian murder. True, London was far from perfect but even so, you didn't feel you were constantly being scrutinised for who you were and what you were. I felt liberated. There were no soldiers, no cops with guns, no barbed wire, no barricades, no paramilitaries. Generally, people looked happy and stress-free. In Belfast, fear seemed to be etched into the face of every one of its occupants.

I changed trains and took the Victoria Line to Walthamstow. Back then it was a traditional east London community that had seen better days, and a magnet for those who were looking to live as cheaply as possible. Immigrant families of all faiths and persuasions were moving in – and then there was the interesting mix of personalities living at Jacqueline's . . .

The large flat was above some shops on Blackhorse Road, close to the Lord Palmerston pub. And just as Jacq had described it, it was a complete madhouse. The three or four rooms that constituted the living space were shared by at least fifteen people and it was a case of sling your sleeping bag down wherever you could find a gap. And in comparison to the working-class Loyalist community I'd grown up in (with the addition of a few Catholic Mod friends), my housemates were a very eccentric, eclectic set of people indeed.

There were Irish Mods, skinheads, punks, ska girls and rockabillies. In one room, a terrible heavy metal band gathered to rehearse a couple of times a week. There was a strange guy called Max, who had the unique feature of having four nipples on his chest. There was an even stranger girl, Cheryl, who was obsessed with Cliff Richard and would stalk him whenever he played in London. There was a revolving door of gay guys and prostitutes who worked the streets of Soho. I'd never been in the company of such a weird and wonderful bunch and I loved every minute of their company.

God only knows how this wild bunch got on, but we did. There were arguments and fights, of course, but by and large we were a functionally dysfunctional community, if that makes sense. On a Friday night we'd all head to Blackhorse Road Station and take the train to Camden, where we'd hit the Camden Palace, the Electric Ballroom and Dingwalls. We must've looked like something out of *The Warriors*, the cult 1979 film, or, at a pinch, an extended version of *The Young*

Ones, which wouldn't have been far wrong, given the state of our house.

I treated my first few weeks of idleness during the day and partying at night as 'settling in', but as my meagre savings were fast dwindling away I realised it was time to find a job. I went down to the Denmark Street Job Centre, just around the corner from Tottenham Court Road, and I picked this particular place for a reason. I'd always had a bit of an obsession with serial killers – coming from where I did, I'd probably mingled with a few – and I knew from reading his life story that Dennis Nilsen, the serial murderer of young gay men, had worked in that very office. After browsing the jobs boards for a while I began chatting up the staff, shamelessly asking them what Dennis was like and where he'd sat. They must've wondered who this strange Paddy was, coming in and asking all sorts of odd questions about their most notorious employee.

'Paddy' . . . of course, now I was in London that's how I was viewed. Most English people made little or no distinction between Irish Catholics and Ulster Protestants. To them we were all Paddies, working in pubs, mending roads or hanging off scaffolding on building sites, wolf-whistling passing secretaries. At first, this shocked me and pissed me right off. Didn't they know or appreciate the fact we were prouder to be British than them? People from Northern Ireland had (and still have) a very keen sense of who might be from the other side of the fence. Evolution seems to have taught us that this is nothing less than a survival technique. In England, though, it didn't seem to matter a damn. Few understood the difference, and fewer even cared. I was astonished, given the constant drip-drip-drip of bad news still coming out of my country. But there it was. I was deemed to have 'Irish charm' and if that got me a few dates with the girls, which it did, I wasn't going to argue the details.

Thanks to the catering experience I'd gained in Belfast I managed to get a succession of temping jobs working as a chef/waiter/barman where necessary. At that time, towards the end of the 1980s, London was booming. The recession of the early part of the decade was over, the Big Bang (the day of stock market deregulation in 1986) had happened, and it seemed that everyone was either stuffing their faces, drinking themselves silly or drugging till they dropped. I was never short of work, and certainly never short of people to talk to. Diners and drinkers would catch on to my accent and ask me where I was from. When I said 'Belfast' they'd look at me with a mixture of intrigue and suspicion – who knows, they might have been talking to a real live terrorist! If they wanted the 'blarney' I was happy to give it to them – it often meant a fair bit extra in tips – but I was always careful to make sure I didn't give too much away.

I was working in a bar one time when I spotted an older guy, probably in his thirties or forties, sitting at the end of the bar. He clocked my accent when I asked him what he wanted to drink.

'Ah, Belfast,' he said, 'a fine city. My other leg's still over there, you know.' And he beckoned me to peer over the bar at the space where the limb used to be. I asked him what happened, already guessing the answer. He'd been in the army and he'd been caught by an IRA booby-trap bomb. I told him which part of Belfast I was from and he realised then that I was a Protestant. Knowing, as a former soldier, that he was safe with me he dropped his guard, I dropped mine, and we had a good old chat that evening.

I also did some temping work in a private members' club near Trafalgar Square. It was all military personnel and there I met a lovely older fella we knew as 'Sir Stephen'. He'd been in the Second World War, was captured by the Japanese and forced to help build the bridge over the River Kwai. His stories fascinated me, as did those of other members who took the time to speak to me. One afternoon I was interested to see a whole crowd of security personnel arrive in the building, complete with sniffer dogs. There was a big event on in honour of some general or other. One of the security guys talked to me for a few minutes before carrying on with his work. Within five minutes the manager of the club came over and generously awarded me the day off. By his tone of voice I could tell that this wasn't a request, but an order. 'Paddies', even red, white and blue ones, weren't welcome in the club that day.

Still, I went with the flow and would frequent the Irish pubs and clubs up in the Archway and Kilburn areas of the city. I did some work in one such bar in Swiss Cottage – the owner didn't care if you were Orange, Green or any other colour as long as you had an Irish accent of some description. On a Friday night the place would be crammed full of Irish builders and labourers, pissing their hard-earned cash against the toilet wall. One night, a smallish fella came in and sidled up to me as I was clearing away a tableful of empty Guinness glasses.

"Scuse me,' he said, in a soft Cork accent, 'd'youse mind if I collect for the prisoners?'

I didn't need to ask what kind of prisoners he was talking about, and which side of the divide they were from. 'You can get to fuck,' I replied, 'and get outta here. How dare you people do that in England, when you're trying to blow the place to smithereens?'

In recent years there'd be a number of high-profile IRA attacks on the mainland, not least the Brighton bomb that aimed to kill as many members of Margaret Thatcher's government as possible, including the lady herself. I wasn't having any of the Provie shite in any place I worked, no matter what the clientele might've thought. For a moment the Cork man stared at me in astonishment and I thought I'd need to use my fists. But he'd obviously clocked my Belfast accent and decided the issue wasn't worth pursuing. No doubt he understood that whatever side I was from, I'd seen a whole lot more trouble in Belfast than he'd ever experienced down in the soft South.

After a few months' temping, I picked up a full-time job in the Montague Hotel in Bloomsbury. The job came with a room of my own, so I said goodbye to the 'Young Ones' in Walthamstow and moved smack into the middle of London. I couldn't have asked for a better location. Not only was the area full of great bars and clubs, but the hotel itself was right opposite the British Museum. Despite my lack of schooling, I'd always loved history and I spent much of my free time wandering around the museum, gazing in wonder at all the collections from so many different cultures.

My work colleagues at the Montague included two guys from

the Irish Republic, Tony and Padraig. At first they were wary of me and my accent, especially when I told them I was from Glencairn. But after a few weeks we all settled down together and bantered regularly on the themes of 'sick Orange bastard' and 'Fenian scum'. Such insults hurled in Belfast would've led to a gun battle; here in London, words were just words.

That said, even an upmarket hotel like this wasn't safe from trouble. One of my fellow chefs was a guy called Phil from somewhere up in the north of England. At the best of times he was one messed-up individual and when his girlfriend (one of the receptionists) dumped him he took it very, very hard. One night they were having an argument in the staff quarters when suddenly he told her that he couldn't live without her. Then he pulled out a huge knife and started slashing violently at his wrists. Blood shot up the walls and sprayed the carpet, causing pandemonium. Needless to say, he was sectioned and taken to a secure hospital, where he remained for a number of weeks. Eventually he returned to work in the kitchen and although I'd previously got on well with him, I was always on edge when working with him, especially with so many sharp knives around.

There were many other staff living in the hotel and I was surrounded by beautiful women from the four corners of the earth. To pull no punches, I was like a dog on heat. Thankfully, the ladies found me acceptable and I must have worked my way round most of the reception staff and other female staff who seemed to like my Belfast charm and accent.

One of these was an Irish girl from Cavan whom I'll name Finola. We hit it off and started seeing each other regularly, despite me knowing that her father was a staunch Republican who would've hit the roof had he known his daughter was dating a Prod. Her family home was in Islington, which we visited in great secrecy while her parents were on holiday.

Sadly, the inevitable happened and Finola became pregnant. I was in no position to become a father, even if I'd wanted to. But I was prepared to make a go of things for the sake of the baby. Finola's Catholic upbringing taught her that abortion was a terrible sin but even so, she knew she couldn't go home and announce to her father that she was having a baby with a Loyalist from Belfast. So the abortion went ahead and after that our relationship fizzled out. We were too full of guilt and remorse for what had happened to continue seeing each other.

I met two people at the Montague who would go on to become good friends, John and Theresa. In time, John would become my clubbing partner and we'd have many adventures on the rave scene. Theresa was another Irish girl, a wild character full of spirit and fun. She always carried a little plastic bottle shaped like the Virgin Mary, full of holy water from Lourdes, and often threw it over us before we hit the town or were being particularly naughty We became very close but often her hyperactivity scared me, I backed away from having a relationship with her and we always kept everything strictly platonic. As the years went by, we went our separate ways but much later I heard that she'd returned to Ireland in the hope of finding someone to settle down with. That hadn't happened, and in despair she stood on the edge of a cliff, drunk a bottle of whiskey, smoked a full packet of cigarettes, then threw herself off. It was a tragic end to a life lived at full speed.

With Theresa's help I took another job at the Imperial Hotel, also in Bloomsbury, and now I had some more money I could afford to move out and rent a place in Paddington with a few mates I'd made. By now, at the very end of the 1980s, the rave scene in and around the capital was booming and I was desperate to be part of it. I danced my head off in various clubs and would pile into cars full of E'd-up ravers, driving at breakneck speed around the M25 to find an acid house party in the middle of some obscure field. It was like my Mod days all over again, except with different drugs and music that was cutting-edge and bang up to date. Those nights out partying were wild, and I knew I'd have to get a job with more regular hours so that I wouldn't miss out on all the fun.

I'd always been a good talker and I was aware my Northern Irish accent, when not being mistaken for the voice of a terrorist, had enough lilt and charm to take me all sorts of places. I had the banter, so I headed in the direction of insurance sales. After all, I'd honed my skills at an early age selling UDA raffle tickets and firewood around Glencairn! I was a natural and when I started work for Royal Life Insurance I began to make more money than I'd ever seen in my life. I could easily afford to fund my lifestyle as a weekend raver and, having an addictive personality, soon got bang into as many pills as I could swallow and as much coke as I could snort.

I needed what was called a 'Lautro', or a licence, to give or sell financial advice so I was sent up to Liverpool for a week's training. Everyone who took the course was accommodated in the famous Adelphi Hotel and we were treated like royalty. I visited the Cavern Club and, as an old Mod, enjoyed the buzz of being in the club that made the Beatles world famous.

I really felt that the world was now my oyster. In a matter of months, I'd come a very long way from Glencairn and the rainy grey city of my birth. Now I seemed to be in this Technicolor world full of beautiful, amazing young people who loved each other and danced like dervishes after dark. And yet, deep down, the old nagging feeling of 'something missing' continued to haunt me. No matter how much booze I drank, pills I necked or coke I snorted, I could never seem to rid myself of this shadow. There were connections to be had in the rave scene all right, but they were facilitated by drugs, and with drugs there is always a terrible price to pay for the high via a terrible comedown. In short, such connections didn't feel genuine. I wanted something deeper, more meaningful, more real. And so the search went on . . .

CHAPTER 16

A room in North London, night-time. The smell of incense is overpowering and I notice that the cushion I'm sitting on is full of dog hairs. Fleetingly, I worry about the effect this is having on my new trousers, but I need to concentrate on what's going on, because this is about to get pretty weird indeed . . .

I'd always been a seeker. From gods to Mods and anything in between, if it interested me I wanted to know more. It was a restlessness born out of my personal circumstances and the life I'd led to believe was 'normal' in Belfast. All around me I could see hatred, bitterness and narrow-minded attitudes. I wanted to experience it all. But I wasn't sure I wanted to experience all of this . . .

Having walked past it several times I'd become interested in a New Age shop in Covent Garden called Mysteries. Once I'd plucked up the courage to go in, I discovered it was packed full of tarot cards, candles, cauldrons, occult books and strange statues of horned gods. I knew I was very much drawn to the darker side of spirituality; there wasn't a lot of it around in Belfast, at least not on the surface, but in London the devil and all his works seemed to be everywhere.

On one visit I'd spotted a handwritten sign in the shop window that asked 'Are you interested in witchcraft? Would you like to learn more?' A London telephone number was scrawled underneath.

'Me,' I thought, 'I'm interested in witchcraft.'

I could see myself casting spells and hanging out with black-cloaked witchy ladies. It wouldn't be the first time I'd dabbled in the world of the strange and the occult. When I was about fifteen, I'd bought a book on astral projection and, highly excited, I locked the front door, closed the curtains in our front room when everyone was out and attempted to float across the ceiling. I sat there for ten minutes, stopping to check if I was doing it right in the book, until a state of extreme disappointment came upon me and I flung the book across the room (at least something was flying), never to look at it again. I considered demanding a refund as it hadn't worked. I even went through a phase of thinking I was a devil worshipper, becoming obsessed with Aleister Crowley and reading everything I could find about him. Also, because my birth date included 666 – 16 July 1966 – I thought I had the mark of the devil. I was a truth-seeker but equally, I was always into instant gratification.

Cautiously, I phoned the number I'd jotted down on the back of my hand. A seductive female voice answered and, after answering a few questions about my interest in witchcraft, I suggested that we meet up. 'King's Cross Station,' said the voice, 'Platform Nine.' Fitting, really, considering the later success of the Harry Potter books.

'How will I know you?' I said.

'Don't worry,' said the voice, 'we'll know you.'

Excited but somewhat apprehensive, I turned up early for the meeting and looked around. The platform was deserted except for a few commuter types rushing for late trains. Then, seemingly out of nowhere, two hippies appeared next to me. A male and a female. We sat on a nearby bench and talked about witchcraft, magic and something called the Kabbalah. That was a new one on me, but it seemed the way they worked as witches was based on this. After about fifteen minutes they stood up as if to go.

'Come to one of our meetings,' said the woman, beaming. 'You can see then what we do – see if it's for you.'

They gave me an address in north London and left. The following week I knocked shyly at a door in Kentish Town and was brought into the incense-filled room. Other people were already there – people with posh accents and expensive clothes. Some of them looked like doctors, lawyers and police officers, and probably were. A smell of marijuana hung in the air, mixing with the incense to form a heady brew. There were two, three, maybe four people all fondling and kissing each other.

After a while the guy who'd interviewed me gave a talk on the Kabbalah and we were required to carry out a few exercises. One was visualising a white globe floating in the air and although I tried I was distracted with what was going on around me. Other people seemed to be getting something out of it, but try as I might I couldn't connect with the thing at all. Here I was, a lad from West Belfast and an ex-Mod, trying to get along with a bunch of New Age freaks. I respected their views but there was definitely something odd going on, something cultish, and I didn't want to delve any further.

I never went back, but the itch that my search for 'something' always produced could never be fully scratched, no matter where I looked. I was doing well in my job – far better than I could ever have imagined – and life in London was great. I'd left 'the Troubles' behind, but my own personal troubles seemed never far from the surface and there were times I'd sink into a deep depression. I'd no idea why this was, or what the causes were other than the rollercoaster of my childhood in Northern Ireland and the crazy, dangerous city where I'd been born and raised. Sometimes there were horrifying reminders of what was going on only a few hundred miles from the bright lights and liberty of London. The lynching of the two British Army corporals who accidentally drove into an IRA funeral party in March 1988 was particularly dreadful. They were slaughtered like animals, and on camera, yet it was nothing short of animals who did the slaughtering. I remember feeling profoundly angry at what had happened, and the old feelings of wanting revenge for such atrocities bubbled up to the surface once more.

And yet there were whisperings from across the Irish Sea of terrible deeds being done by people I knew, good Loyalist friends of mine that I'd grown up with and met through the Mod movement. Some of these were guys who'd joined the UDA at the same time as me, and at the start had been in it for the craic. But they'd taken it far, far further than I could've ever imagined, becoming involved with some very dangerous individuals in and around Loyalist West Belfast and taking part in the killing of innocent Catholics, and fellow Protestants too. I could hardly believe it was the same boys I'd known in my youth; kids like me who'd befriended Catholic Mods and dated Catholic girls. I could understand their desire for revenge on the IRA, sure. But killing random guys in pubs having a quiet drink? To my mind that was deeply wrong and unjustified, and I breathed a sigh of relief that I wasn't over there and caught up in all the horror.

The eighties became the nineties and we moved into the final decade of the millennium. There seemed no end to the violence in Northern Ireland. If anything, those few years before the peace process started appeared to be some of the deadliest in the whole of the thirty-year conflict. The tit-for-tat shootings and bombings on both sides were deeply disturbing, highlighting a whole new level of savagery. Enniskillen. Greysteel. Warrington. Deal Barracks, Kingsmill, Teebane. Loughinisland. And many others. I didn't know it then, and nor did most people in Northern Ireland, but it seemed as if both Loyalist and Republican terrorists were trying to kill as many of the 'enemy' as possible before they accepted the inevitable and would finally sit down to talk peace.

By now I was living in a shared house near Holloway Road with Peter, a Scottish friend and his mate Alan. Alan was also a Scot, and was a Republican supporter who hated Loyalists and Loyalism. He and I were never quite going to see eye to eye about certain things and although we'd banter about our differences he could get very nasty, which pissed me right off.

He was another who had a lot of opinions about Northern Ireland without having had to suffer the difficulties of actually living there. He knew nothing apart from what he'd watched on the telly or read in books, safe in a Glasgow library.

Peter and I were very close; so much so that people often mistook us for brothers when we were out and about. We both had a love of the rave scene, dropping Es and clubbing. I was also spending lots of time with Theresa and John. I was still working in sales jobs, with a bit of bar/hotel work here and there, and I was making good money. However, I was always spending it faster than I made it and was always chasing the next job and dollars to pay for my never-ending party lifestyle.

As I mentioned, the events in Northern Ireland during this period disturbed me, but none more so than the bombing of Frizzell's fish shop on the Shankill in October 1993. That Saturday afternoon I'd been around the pubs and clubs of Holloway Road with David, my brother. He'd also had enough of the Troubles and somewhere around the turn of the decade had decided to join me in London. Although he was the youngest of us, he was always independent-minded and quickly made his own life in the city. However, we saw each other regularly.

David was living in a shared house near Kilburn and was working in the building trade. We often got together for a piss-up and blowout and I was forever leading him astray. Never have two brothers been so different in every aspect and yet we have always been very close.

Anyway, I went home to shower and get ready for the evening

session. I turned on the news to hear reports of a bombing right in the heart of the Shankill. My whole world seemed to stop at that moment, and as the story unfolded I felt a panic rising in my heart and soul. I had sisters, cousins and friends living and working on the Shankill. In addition, everyone would have been down the road shopping and getting ready for the weekend.

I tried phoning Mags and Jean and couldn't get through. I tried Linda and Wee Sam (who, by this time, was known as Sexy Sam – don't ask) and I just couldn't get through to anyone, no matter who I called. As the evening wore on, I was thinking the very worst, especially when news of the fatalities started coming through. I sat in stunned silence, realising I had known many of the victims and their families and I felt an overwhelming need to get back to Belfast and be there for my people and family.

Having grown up in the Troubles, there are certain events that have stayed with me forever and among the many I had lived through, the Shankill bomb was almost the most personal for me. It was a direct attack on my community, and I hated the IRA more than ever that day.

Eventually, I got through to Mags and she assured me that everyone was fine and I had nothing to worry about. Apparently, Pickle and some of my other cousins were down near the bomb when it went off and helped with the rescue effort.

Michael 'Minnie' Morrison, his girlfriend and young child were three of the victims. I had been through secondary school with Minnie and knew him and his girlfriend well. Coincidentally, I also knew the bomber's brother, having been through the YTS scheme with him, as I've mentioned. The Shankill and everyone in Belfast and beyond connected with this part of the city united in grief for this atrocity. Although I remained in England, I was in daily contact with the family, sharing the grief and sorrow as the dead were buried and the community I loved and missed tried to pick itself up again.

As siblings we're all very different but we're supernaturally close, I think because of the loss and trauma we suffered as children. When something happens to one of us we all feel the hurt deeply. Which is why, when the police came knocking on my flat door one evening, I nearly had a heart attack on the spot – and not just because the whole place smelled of weed.

By the looks on the officers' faces, they hadn't called round to bust me for a couple of spliffs. One policeman asked me to identify myself, which I did, and then, as gently as possible, he said that he had some bad news about David Chambers, and could they come in?

There were cigarette papers and tobacco all over the place but I didn't give a shit. Panic rose in every part of my body as I led them into the front room. They told me to sit down and brace myself. My stomach turned to water as I took a seat and one of them said that David had been in an incident and was currently in Whitechapel hospital and they were going to take me directly to see him.

I grabbed a coat and made my way to the police car. On the way to the hospital the officers explained that David had got into an altercation with some youths on the Tube and had been stabbed. He was currently in surgery and that's all they could tell me at that moment.

By the time I got to the hospital I was in a real mess. The policemen led me into a room, where a surgeon explained that David had been stabbed multiple times and had gone into cardiac arrest at the scene.

'I should be honest now,' the surgeon said, 'and tell you that we're fighting to save his life. We are doing our best and we'll keep you informed of our progress when we have a moment. In the meantime, please try to relax and if you need to call anyone, there is a payphone just down the corridor here.'

The phone calls to Margaret and Jean were the hardest I've ever had to make in my life. Their distress triggered a wave of emotion in me, and the three of us sobbed down the line. I told them that David had a slim chance of pulling through, and that they should get over to London immediately. We all understood the irony of the situation: a young fella like David leaving one of the world's most dangerous cities, only to be stabbed in London for no apparent reason.

While the surgery was taking place, I sat outside and smoked myself to death, cursing the gods and the fates for putting us through this latest ordeal – as if we hadn't been through enough. My kid brother had a massive heart and would never hurt or do wrong to anyone. I couldn't understand how he had ended up in the state he was and who would want to hurt him. I was beside myself with fear and anxiety. When he finally came out of surgery, they said he was in intensive care and I should get home and grab some sleep. They would call me if there was any change in his condition.

I went home and watched the news. They were reporting on my brother's stabbing and I felt detached from it all as I sat watching the phone, praying that it wouldn't ring in case they were calling to say David had passed away. It was the longest night of my life.

Next morning I met Margaret and Jean at the hospital. The three of us looked weary – those two from the travelling and all of us from stress and worry – and we sat about for ages not knowing what was going on. Eventually we were brought into the intensive care unit, where David was wired up to what seemed to be dozens of machines. He was in a coma but the doctor said the surgery had gone as well as expected and they were just monitoring him to see when or if he would wake up. We sat holding his hand, crying and once again cursing the gods.

Then something amazing happened. David's eyelids flickered briefly before opening fully. He stared at us and a huge fat tear rolled down his cheek. He squeezed my hand and at that moment I knew he was going to survive. Begrudgingly, I apologised to the gods and thanked them for being kind to us.

His recovery was slow and even now he still carries the physical and emotional scars from that day. When he was fit enough to speak, I got him to tell us exactly what had happened. I had also been speaking to the police, who helpfully filled in some of the gaps.

David and his white South African friend Steve had been on a Tube travelling into central London for a few drinks when a group of four or five young black guys got on. They caught Steve's strong accent and had started to abuse him. The argument turned violent and Steve ran down the train, leaving David alone with the young fellas. They beat him up, stabbed him multiple times and left him for dead before running off. David had had multiple heart attacks and was bleeding profusely before the helicopter arrived and took him to the hospital.

It turned out that the guy who had stabbed David was out on parole for another violent attack and had gone missing. At the time of the attack police were hunting for him. Eventually, several people were arrested and charged with attempted murder. As a family, we waited anxiously for the court hearing. When the time came for the trial we sat in court every day, making sure we let the scumbags know how we felt. I was often overcome by my emotions and hatred for these people and at one stage I was almost thrown out of the court. If I could have got my hands on the main perpetrator, I wouldn't have been a pacifist for much longer. This man was sent down for eighteen years after being convicted of attempted murder, but no doubt he's long out by now and making someone else's life a misery.

In all of this, there remained the unanswered question, the one that had nagged me for years. Where was our mother and why had she abandoned us so suddenly? Margaret, Jean, David and I had been through plenty by then, collectively and in our own lives, and by and large we'd remained strong and resilient. For me, though, this missing piece of the jigsaw was one that had to be located and, if possible, fitted back into its rightful place. Only then would I feel at peace and complete.

CHAPTER 17

The world of sales can sometimes involve periods when you're between jobs. Salespeople are restless types and I was definitely in that category. I've always been a natural salesman and could sell sand to Arabs if push came to shove. If I felt bored or under-paid, I'd quit, then look around for another opportunity. If one didn't appear immediately I'd go back to temping in pubs and bars. Work in this field was plentiful, easy to come by and fun.

This was the position I found myself in during the early part of 1994, when I landed a job at the King's Arms pub in Covent Garden. I was in my late twenties by now but still raving like a madman. Life was one long drug-fuelled party and I was constantly at the pills and the coke. It seemed everyone around me in London was doing the same thing. But I could hold a job down well enough, particularly a pub job where you needed something to keep you up during the long evenings serving customers of all types and in all states of intoxication.

I got the position in the King's Arms via a friend, and I was told that I'd be covering catering shifts for someone called Simone. She was also a part-timer in the pub; the rest of her time she earned her living as a professional dancer. I hadn't met her, but apparently she'd trained at the Ballet Rambert and by all accounts was a lovely and beautiful woman. At that time she was working away in Holland and I hoped she wouldn't come back, because that would mean my hours would be cut.

I loved working at the King's Arms. The owner was an elderly lady called Lilly, straight out of central casting's list of cheeky cockney characters. She dripped gold jewellery and her speech was peppered with rhyming slang. Lilly lived above the pub with her little dog, which the staff hated because it would piss and shit all over the place and we'd be responsible for cleaning up after it.

We were also required to take it for regular walks around the block. One time, after a particularly soggy clean-up operation, one of the barmen took it out. Five minutes later the dog came back completely soaked. I was surprised, as it was a gorgeous sunny summer's day.

'I needed a pee while I was out,' said the barman under his breath, 'so I tied up the little shite down an alleyway and pissed on him. That'll teach him.'

I laughed my head off at that, and thereafter the dog was very reluctant to go whenever Lilly asked the barman to take him for a walk.

It's a good job Lilly never found out because she was very old-school and had what we might call an 'interesting' selection of friends – thieves, gangsters and other assorted villains among them. On Sunday nights, when the pub was quieter than usual, they'd gather in the upstairs bar and gossip about all the local goings-on.

Not that the pub itself was without incident. There was often a bit of coke knocking about the place and various members of staff, including me, would hoover up a few lines to help us get through the evening, particularly at weekends when the place was rammed. On Fridays, when the pub was at its fullest and maddest, we'd drop Es, turn the music up and party as hard as the customers. We were all having the time of our lives – and the staff were getting paid for it!

Because it was located close to so many great theatres and other venues, the pub's regulars were a mad mix of bohemian arty types – including actors, writers, dancers, stage crew. There was a lot of passing trade too – pre-theatre drinkers, the post-work crowd – so there was never a dull moment. Before working in the pub I'd never darkened the doors of any theatre, except maybe for a gig or two, but talking to the arty crowd sparked my interest and I started to see a few West End shows, courtesy of customers who'd offer me free tickets. My cousin Pickle had by now also escaped Belfast and was working on the refurbishment of the Royal Opera House. He and I went there for a few shows and the pair of us would wonder how we'd ended up in such a prestigious venue. I was moving in circles and doing things I'd never dreamed possible. It was a far cry from the tribal world of my childhood in Glencairn and Belfast.

The pub regulars included a guy nicknamed 'Rolex Reg', a dodgy East Ender who always carried a briefcase full of fake watches and other knocked-off gear. He was often found in the corner in meetings, whispering to shady-looking Bulgarians and other Eastern Europeans. There was Maggie, an old girl well past her sell-by date who stank of pee and got pissed every night alone in the corner. At the bar sat John, the boring manic-depressive who would send the devil to sleep with his conversation. There was also a beautiful Japanese dancer who was in love with me and use to buy me really expensive presents, even though I showed no interest in her.

Among the more famous customers were the cast of *The Detectives*; screenwriter Stephen Knight (who created *Peaky Blinders* and *Who Wants To Be A Millionaire?*), comedian and writer Barry Cryer; TV star Phillip Scofield and none other than Teletubbies' 'Tinky Winky' – the actor Simon Shelton, a lovely guy who died tragically young. Famous faces were in and out all the time but for me, the biggest buzz ever was when actor Gary Shail came in one day. He played the drug-dealing Spider in *Quadrophenia* – the film that seemed to echo many aspects of my life as a Mod in Belfast and provided the soundtrack to my antics during those times. In fact, my Belfast Mod mates used to occasionally refer to me as 'Spider' because of my ability to lay my hands on drugs. Gary became a regular and I never got bored with chatting to him at the end of the bar. I only wish I'd taken a picture of us together to prove it!

I'd often hit the town with friends when my shift was finished, and inevitably I'd need drugs to get myself into the party mood. One day, I'd arranged to meet my pal Peter after our shifts were finished at about 6 p.m. We agreed that we'd drop a couple of acid tabs around 4 p.m., so that we'd be coming up just as we set off for our night out. As the end of my shift approached, I could feel things starting to get slightly weird – not surprising, given I'd dropped two microdots. Still, I was used to this, and looking forward to the experience, when Bob came running over and told me that a member of staff had suddenly called in sick. There was a big party due in the upstairs bar, he said, and I'd have to stay on to cover the absence.

I smiled at Bob as I watched his face turn into that of a giant spider's. The spider was now insisting that I get upstairs ASAP and start preparing the bar for the party, which would be starting in thirty minutes. I was too wasted to argue with Bob the Big Spider, who looked at me quizzically and asked if I was all right.

'I'm fine,' I lied, tripping my face off. 'I'm a wee bit knackered, though. I might just take a line to get me through.'

I knew that wouldn't be a problem. I was hoping that the coke might speed me through the trip, or at least make it more manageable. Now I felt more confident I could get through this, I asked Bob what the party was for.

'Oh,' he said, 'it's some old copper retiring. CID. There'll be a lot of Old Bill in tonight. So be on your best behaviour, eh?'

Bob cheekily tapped the side of his nose. I could've died at that point. I felt my heart racing and my mouth was as dry as an Arab's sandal. There was nothing I could do but get on with it and try to act as normally as possible.

The next four hours were a supreme test of mental strength. The two microdots were taking me to places far out of this world and yet I had to serve a room full of peelers with as much charm and sobriety as I could muster. In short, it was very bloody difficult and there were moments where I knew I was losing the plot completely. I was tripping my very bollocks off and how those eagle-eyed CID officers didn't spot it I've no idea. I kept a pint of lager close by and took regular sips, hoping that if anyone saw me acting strangely they'd just assume I'd had a drink or two.

In the midst of all this madness arrived Rolex Reg, who plonked himself at the end of the bar, opened his case and started touting his bent watches to various coppers. This really tickled me and I went into a fit of laughter that seemed to go on and on and on. Bob noticed me and, assuming I'd had a little too much coke mixed with lager, said that I could leave early, and he would finish up. I've never been so grateful to get out of a pub. I grabbed my coat and somehow managed to track down Peter. Far from going home to sleep it off, I necked a few pills and partied the rest of the night away in Soho in a state of advanced hilarity.

I loved Soho. Now, it's an upmarket area for tourists and the wealthy, but even in the early 1990s it still had plenty of its old underworld charm left. I went to many lock-ins in shebeens and secret bars above and below the shops and restaurants. These drinking dens were full of gangsters, druggies and their dealers, thieves, prostitutes, writers, actors and all the rest, and I spent many a night in such places getting wasted and meeting the most weird and wonderful people.

Soho was also full of homeless people and occasionally I'd stop on my way somewhere to give one of these poor folk the price of a cup of tea or a fag. One afternoon I passed a guy lying in a shop doorway in Tottenham Court Road. Something about his face rang a bell with me and as I stooped down to pass him a fag the recognition hit. It was Biff, the big Glencairn skinhead who'd chased me and my Mod mates through Carnaby Street before he realised most of us were good Loyalist lads.

'I remember you,' I said. 'Remember that time you nearly battered me? I was a Mod. Then we all went for pints afterwards.'

Biff looked at me in total confusion. 'I dunno, mate,' he said. 'I was a skinhead, yeah, but . . . it was a long time ago. I got messed up into smack after that. I've not been home to Belfast for years. I'm just here now and . . .'

His voice trailed away. My heart went out to him. I was suited and booted that day, probably on the way to some sales job interview, and looked like I'd never seen a place like Glencairn, let alone grown up there. I walked away knowing that it could've been me lying there had my life gone in another direction. After that first encounter, whenever I was in that part of central London I always looked out for him and if I found him, which I did on a couple of occasions, I'd share a fag or two with him and slip him a few quid. Later I lost contact with him and never saw him again, but I often think of him and hope he found his feet again and somehow turned his life around.

Fate can be very fickle, as well I know. I've had some terrible luck in life, but also moments when good luck has been handed to me as if from heaven. One of those came at the King's Arms in April 1994 and really, it came as a result of possibly losing my job. As I mentioned, I'd taken over the chefing/bartending role from a girl called Simone who was away dancing in a show in Holland. From time to time the other staff would mention her, and the terms 'beautiful', 'gorgeous', 'great personality' would be bandied about. Now, at that time lots of dancers from the nearby theatres came into the pub and seeing beautiful women from all corners of the globe was nothing new to me. All I cared about was that this Simone wouldn't come back too soon, and that I would be able to continue my party lifestyle and enjoy my job at the pub. I liked mixing with all sorts of people – the kind of people you'd never meet in Belfast – and I didn't want to stop having fun.

With my crew, I pubbed and clubbed it all over London. Myself, Peter, John and Theresa particularly enjoyed going to gay clubs because the music there was better than anywhere else. These places were an experience I certainly wouldn't have had back in Belfast, not then anyway. Theresa was a good Catholic girl and never took drugs, though she more than made up for it with her red wine, which she loved. We'd splash out on special occasions and get in bottles of champagne, which seemed to send Theresa to new levels of craziness. As she danced the night away, even those of us pilled up on everything couldn't match her. She always dreamed of meeting Mr Right, which I think she hoped might be me, but there was no way I was into settling down. Theresa was like a big sister to me and I adored her, but a serious relationship was out of the question.

Finally, the day came when I was told that Simone was back from Holland and would be taking up her old job again. I was disappointed, but took it on the chin and worked a normal day, watching the clock ticking round to 5 p.m. so I could get out of there and start partying. About an hour before I was due to finish a group of four dancers came in for a quick drink before their evening show. Among them was the most beautiful girl I'd ever set eyes on. She was mixed-race, with dark hair and eyes. She had a fantastic dancer's body and a wicked laugh. I was totally, completely and utterly smitten.

She came up to the bar and ordered a drink. For a moment I was dumbstruck, then I started slabbering, just rattling on about nothing. She looked puzzled for a minute, then asked me where I was from.

'Hi there,' I said, 'I'm John, I'm from Belfast, I'm here part-time.'

'Ah,' she said, 'I've heard about you. I'm afraid I've got bad news for you. I'm taking over your job from tomorrow.' She stretched out her hand. 'Hi,' she said, 'I'm Simone.'

Well, you could've knocked me down with a feather. Here was the woman who was about to put an end to all the fun I was having, and I'd completely fallen in love with her in an instant.

'What's the matter?' she said, 'Are you upset?'

I realised I'd been staring at her, gobsmacked.

'Ah no, no,' I replied, slabbering again. 'No, that's grand, no hard feelings about the job, eh?'

She smiled with her eyes. 'As long as you're OK about it,' she replied. 'Anyway, I think we'll be working a few days together for the rest of the week, so maybe we'll get to know each other a bit.'

She smiled again and I could've died on the spot. I went out that night as planned but I couldn't get this woman out of my mind. She ticked every single box and I couldn't wait until work came around again so that we'd be able to spend a bit of time together. I'd always been pretty lucky with girls but I'd never been one for spending a lot of time charming them and chatting them up. I figured I'd have to put in a lot of work if I wanted to make a good impression on this one – and more than anything else, that's what I wanted. From the moment I saw her, I knew she was the one for me.

When I set eyes on her again the following day I knew I had to overcome my natural shyness and try and get to know this stunning girl better, so I took a deep breath and turned on all my Belfast charm and patter. Before long we were chatting like old friends. Gradually, I learnt more about her. Her mum was of Indian descent and her dad was white British. When she wasn't travelling as a dancer she lived in Norbury, south London with her parents and brother. I was smitten, but I was too shy to ask her out. Luckily, she took the initiative and asked me if I wanted to take her for a drink. Needless to say, I grabbed the chance with both hands and within a few days we were going out.

Unlike the other girls I'd dated in London, Simone was a keeper; any fool could see that. I was walking on cloud nine, and we spent almost every moment of our free time together. We visited the illegal after-hours drinking clubs in Soho and had many a crazy night just getting to know each other and falling head over heels in love. I knew I was a jammy so-and-so and to this day people say I'm punching above my weight. I just smile and say, 'I know!'

One of those nights in Soho stands out and is imprinted on

my soul forever. We were in a bar, getting drunk and enjoying each other's company and we had stepped outside to have a cigarette. It was pouring down with rain but I didn't care: I was with the girl of my dreams and the world was all good. Then from somewhere The Pogues' 'Rainy Night in Soho' came on and I knew at that moment that I wanted to spend the rest of my life with this beautiful woman.

> *I took shelter from a shower*
> *And I stepped into your arms*
> *On a rainy night in Soho*
> *The wind was whistling all its charms*

Within weeks we were living together and perhaps for the first time ever I started to think about the direction my life was taking. In the past, I'd let things happen to me and, good or bad, had just accepted that was what fate had decided. Also, my mum's continued absence in my life seemed to prevent me from being completely happy. Now I realised that while I'd been incredibly lucky to meet the love of my life, from now on I had to make my own luck. If I wanted to keep Simone I needed to settle down, stop my drugs-and-partying lifestyle, work hard and hopefully have a family one day. This was the first time I had ever felt that way and I knew that my 'Brown Eyed Girl', as I called her, wanted the same. For once, fate and the stars had aligned in my favour and been good to me.

At first we moved into a large apartment in the Angel, north London, above a pawn shop. We shared the house with people from around the world. It was a cool place to live and we had some good times. Once we had a party and it was a crazy affair. We had a DJ and I was so wasted that at the end of the night I got my coat and said my goodbyes to everyone. I'd forgotten I was in my own house.

Shortly after we met, Simone started working with a dance company called Union Dance, which was funded partly by the Arts Council. This was her dream job as she had trained at the Ballet Rambert in contemporary and ballet and Union Dance got to perform throughout the UK and all over the world. It seemed that the stars were aligned for her too, because just before meeting me she had gone to a fortune-teller. She'd been told that her life was going to change and a 'Knight of Cups' (a card from the tarot pack) would enter her life and things would be wonderful. She always said I was her Knight of Cups . . .

The world Simone lived, moved and worked in was far removed from anything I had ever experienced. Before I knew it, I was going to dance performances and learned to appreciate and enjoy most forms of the art. I always got a buzz while watching Simone perform and hearing others around me compliment her and the dance troupe.

We decided to move to south London and while we looked for our own place we went to live with Simone's mum and dad in Norbury. Obviously, I'd been nervous about meeting her parents for the first time and my natural shyness was threatening to call the whole day off, but I sank a few beers and, fortified, I stepped into their world. I had nothing to worry about; they were so kind and nice to me that I felt welcome from the very start.

Simone's mum's Indian heritage fascinated me and I was

mesmerised as she told me stories of her childhood in British Guiana and her mother's upbringing in Kashmir, India. I loved hearing her tales, including those about her grandfather, who was a witch doctor. Even better for me was that she made the best curries I have ever tasted in my life, even making her own naan bread and raita. I was in heaven.

Royston, Simone's dad, was a beautiful, gentle soul and like me he had lost his father at ten years of age, which gave us a special connection. He was laid-back and so easy-going and he and I would often go down the pub where we'd sit for hours, chatting and playing the slot machines. He was a delight to be around. Also, this part of London was very multicultural, and I loved the diversity and feel of the place. I embraced all those around me, as I got to know and love Simone's mum's extended family.

After so much chaos and so many troubles in my life, finally I was looking forward to a honeymoon period that I hoped would last for the rest of my life. While my demons still stalked me and overwhelmed me from time to time, the difficult past that had shaped me in so many different ways seemed to be receding into the distance.

Then, one afternoon, I got a call at work from my sister Margaret. She sounded tearful, and immediately my hackles went up. As I've said, when one of us gets hurt we all feel the pain.

'No, John,' she said, 'it's nothing bad. It's just . . . '

'Just what? Come on, Mags, tell me for God's sake!'

'I'm in shock, John. I really am. I've been passed a letter. It's addressed to you and I need to read it to you over the phone.

Are you sitting down? Please sit down now, John. You're not going to believe this . . .'

CHAPTER 18

An hour or so after Margaret had hung up, I was still unable to stand. She was right. I couldn't believe what I'd just heard. The wind had been totally knocked out of my sails. Of all the news I thought I'd receive – the death of a sibling, a friend or a loved one killed by a bomb or a bullet, an acquaintance sent to prison for some terrorist crime – this was the news I least expected.

But it was what I'd been waiting for all my life. And it had come about by the most incredible coincidence. If I thought I was dealt a lucky hand when I met Simone, this information seemed to have been gifted to me on a golden plate from on high.

It appeared that an old schoolmate from Glencairn, Martin Burns, had been on holiday in Florida. One evening he'd met a couple in a bar. The man was American but his wife was originally from Belfast. As Northern Irish people invariably do, they got talking and it transpired she came from the

Falls Road. Martin said he was from Glencairn. No matter. Everyone was on holiday, having a good time and sectarian differences didn't matter.

The woman then asked Martin whether he knew many people in and around the Shankill. When he said he did, she asked him if he'd ever come across the Chambers family.

'There'd be four wee children,' she said. 'Well, not so wee now. In their twenties or thirties, I'd say.'

Martin was surprised. 'Yeah,' he said, 'I know them right enough, if it's the same ones. John Chambers is my mate. He has two sisters and a brother. Their daddy died years ago. Dunno what happened to their mammy. Disappeared or somethin'.'

The woman fell silent for a moment, then tears pricked at the corner of her eyes.

'John Chambers,' she said. 'That'd be the daddy's name too, right?'

'That's right,' Martin said, 'sounds like the same lot. You know them, then? Small world, eh?'

The woman introduced herself as Philomena, mentioning that her maiden name was McBride. Then she told Martin that she must be our auntie.

'My sister is your friend John's mother,' she said. 'She's been trying to get in touch with her children for twenty years or more, but somehow it's never happened. I can't believe I've met you. Are you still in touch with John?'

Martin nodded. 'Aye, so I am, but he's over in England now anyway.'

'Then may I give you a letter to take home to Belfast and pass on to his family?'

Shocked, Martin agreed to the request. Philomena wrote the letter and passed it to Martin the following day. He brought the letter home and handed it to Margaret. This is what it said:

Dear John,
I hope this letter finds you well and apologies if I have the wrong person.

You obviously don't know me but my name is Philomena McBride and although I now live in Boston USA I am originally from the Falls Road. A few days ago I met a Belfast couple in the local bar and naturally we got talking. When I heard they were from the Shankill Road I felt goose pimples run up and down my spine. You see, my sister, Sally McBride, married a guy from the Shankill Road, John Chambers, in the early sixties and they had four children together.

At the time the Troubles were at their height and as you probably know it was unusual for Catholics and Protestants to marry, as this was frowned upon by both communities.

The strain of coming from a mixed marriage was too much for them and they eventually separated and all the children stayed with their father in Belfast and my sister came to England to start a new life. The break-up was very hostile and my sister was denied access to the children and lost contact with them and has not seen or heard from any of them for twenty-five years. In fact, all contact with members of my sister's family was denied and we have been trying to find the children ever since.

I asked Martin if he knew the Chambers family I was

*amazed when Martin told me he went to school with you
and he knew your brother and sisters. John, I think you
are my sister's son (that makes me your aunt) and I am
including my telephone number and address and would be
over the moon if you would contact me. I will understand if
you don't wish to speak to me but my sister has always loved
you all and has spent a lifetime searching for you. Even to
know that you were all well and happy would mean the
world to her.*

Love, Philomena McBride.

At the bottom of the letter was a United States phone number, which Margaret advised me to write down. As the oldest sister, she was naturally concerned for my welfare. She knew I'd been searching for our mother for so many years, and in vain. She understood how much this long-lost connection meant to me, even though I'd not really known my mother at all. She acknowledged the hurt that the separation had caused us all, in so many different ways.

'John,' she said, 'I know you'll be thrilled by this. And I know you'll want to find Sally now. But please go carefully. It might not be what you hope it will be. That letter says she tried to find us, but was blocked. Now I wouldn't know any of that for sure. All I know is that if I'd been separated from my kids, I'd have moved heaven and earth to find them again.'

I nodded. I knew what Margaret was saying. She and Jean had the stronger memories of our mother, and her disappearance hurt them both very badly. They felt a tremendous amount of anger that four children could be left in this way, and even though they understood how dangerous it might have been for Sally McBride had she stayed married to a Protestant, they still couldn't ever imagine abandoning their kids.

I respected my sisters' point of view. But I had to know the truth. I had to meet the woman who'd walked away from us all those years ago, and I needed to know what she looked like, how she spoke, who she resembled – and why she left us. There was no way I could let this rest now, not after such an incredible twist of fate. The universe had called – now I had to answer that call.

For a day or two I couldn't bring myself to ring the number. I stared and stared at it. Simone understood what I was going through. By now I'd explained the whole dynamic of the family situation and she'd been as shocked as I was when she'd heard about the letter.

'Just take your time, babe,' she advised. 'This is really big news for you and you shouldn't rush anything.'

That was true, I knew. That said, I've never been the world's most patient man. I like it when things are happening. A couple of days later I worked out the time difference between London and Boston, then rang the number when I imagined Philomena might be in.

She cried when I told her who was calling. I cried when I heard the voice of Philomena McBride, my aunt and the sister of my mother. I'd never been as close as this to my 'other' family, the one I knew next to nothing about. Philomena gave me some details which confirmed that, yes, we were related.

'Is she still alive?' I asked. 'Sally. My mum. Is she alive or dead?'

'She's alive, John,' she said. 'She's OK. She's living in England, somewhere up north. I can find her address for you.'

'And her phone number?'

'And her phone number, yes. If you want to speak to her. She's been looking for you for a long time, you know. I've told her about meeting Martin and the letter, and she wants to know that you're all OK.'

'We are,' I said.

Well, OKish. It hadn't always been easy, far from it, but we'd survived. There would be time for all that later on.

'And she wants to know if you'd be willing to meet her?'

In response I let out a huge sigh, both of relief and fear. Relief that I would eventually come face-to-face with the woman who gave birth to me, but also fear that for the second time, I would be rejected. I started to cry, and found that I couldn't stop. Philomena was crying too. The whole thing was racing along on a rip tide of emotion. I hardly knew what to think, only that I couldn't stop now. Whatever happened next, for my own peace of mind I had to meet this woman.

'I think the best is that I get Sally to call you, John,' she said. 'Then you both have time to prepare. If you give me your number, I'll set something up. How does that sound?'

I agreed, and within a few days a date and a time was set. At the appointed hour I sat by the phone, willing it to ring and wondering if it ever would. When it did, right on time, I nearly jumped off my chair.

'Hello?' I said

'Hello? John?'

'Is that . . . you?'

'It is. It's me. Sally. Your mum.'

'Mum.' A word I always prayed and hoped I'd hear from the lips of the woman who gave birth to me, but never expected I would. Now she was just a breath away.

'Oh my God. I can't believe I'm talking to you . . .'

'I know. I feel the same way. Sweet Jesus, I never dreamed this would happen.'

She still had her Belfast accent, though softened by her time in England – just as mine was now. I asked her where she was, and how she was.

'I'm fine, John,' she said, 'just fine. I have a life up here in Lancashire now. I have a nice fella that I've met, and my job's good. But oh my God, have I missed you four. How are yousc all?'

I filled her in with some basic details but I was wary of saying too much. Years of living under the shadow of the Troubles had taught me that. Also, I didn't want everyone else's lives exposed so fully just yet. Margaret, Jean and David were all struggling to absorb this momentous news; they would have their own ways of dealing with it. I just wanted to know that she was safe and well, and to tell her that we, her children, were OK too.

We laughed and we cried. We talked for what seemed ages. Occasionally I heard the sound of coins being slotted into a box. There's a sound you never hear now.

'Are you at a payphone? Don't you have a phone at home?'

'I do,' she said, 'but . . . it's probably just easier this way for the minute.'

Then I realised – she didn't really know who she was talking to. Yes, I was John Chambers, her son, but aside from that she knew nothing about me. For all she knew, I could be some mad sectarian killer bent on revenge for the fact that his mother had abandoned him as a wee boy. By ringing from a callbox she too was being cautious. Whatever had happened to send her away from Belfast, it still must have scared her witless twenty-five years after the event.

We talked and cried and talked some more, before agreeing that she and I should meet up. Before she went, I warned her that her daughters may not feel the same way about her as her sons did.

'I understand, John,' she said, 'and I have to accept that. I can't blame them. But if I can just see you, and perhaps David, then I'll be happy. Maybe in time things will be different.'

David had even fewer memories of Mum than I had, and perhaps for that reason he agreed to come with me to meet her. To him, she was just a word, a name. Even so, he had suffered just as much as the rest of us for the fact of her absence and, like me, was looking for answers.

We met at Euston in mid-January 1995. The UK was in the grip of one of its coldest winters in years. Outside, heavy snow was falling and the landscape was covered in a thick blanket of white. I watched silently out of the carriage window as the train gathered speed, scenery flashing by in a blur of white and grey. Opposite, David snored quietly and I was glad of the silence. I needed to prepare myself for what was to come.

I watched as we sped by houses built along the line and thought of the families inside them. Many would be close-knit, happy and functional, with parents who could get along and – in this part of Britain, at least – would never be torn apart on the grounds of religious differences. Yet despite many things, not least the day-to-day madness of living in Northern Ireland, mine was a functional family. There was love, warmth and respect. But of the two people who'd brought this family into being, one was dead and the other had been missing for too long.

Now it was time to confront the ghosts of my past.

David slept on, oblivious to the blizzard of thoughts and emotions swirling around my mind. He was still a wee baby when Mum had left. It was hard to believe that a mother could simply abandon a child of just a few months old, but in the war zone that was Northern Ireland at the start of the 1970s, anything was possible. I didn't understand her actions; neither did I condemn her. She was just doing what she thought was right for us and for her. Had she stayed, she might not have even lived to see us grow up. Had she survived and raised us instead of Dad, we'd most likely have been Republicans living close to the Falls Road. That was mind-boggling, given we'd had exactly the opposite upbringing.

Too many questions, not enough answers. For years I'd tried to learn more about my mother but had been stonewalled by family who simply refused to discuss her. This too I understood. They'd raised me and my siblings, nurturing and caring for us, especially when Dad died. They'd tried to create stability in the midst of chaos. Difficult questions about a Catholic mother played no part in strengthening that stability. It would be best just to forget her, I was told, and let sleeping dogs lie. Nothing good would come of trying to find her. They didn't understand that whatever she was or whatever she'd done, she was still my mum; she had brought me into the world and I missed her deeply. The nagging feeling of loss would never be healed unless my questions were answered.

I pulled the folded piece of writing paper from my pocket and, for the thousandth time, read the words. '. . . *My sister has always loved you all and has spent a lifetime searching for you.*'

Neither David nor I knew what to expect. What would she look like? Who would she look like? Would she even turn up? David yawned, stretched and stared out of the window. We'd just left Wigan and with only a few minutes to go before our final destination we started to gather our bags along with our thoughts.

The metal-on-metal screech of the train's brakes being applied signalled the end of the line for us. We made our way to the door and I watched as the train slowed by the platform. Just before it came to a halt I pulled down the window and reached for the door handle, opening it a crack as the train finally stopped.

'This is it,' I said, turning to David. 'the moment we've been waiting for.'

'I'm shaking like a bloody leaf,' he replied. 'D'you reckon this was a good idea, John?'

'Too late now, mate,' I said. 'C'mon, let's do it.'

We stepped down from the train. The platform was completely deserted, except for a solitary figure waiting at the far end by the exit steps. Bags slung over our shoulders, we walked towards it. As we approached the steps there was no doubt in my mind. She was the spitting image of my sister,

Jean. Short and blonde, with a glint of mischief in her eye. She hesitated, then half-walked, half-ran towards us.

'John! David! My boys! Jesus, my boys are here!'

We didn't quite fall into her arms – there was far too much to discuss before that level of intimacy – but I could tell by her tears that she never believed this day would happen. And in truth, neither did I.

'I'd have recognised you anywhere,' she said, appraising my face. 'You're the spit of your daddy. I can see him standing here in front of me right now.'

I smiled, wondering if she even knew my father had been dead for almost twenty years. But we would deal with all that later. For now, we would just drink in this one-in-a-million moment, born of so many troubles and tears. Fate had conspired to keep us apart during the worst of times. Now, reunited by the most incredible coincidence, we who had been separated by hatred and division for a quarter of a century would finally get to know each other once more.

CHAPTER 19

We sat in a nondescript pub on the outskirts of Preston – me, David, Mum and her husband, Denis – and stared at each other in disbelief

'Tell me this is not happening,' said Mum. 'Tell me it's just a dream. Two grown men sitting here. My wee boys. I wanted this day to come for so long, but I never thought it would.'

'Neither did we, Mum,' David said. 'It's been so long. I don't even remember you, to be honest.'

This was painful to hear, but truthful. Tears welled up in Mum's eyes. Denis leaned across and held her hand. Her pain was obvious for all to see. I didn't want to push anything too hard, yet I had so many questions I wanted to ask. I'd already filled in some of the gaps – Dad dying, our upbringing with other people, my escapades as a Mod and getting mixed up with the paramilitaries. I could tell she was shocked at that last part, and wary too. I told her that my involvement had ended years ago and that I'd never done anything while a member, but how did she know what I was saying was true? After all, she knew nothing about us.

'We missed you, Mum,' I said. 'All of us. We needed you. We were in a mess without you. We thought you were dead, you know.'

'I was, in a way,' she said. 'I had to leave. I don't know what would've happened to me – to all of us – if I'd stayed. It was the hardest choice I ever had to make. I tried to contact you, but . . . I couldn't. I was warned away.'

I could believe it – many couples in mixed marriages faced threats and violence from the paramilitaries on both sides and mixed couples had been killed in the maelstrom of sectarian violence.

She started to cry. Gently I put my hand in hers and squeezed it. In a strange way, I felt like the parent now, the one who needed to give comfort and reassurance.

Slowly, she started to tell us a story. She was one of seven – six sisters and a brother – and her mother Jane died tragically young while giving birth. Mum and her siblings were brought up by their father, my granddad Christy McBride, who I never got to meet. There were also two other sons but they died of TB when they were only a few years old. Ironically, my great-granddad on Mum's side was a Protestant who came over from Scotland and settled in Sandy Row.

Then there was the start of the Troubles, the fear and violence growing daily, and the danger of being in a mixed marriage in a vicious sectarian conflict. At first, she and Dad lived in Ardoyne, which was mixed back then, but Dad didn't feel safe there and they moved down to Little Distillery Street so they could be near my grandparents and Mum's family, who lived on opposite sides of the sectarian-divided street. There, amid all the rioting and violence, Mum had a nervous breakdown. She had no idea what might lie ahead for her in Belfast, only that she could stay no longer.

'I left with only the coat on my back,' she said, 'but I took a few things of yours, just as keepsakes. Photographs, toys, some wee bits of clothing . . .'

'You took some of our baby clothes?' I said.

'Aye, wee jumpers, shoes, that kind of thing. I still have them. I'll show you next time you come up. You will come up again, won't you?'

I reassured her that I would. She desperately wanted to make this work and keep us close now that we had been reunited again. She wanted us to know she hadn't been a bad mother. I had some sympathy with Margaret and Jean's view that under no circumstances would you leave your kids. Equally, I could see that Mum did what she thought was best for all of us, herself included, in the extraordinarily violent atmosphere that was Belfast in the late 1960s.

'I knew your father had died, you know,' she said. 'My family told me. I came over . . .'

'To see us?'

'To see you, and to maybe get you back. I couldn't see you. I wasn't allowed. But I asked social services about having you back. They contacted your dad's family and the answer was "no". That the family would be looking after youse all now.'

Apparently, a Catholic social worker visited Grannie and Granddad up in Glencairn and went back to tell Mum and her sisters to forget about us as we were living in a Loyalist shithole and there was no hope for us. At some stage there was another attempt to get us back, but after a few meetings it was decided that we were better off with Grannie and family in Glencairn and thus we were left where we were.

'At least you tried,' I said, trying to comfort her.

'I did,' she replied sadly. 'But I got nowhere.'

'How strange,' I thought, 'that I was thinking about Mum so much after Dad died and there she was, probably less than a couple of miles away from us, trying to get us back.'

Mum said that after that she tried to put everything behind her. She lost contact with her family in Belfast and had already moved up north, where she met Denis. He was English, a committed Catholic, and a lovely man. His religion didn't matter to me. Although I'd only just met him, I could tell he was the right man for Mum and I hoped I would establish a good relationship with him over time. He was one of those rare folk who everyone loved – no one had a bad word to say about him. From the start he treated me and David like a member of his own family, which considering we were two Loyalists who had turned up out of the blue was testimony to his character. His kindness and generosity of spirit filled us with joy and we loved being around him, although no one would or could ever take the place of our dad.

I was also curious to know if Mum had ever had any other children and this thought both troubled and intrigued me. I'm not sure how I would have felt if she had; no doubt jealousy and anger may have come into it. She hadn't looked after us and the thought that she might have had other children and brought them up would have left a bitter taste in my mouth.

She assured me that she had never considered having any other children.

'I have four children, John,' she said. 'That's enough for me.'

Straight away, I noticed Mum was sketchy about the details of her disappearance. It was as if she'd tried so hard to bury the painful memories that she never wanted them excavated again, not even for her own children. Belfast people are open people in many respects but very closed in others, and I sensed there were things she wasn't telling me – and might never explain.

In a way, that was fine. I understood that her life, and the decision she'd made, had been very hard. If she had secrets she wanted to keep close to her chest, there wasn't much I could do about it. I saw no reason to push her. She was evidently pleased to have me back in her life. Could I ask for more? Not at this stage. And did I really want to know more? In truth, my mind screamed for answers to the questions that might explain why she had abandoned us. But I had spent so much of my life missing her that I pushed these thoughts away and made a decision to accept things for what they were and to enjoy every moment of getting to know my mum again and let the past stay in the past. Sometimes this was very hard; after all, I'm only human.

Despite the many difficulties encountered as a result of her leaving and my dad's death, we had grown up with a warm and close family on Glencairn. Yes, those days were wild and chaotic, but the love of my grandparents, aunties, uncles and cousins was never in doubt. I'd had a deprived childhood, but it was certainly not short of love. The miserable time spent with Alistair and Betty aside, I'd felt secure and happy. Nothing could or would change that.

The connection between Mum and me was instant. We wanted to meet again. I told her about the incredible, beautiful woman I'd met, and how we planned to spend the rest of our lives together. Mum was pleased that I seemed to be settling down and we parted with a promise that we would be part of each other's lives for as long as they lasted. We kissed, embraced and said our goodbyes. David and I returned to London in a hazy daze – life would never be the same again for any of us but at least we'd found what we'd been looking for.

After that first meeting we went up as much as possible, spending almost every holiday and long weekend with Mum and Denis. That first year she invited David and I up to spend Christmas with her and it was the most wonderful time in many a long year. She made a special effort and on Christmas Eve all Denis's family came around for the party that Mum and he held each year.

I missed Dad and I thought of him, as I always do at Christmas and on other special occasions, and there was a part of me that was jealous thinking of Mum having so many Christmases with Denis's family while we were 'orphans' in Belfast. The ghosts of my past were still close, whispering in my ear.

Nevertheless, that Christmas Mum bought David and I sackfuls of presents. Mine included a typewriter because she knew I was interested in writing. The day was wonderful, and my soul was extraordinarily happy. I felt like a child again and was pleased my brother was there to share the experience with me. Denis, being a good Catholic, asked that Mum, David and

I attend Midnight Mass with him and I thought, 'Why not, if it keeps him happy?' If my mates from Glencairn had seen me in a Catholic church they'd have been astounded, but I'd come a long way from the entrenched prejudices of my childhood. Never again would I judge a man by his religion or culture, provided the god they worshipped and the political system they followed was peaceful and respectful to all others.

Although I had long moved on from my childhood Christian days, God still meant something to me and to this day I find churches and religious services soothing to my soul. I love choir music and hymns, although I can't hear 'Amazing Grace', the hymn played at Dad's funeral, without getting a lump in my throat.

Mum's reappearance triggered conflicting emotions in me. I was overjoyed and delighted to find the piece of the jigsaw that had eluded me for so long, yet the act of discovering her reawakened very painful emotions from childhood that I'd only addressed by suppressing them with whatever was available – drink, drugs, mayhem and chaos. Now I was heading towards my thirties and I'd met the girl of my dreams. I knew I should be settling down and thinking about a different kind of life, but demons continued to haunt me, and I made yet another half-arsed suicide attempt – this time with pills. Quite a lot of this was down to difficulties with gambling – I am the classic addictive personality – and after one big loss I felt I'd let myself and everyone else down. Simone was away at the time, dancing in Turkey, and I felt alone and helpless without her. So in a drunken fit of madness I necked some pills and ended up with a stay in a mental hospital.

This was a very brief visit but it was enough to make me realise that I had a lot going for me in life, and I'd be a fool if I let the darker, destructive side of my personality have its way. When Simone came home she made me join Gamblers Anonymous and I went along and sat in the 'Chair of Truth'. Thankfully, with their help I eventually beat the gambling addiction and apart from the Grand National I never bet these days.

I also agreed to take a course of anti-depressants combined with counselling, and I can only thank the NHS for the help and support they gave me – and continue to give me. I still have my off days when I feel nothing is right with the world and I wonder whether being prone to depression is hard-wired into my psyche. I'm something of a prisoner of my past, physically (with my bad leg) and mentally too. That said, very few of us are dealt a perfect hand in life and making the best of whatever you get, even if it's difficult at times, is probably the best and only way to deal with it. I work at it, reminding myself every day that I have so much to be grateful for.

I realised that I needed to stop moonlighting in and out of bar and sales work and settle down to something regular. I joined a market research company in Victoria and after a few weeks' training I was promoted to a supervisory role. This involved the training of new staff on the ins and outs of market research and supervising the various shifts. I enjoyed the work but the pay wasn't great, so I ended up working for a print advertising company in Croydon that worked on a range of magazines, including *Football Monthly* and *Dream UK*, one of the country's biggest-selling dance music magazines – right up my street.

I took great satisfaction in learning to be an ad exec, cutting deals with some of the biggest advertising agencies in London for the various titles I worked on. I was flying again and punching way above my education level as usual. Simone's career as a dancer was taking her across the world and we'd settled into a blissful existence where we had the time and money to really enjoy ourselves. My contact with Mum was regular and we visited Lancashire when we could. On one of the early visits Mum brought out the baby and toddler clothes that she had kept for all the years she had been without us. Seeing those, along with the few snaps she had of us as children, was very emotional indeed.

Mum and Denis owned a canal barge, of all things, and when she invited Simone and I for a week's holiday touring the Leeds–Liverpool Canal we jumped at the chance. We had a lot of fun chatting, drinking, eating and seeing the sights. Spending time with Mum made me realise that it's never too late for anything: time can heal even the most turbulent events, such as those Mum had experienced when she left Belfast and her children behind.

The best holidays of all were the ones we spent by the Toward Lighthouse, in Dunoon, Scotland. We were staying in a deserted cottage, right by the lighthouse. We were right beside miles and miles of secluded beach and we spent long hours walking around, collecting shells and crabbing. One year we went there for New Year's Eve and although it was absolutely freezing, the beach looked beautiful blanketed in snow. One afternoon we took a walk along the beach and for some reason Denis and David decided they were going to strip off and go for a swim in the sea. 'Utter madness,' was my reaction when they asked me to join them. It was bitterly cold and the sea looked angry and dangerous. Anyway, I held their clothes and watched while they went for a quick dip. My balls were in my stomach just thinking about it.

On summer's days we would have a barbecue by the sea and play bowls at the front of the cottage. In the evenings, the drink would come out and we would spend hours playing Trivial Pursuit. Denis, who seemed to know everything about everything, always won. The games would be forgotten the more drink we had and when we were nicely in our cups Mum would put on her Irish tunes and we'd have a good old sing-song. I remember me and Denis singing the traditional Irish song 'The Fields Of Athenry' at the top of our voices and I came to know the words off by heart. Thank God my mates on the Shankill and in Glencairn couldn't hear me.

At the time, the late 1990s, Northern Ireland was very much back in the news. Years of secret meetings, and a realisation by all sides that no one was ever going to 'win' the Troubles, had brought about the Good Friday Agreement. I was still in touch with my mates – those in prison as well as those on the other side of the wall – and I kept a close eye on what was happening in my hometown. I'd go home three or four times a year and of course always for 12 July. The Twelfth was still my favourite time of year and a great celebration of my cultural heritage.

While Simone was busy working in the dance world and travelling all over the place, I was plodding along in my new career. One day she told me she was pregnant and my whole world changed in an instant. We hadn't planned for a baby, but the news filled us both with happiness and we started building our nest for the arrival of our little bundle of joy. In October 1999, Simone gave birth to a beautiful girl, who we named Autumn (after The Small Faces' song 'The Autumn Stone' – once a Mod, always a Mod!). Her birth date was two days after my dad's, which made her feel extra-special.

Although I had always been good with kids and had been around for the births of my first three nieces, parenthood was a learning curve for both of us. As we were both working, Simone's parents played a very active role in Autumn's early years and she was always especially close to them. Roy, her grandfather, was keeping her entertained one day in Norbury Park when little Autumn was spotted by a talent agent. Her looks and personality earned her many subsequent child modelling contracts with organisations including George at Asda and Marks & Spencer, among other well-known brands.

Three months after Autumn was born, Simone was booked in for a series of shows on Broadway, New York. As she was still breastfeeding, we decided I should string along too, and look after the baby while Simone was dancing. It was mid-February and across the city the snow was thick on the ground. I was absolutely freezing but I took a well-wrapped-up Autumn out sightseeing and discovered all the wonders of New York. Less than two years later I watched in horror with the rest of the world as the Twin Towers that I'd marvelled at collapsed during the 9/11 attacks. I was horrified and saddened. The lessons about terrorist conflict that had been so hard-learned in Northern Ireland seemed to have been completely forgotten, and tragically we were entering a new age of conflict and bloodshed. The attacks disturbed me greatly. Will we ever learn to put down the guns and live in peace? Anyone who lived through the Northern Ireland conflict would tell you that it's the best way, but no one else seems to be listening. How sad for humanity.

Mum, of course, was delighted by the birth of her 'first' grandchild. It wasn't her first, of course – there were others in Belfast, but she'd never seen them. She doted on Autumn (and later our son, Jude) and so did Denis, who I'd come to love and respect as one of the kindest, most helpful and thoughtful of men. In early 2002, Mum told me the terrible news that he had cancer and again, I was angry with God for bringing trouble to this devout Catholic who never missed Mass. Ironically, although Mum was a Catholic she rarely, if ever, went to Mass, saying that her religious beliefs were 'between me and Him upstairs'. Denis would roll his eyes but he'd never criticise her, preferring to get on with his own religious practice.

Bravely, he fought the cancer but the battle couldn't be won. We were devastated. Losing him was like losing another parent and it was dreadful for Mum because Denis was her rock. And yet, Denis's death crystallised a thought that had already been playing around my mind: that as a family, we should move up to the north of England and be closer to Mum. At the time I was getting into trouble with gambling again. This time it was online stuff and I was in a mess. I was earning good money but it was disappearing into a black hole of my own making. Simone, Autumn and I were spending enough time going up and down the motorway from London anyway, and a move felt like something of a new start for us all.

For the first six months or so we lived with Mum while

we found our feet and established ourselves in the small town just outside Preston where we still live. As ever, such a big change came with its challenges, but we settled into our new life well, particularly Simone, who used her dance and fitness experience to train as a yoga teacher and become very successful at it. She gave birth to Jude and we also got married in Lancashire. Of course, we spent a huge amount of time with Mum and although the years we were apart could never be re-lived, at least now there was a great relationship and a sense of a wrong righted.

When we first moved up north, I got a really well-paid sales job, earning more than a grand a week, and this enabled us to get a lovely wee terrace house. It was Mum who pushed for us to get married and we had a luxury wedding. For the first time ever I got to meet all Mum's sisters in one place and I really enjoyed this. Mum was proud to show her sons off to her sisters and was proud of the way we'd turned out – and that we hadn't been too fanatical in our Loyalism.

Around 2007, the year Jude was born, I had two more serious fractures to my right femur and knee within a three-month period and the pain was indescribable. This meant I spent a considerable time in hospital. I hated it and couldn't wait to get out and back to Simone and the children. These breaks set me back years with my leg, causing me no end of pain and misery and to this day I must be very careful as my right leg is very weak and the smallest wee knock could cause another break.

Despite our increasing physical and emotional closeness, Mum never really explained in detail the circumstances of her leaving. She'd talk a bit about her life in London, and how she'd met Denis and moved up to Lancashire to work in a factory. She said she'd had a nervous breakdown and, of course, that she'd attempted to get us back, but if I ever probed further Mum would simply close down. She found the whole thing far too painful to talk about and no matter how I tried, the events of 1969–70 had been placed into a box marked 'Never to be opened'.

Mum was very stubborn and after our first meetings she refused to discuss the circumstances of her leaving Dad and us. At the time I just had to accept this and put into the back of my mind, where it festered for years, until one night after a few beers I demanded to know why she'd left us and never tried harder to find us. She got very upset and told me that we had dealt with that when we had first met and she had nothing more to say about it all.

This was hard to swallow. I felt I was owed an explanation and, to be fair, I did get a partial one. But I think – as we four siblings all do – that there is more to the story than meets the eye. She was told, in no uncertain terms, that she wasn't welcome back and couldn't have anything to do with us. Even in the pressure-cooker environment of Belfast during the Troubles, this was a major decree and, obviously fearful, she took it seriously. What else might have happened between Sally and John that caused such a violent and permanent rift? We simply don't know for sure, and over time I learned not to ask. Mum's reaction was too upsetting. After everything that had happened, I didn't want to lose her again.

CHAPTER 20

The years went by. We settled into life in the north-west of England and found it to our liking. The kids missed their grandparents in London but were lucky to have another grandparent – albeit one I never expected them to have – close by and keen to play a big part in their lives.

As I got to know her, I discovered that Mum was a practical joker and had a wicked sense of humour. She never let the facts get in the way of a good story and she could tell a great tale that hooked you from the beginning. Her laughter was infectious.

She'd been this way from childhood, it seemed. She said of herself that she was 'a cheeky wee so-and-so' and often pulled pranks and tricks on her sisters. Once when they were out in Bangor, an Orangeman offered to give them a lift back to Belfast. They piled into the car and enjoyed the free ride home. Just as she was getting out of the car, Mum turned to the driver and said, 'Thanks for the lift, mister. By the way, I'm a Fenian from the Falls!' Then she ran off at full speed!

Mum and I had a few minor fall outs over the years but nothing too serious and she was always there when I needed her. She was very headstrong and set in her ways. Once she had made a decision there was no going back and she could be infuriating sometimes with her stubbornness. Neither was she your typical little grannie sitting at home, baking and knitting. Every evening she'd have a few whiskies and watch the telly, particularly *Coronation Street*. Whenever I hear the famous theme tune now, a kind of sadness washes over me for the wasted years I never got to spend with Mum and all the things we missed out on.

What surprised me most was how well she got on with the kids. She had an enormous amount of love and affection for them, which they gave back to her in spades. To Denis's family she was known as 'Aunt Sally' and they worshipped the ground she walked on, as did Autumn and Jude. When I saw her interacting with children, I thought of how difficult the decision must've been to abandon her own kids, and how she must have been racked with guilt ever after. She seemed to overcompensate where children were concerned, and if they were around would focus on them to the exclusion of almost everything and everyone else.

She was a joy to watch as she wound them up, played jokes on them, told tall stories and took part in silly games. She was a natural around children and when I saw her so involved it only reinforced what I'd not had. She never talked down to them and would have them captivated as she told them she used to know a leprechaun back in Ireland. She'd have them believing she knew where the pot of gold was and they would go into the garden and try to help her find it. She'd often hide gold chocolate coins in the garden and the kids were delighted when they discovered the treasure.

Not surprisingly, the one thing Mum and I did not agree on was politics. It never came between us, but she was a natural Nationalist and was never hesitant in expressing her views, which could occasionally spill over into out-and-out Republicanism. Although she was married to an Englishman she was always bitching about the British, the Loyalists and the Prods while sticking up for the Nationalist community in Belfast. This amused and appalled me in equal measure and although I tried hard to see her point of view, a political reconciliation wasn't really on the cards. She told me that when she and Denis visited Belfast they often spent time in the Nationalist pubs and clubs along the Falls Road. Despite being a Catholic, Denis's English accent was quickly noticed and he told me he stood out like a very sore thumb. Although he enjoyed visiting the city, I think he was never sorry to say farewell to West Belfast. All that said, Mum was as appalled and angered as anyone over IRA and Loyalist killings and she was a big supporter of the peace process. She'd had enough of a taste of the Troubles herself to know there could be no going back to the days of tribalism and terror.

Mum and Denis had been heavy smokers for most of their lives, but had managed to quit for a number of years. That was until Denis contracted terminal cancer. He didn't see the point in stopping and so he and Mum took it up again. Denis's death didn't deter Mum from the fags but I could see that, over time, they were having an effect on her. She'd had bouts of serious illness, during which I'd urge her to go to the doctors.

'Away with you, John,' she'd say, a fierce look in her eye. 'I don't trust those people. Dragging you in and testing you for this, that and the other. I'm fine, so stop fussing. And anyways, I don't want them doctors sticking things in me.'

'But you're not well, Mum.'

'I am well. Don't you tell me how I feel!'

'You're not well. It's obvious. You're coughing your lungs up and you can hardly breathe. Go and get yourself checked out. How do you know what's wrong with you if you don't go?'

'I've told ye – there's nothing wrong with me. So shut yer bake – maybe you should stop smoking too.'

Well, she had a point there but even so, she was looking ever frailer with each week that passed. During Christmas 2017, she took a flight to my brother's place in Ireland and became very ill in the airport. She had to be wheeled on to the plane (there was no talk of giving up and going home) and when she arrived back in Lancashire after the break I insisted she went to the doctor's. She was in chronic pain and had stopped eating. A series of tests were run and less than forty-eight hours later she was contacted by the hospital – could she come in please, there was something she needed to know.

It was cancer, of course; lung cancer. She took it as well as she could, which was with courage and resilience. Maybe she knew that after all the trauma she'd endured, she wouldn't live much beyond seventy years old.

I was in pieces. I was devastated and angry. All these years without her, and now she was being taken away again, this time permanently. I didn't want her to die, and I didn't want her to suffer. I was all for more treatment but I didn't want her pumped so full of drugs that she didn't know who she was, or who any of us were. There were several moments when she seemed at the point of death but somehow rallied. Belfast people are tough.

Even so, there came a point where the end was in sight. In June 2018, I was in the local hospital's cancer care unit with her as she underwent yet another round of tests. The news wasn't good – the cancer had spread from her lungs to her breast and most worryingly to her spine. The prognosis was six months at the most.

When I heard the news, I went into meltdown. Excusing myself, I went to the toilets, sat down, put my head in my hands and cried like a baby, sobbing uncontrollably. My heart was broken all over again and I didn't know if I would be strong enough to deal with watching Mum die in front of me, after everything we'd been through.

After the initial shock, I pulled myself together and made it my duty to comfort Mum as much as possible. I grasped at anything positive, talking to her about the various treatments available, and told her that she shouldn't give up and that we were going to fight this together. In my grief and sorrow I was clutching at anything and I attended the next few hospital appointments with her, asking the doctors what could be done to help her.

At one of these appointments I rattled on, wondering if we could put the cancer into remission or cure it altogether. In reply, a doctor discussed different treatments and how long extra she might have if she took these tablets or that round of chemotherapy. She sat in bed, the doctor and I on each side, and listened silently as we talked through the options. Then she raised her hand.

'Stop,' she said, in the voice I'd come to recognise as her 'serious' tone. 'I've heard enough. John, I don't want any treatment. I've told ye that until I'm blue in the face. I just want to die. That's all.'

This broke me all over again as she was so stubborn and once she'd made her mind up about something, that was final, even when talking about treatment to prolong her life. She wanted to go home and die in her favourite chair, surrounded by those she loved.

Surprisingly, Margaret took the news very hard, though I knew she would feel some sorrow at her passing. Throughout the years I'd always kept Mags up to date with our life up north and with Mum and she was always interested to hear about her, but never felt the need to meet her. There were times I could see she was in conflict about this and in the beginning I thought that Mags might be able to forgive and forget the past and make contact with Mum. But this was not to be, and I trusted and respect both my sisters' choice in this matter.

To their credit, they have never judged or criticised David and me for wanting to get to know Mum again and this is testimony to their true love for us. They've put their own feelings aside in order to stand by us no matter what our choice was, even with something so monumental as meeting our estranged mother. Other families could have gone to war, but we four have been through so much together that nothing could ever come between us and that stands to this day. I know for a fact that my sisters would fight to the death to care for and protect us and that is a very special connection.

They were both older when Mum disappeared and therefore have more memories of her. Like me, they have a very strong sense of family and that unbreakable connection through love and shared history. And, like me, they would move heaven and earth for their children.

I understand this too. However, having her in my life was the only thing that would make my restless soul content and I was able to put feelings of anger and resentment aside for ever and enjoy having her around me.

After our first meeting, Mum held out hope that Mags and Jean would come round, but as the years ticked on she let go of this dream and we barely spoke about it until the last few months of her life, when she was full of regrets and guilt over what she'd done. I could never judge her over this, and I comforted her with stories about Mags and Jean's life back in Belfast. I think she was ashamed of herself in many ways.

Eventually, Margaret did feel the need to reach out and she wrote Mum two letters. She treasured them and slept with them under her pillow every night, which made me sad for the lost opportunities over the years. The joy these letters brought her was a ray of sunshine in a sea of misery and it soothed my soul and hers a little. I wish Mum had taken the opportunity to write write both Mags and Jean letters to apologise and try and explain why she had thought the best course of action was to leave us with our father's family in Belfast. Near the end, I know that Mum was considering writing to them. But by the time she was ready to write, she was too weak and drugged-up and although we made several attempts she was unable to concentrate for very long. I wish she had done so, to give them both a bit of closure on events that had shaped our whole lives, but I think she was afraid of being rejected by them both.

That said, she came to my brother's wedding in the Republic of Ireland and got to meet some of her grandchildren from my sister's side. Although they spoke to her, they didn't make a long-term connection and played no further part in her life. The sadness of this situation weighed heavily on me and in the beginning I tried to build bridges, but the foundations weren't strong and this all came to nothing.

As Mum grew weaker, I spent more and more time with her in the house. Watching her fade away in front of me was so sad. I would sit with her and, holding her hand, would chat about the few happy years we had been lucky enough to spend together. I spent many a night sleeping over and helping to look after her and near the end helping her to the bathroom, which she found hard as she had always wanted to keep her dignity until the last.

Maureen, my mum's only surviving sister, and Jeanette, her daughter, came over for a long weekend in August 2018 and it was a joy to meet and spend time with them and find out that we had so much in common. Maureen remembered every little detail about us all when we were babies, and like Mum she had never thought the day would come when we'd meet. They both gave me and Mum much support and I will be forever grateful for this. She is a wonderful lady and I only wish I'd got to know her sooner and had spent more of my childhood with her.

My cousin Jeanette and I hit it off immediately and within a few hours we were laughing and joking as if we'd known each other all our lives. Once again, I was sad at the missed times we should have spent together. She was a Nationalist through and through, and my eyebrows nearly shot through the ceiling when she whipped out her phone and showed me a picture of her and Gerry Adams. You could have knocked me down with a feather and I was momentarily unsure how to react. I have strong feelings about Republicanism and the IRA, yet I couldn't let this come between us. We'd all suffered enough due to the Troubles ripping our families apart and I was old and wise enough to accept her for what she was – just my cousin. I know we will never agree politically but I respect her views and we never even speak about politics, which is probably the best course of action.

Also, Jeanette has a wicked sense of humour. The two of us got rolling drunk when she was over visiting and I had a great time with her and her mum. My mum was delighted that we were all getting along so well and it lifted her spirits to see Jeanette and me getting on like a house on fire. I was on the gin, and needless to say I got very emotional about everything and before I knew what was happening I was sobbing my heart out to a shocked-looking Jeanette in the garden. To her credit, she dealt with it well, comforting me and making me feel better. Mum just rolled her eyes; she knew how emotional I could get and had seen it a thousand times before. In her inimitable way she told me to pull myself together, which I did.

For the first few weeks I could hardly tell that Mum was ill, but it crept up on her gradually and one day I looked at her and could see that she was tired. She wanted nothing more than the pain and struggle to be over. She became very ill on a few occasions and once they took her to the hospital after a terrible night of pain. However, the next day she refused to stay and against the wishes of the doctors and threats from the nursing staff to call the police, she went straight home and into her favourite chair, proclaiming that she wouldn't move again until it was all over.

One night, she was so poorly that when the Macmillan nurses and doctors came they told me they had to get her to hospital or the event could be terminal. But Mum point-blank refused to budge from her chair and after filling her with medication the doctor left. I could tell he wasn't happy with the situation. We got Mum into bed and I held her hand as she drifted in and out of consciousness. Once she woke up and looking me straight in the eyes asked, 'Am I in heaven?' My heart broke for her. At that point, and for the first time, I accepted that she was really dying, and would pass away very soon.

At one point we offered to get a priest in for the last rites. Her reaction made me think she'd have a heart attack. 'No way!' she shouted. 'I'll deal with Him upstairs and no one else.'

At the end she was confined to her bed and with Margaret's letters underneath her pillow she looked ready to make the journey from life to death. I knew it was near and I was trying to be strong for her.

But there was a bit of life in the old dog yet and as I held her hand, she drew it up to her mouth and after a gentle kiss suddenly started sucking on my finger as though it were a fag. She wanted a fag to see her on her way. It looked so comical that it brought a smile to my face and I'm glad this is one of the last memories I have of her.

After the Macmillan nurses had cleaned and medicated her I held her hand and looking out the window I saw a little robin redbreast sitting on a branch. This touched me beyond words, because after Denis died she had often said that when a robin visited her that it was Denis coming to say hello. This time he was coming to take her hand and lead her home to him, and everlasting companionship.

Suddenly, she gently squeezed my hand and we stared into each other's eyes. At that moment, a light seemed to go out and I knew she was gone. At that moment, a little light in my soul also went out, and I knew my life would never be the same now that the woman who had in one way or other dominated my existence had left me forever.

Our joint journeys through the trials of life had finally come to an end. The mother I had lost, found and now lost again. I pressed my forehead to her hand, still warm, and wept. I wanted to drag her back into this world, right back to the beginning of my life, and make everything all right again. I wanted a re-run of our relationship so that she was at the centre of my childhood. I wanted to rewrite history and wipe away all the pain, loss and suffering that we'd experienced as orphaned children growing up in one of the world's most violent cities.

Of course, I could do none of these things. Her loss was as raw as it was when she'd left us all those years ago, and I would have to go through the grieving process all over again. This time, however, the sadness was tempered with relief; relief that she was no longer suffering from cancer, and that she no longer would suffer the psychological torment that had haunted her ever since she made her momentous decision to leave the city of her birth and the children she loved dearly.

Mum's family came over from Belfast for her Roman Catholic funeral. Margaret sent over a beautiful bouquet of flowers, which had pride of place on her coffin. David and I got to spend some time alone with her just before she left the house and we slipped Margaret's letters under her pillow in the coffin. The local priest, Father Jonathan, give a beautiful sermon. There was a big turnout for her and when they played 'The Fields of Athenry' I surrendered to the emotion that I had been trying to suppress and the tears blinded me at the finality of it all. But she had a good send-off and back at the wake we all got stinking drunk (Belfast style) and remembered the life and times of Sally McBride, my mum.

A couple of weeks later we retrieved Mum's ashes and buried them in the churchyard, beside Denis. Just being there gave me a sense of peace and, although her death had hit me very hard, I was grateful to have spent the years that I did with her. It never quite made up for losing her when I was a child, but at least we could come to some sense of reconciliation. And that, as all Northern Irish people know only too well, is often the best we can hope for. I like to think she's up there somewhere, keeping an eye on me and telling me to pull myself together when life gets on top of me. Despite everything, I know my life was much richer with her in it, and I wouldn't change that for the world.

So goodbye and goodnight *my* mum, until we meet again. And I hope you aren't giving 'Him upstairs' a hard time. Love you beyond words and Rest in Eternal Peace until we are together again.

EPILOGUE

'The past is a foreign country;
they do things differently there.'
LP Hartley, *The Go-Between*

EAST BELFAST
Early July 2019

I'm standing in a side street just off the Albertsbridge Road in the heart of Protestant East Belfast. I've enjoyed a pint or two of Harp in the nearby Harland and Wolff social club, a stone's throw away from the iconic cranes Samsung and Goliath who watch over the good folk of Belfast, and I'm waiting for a riot to begin.

I often visit this part of Belfast when I want a change from my normal drinking dens around the city centre and on the Shankill. I'm over for a few short days, doing research for and working on the book you are now reading. I'm also taking time out to visit family and friends in West Belfast and enjoying all the glitzy attractions the now-peaceful city has to offer. It's also close to the Glorious Twelfth and I'm looking forward to watching the big Loyalist parades that converge on the city and fill my heart with pride in my culture and traditions. Try not to judge me too harshly on that; it's part of my DNA and today I love and respect all mankind, regardless of religion or political background. And it's good to be able to stroll around the old place without constantly having to look over my shoulder.

Yet, despite a peace process that has lasted twenty years, some things never change and when I get a whisper of trouble brewing in East Belfast, something deep within me stirs, compelling me to take a closer look and revisit memories of a childhood that traumatised me, leaving scars that can never heal completely. Like so many others.

It's all to do with one of the huge bonfires being built across the city to celebrate the Twelfth. Although this one is in a heavily Loyalist part of town, it's been constructed close to a sports centre. The Sinn Fein-dominated Belfast City Council believes this is intimidatory, because Catholics might use the sports centre, and have ordered it to be torn down. The local Loyalist population are furious: they suspect Sinn Fein's motive is purely sectarian as few Catholics, if any, are likely to use the sports centre. Nonetheless, contractors have been appointed to bulldoze the bonfire and a tense stand-off is about to begin.

I persuade Billy to drive us over to see what's going on. I can't help it. I live a very quiet existence in England now. The mad drug days and chaos of my late twenties and early thirties are long behind me and now I prefer the occasional gin and tonic and a good movie night in with Simone and the kids. Yet while I'm a peace-loving fella, I have a primal response to the mere mention of a riot. I don't want to take part in any violence, of course, but also I don't want to miss seeing something that was an everyday part of my existence thirty-odd years ago. It's like watching history repeating itself, and I'm a big history buff.

After the pints we walk across Newtownards Road and head to where the trouble is brewing. There's an odd atmosphere in the air; the crowds milling around the streets and close to the semi-built bonfire sense something is about to happen. The feeling is almost carnival-like, yet it's stoked by years of anger and resentment.

Billy is uneasy. He still lives in the city and knows that beneath the shiny surface of post-Troubles Belfast there are still many bitter memories lurking; memories that can easily translate into flashes of violence. He keeps himself to himself, and away from all this. Me, I'm now a tourist in my own past. I don't want trouble – and yet I'm drawn to it like a moth to a flame.

From nowhere, a gang of intimidating masked men appear on the scene. There is cheering as they move in loose file, placing their hands over any cameras or phones recording their presence. Beneath the masks they appear to be young guys. No doubt, somewhere in the shadows, there are older men directing this, just as there always were. I've been there myself and I know how this works.

One of the lads pulls a can of spray paint from his jacket and starts writing words along a nearby wall. It's a warning to the contractors: if they try to pull down the bonfire there will be trouble. If I was the appointed contractor, I'd be turning around now. Even so, there are rumours they will turn up, flanked by police Land Rovers, and attempt to carry out the job. If this happens, there really will be trouble.

'C'mon, John,' Billy says, 'I think we've seen enough now, don't you?'

'Ach, give us a minute, will you?' I reply. 'This might get interesting . . .'

'It won't,' says Billy firmly. 'The peelers won't turn up till after midnight, if they show up at all. We're wasting time standing about here.'

I'm still reluctant to leave. When you grow up in a place like Glencairn or the Shankill, or the Falls Road, your whole life is dominated by conflict. Because you are in that tribal environment, the community think and act as one. You have to grow up in that kind of environment to really understand the normality of the madness. And though I've left that madness behind – just as I hope most of my fellow countrymen and countrywomen who lived through that period have too – I'm still drawn to the echoes of it.

Kids are kicking bottles and stones around and there's a notion that the bonfire might be set alight early, just to piss the council and police off. But that doesn't happen. Instead, from the sky above comes the familiar whup-whup-whup of helicopter blades. It isn't the army these days, but the police, yet the effect on me is electrifying. For a moment I could be a teenage tearaway back on the border with Ardoyne, battling the local Catholics before being shouted at to go home for my tea.

When I look back at my early and teenage life growing up

in the brutal war zones of Loyalist West Belfast, the past seems more like a different planet, let alone a different country, and back then in the playgrounds of my childhood they certainly did do things differently.

The legacy of those times is more than 3,500 lives lost and around 50,000 injured, plus countless families and close ones left with a lifetime of never-ending grief and sorrow. Was it all worth it? I don't think so. As a pacifist, my heart bleeds for all innocent victims of the Troubles regardless of political or religious background, and I pray for everlasting peace in Northern Ireland and a better future for the generations born after the Troubles and those yet to come.

Life's hard enough to get through without worrying that you will be abused, ridiculed or worse because of your religion, creed or nationality. And in Northern Ireland during the worst years of the sectarian slaughter it seemed that the killings would go on forever, and everyone suffered in their own personal way due to the horrors that ruled and ruined our daily lives for so very long. We were all pawns trapped in a nightmare that lasted thirty long, savage years. Thank God those dark days are behind us now, and I hope that anyone contemplating a return to war will get the message – loud and clear – We Want Peace.

Billy gives my walking stick a gentle tap. 'That leg o' yours must be feelin' it, standing around all this time. You know, if trouble starts, you'll not be able to run so quickly . . . and I won't be stopping to carry you back.'

I contemplate this for a moment. I have a wife and two kids at home, none of whom have grown up in this kind of environment. And thank God, too: riots and violence and murder were why I left it in the first place, to start a new life somewhere peaceful. I lived through a nightmare I'd never want to inflict on my nearest and dearest, especially my family. When I made the monumental decision to leave Belfast and the Troubles behind, I left part of my heart and soul in the streets of my childhood. Despite the madness and pain, Belfast will always have a special place in my heart. It made me who I am. Now England is my home and I'm happy and grateful for everything I have. Had I remained in Belfast I'm sure my story would have had a very different ending and it's possible I would not be here to share it.

When all is said and done, I know I made the right decision to escape the Troubles and I have no regrets about leaving the place. I just wish it was a choice I never had to make in the first place.

The scene playing out before me now has lost its appeal and I'm silently grateful I'm no longer part of it.

'I wouldn't say no to another pint,' I tell Billy.

'There's a good pub around the corner,' he replies. 'You can buy me a Harp. Will we go?'

I nod and we turn away, leaving whatever troubles – with a small 't' – may or may not be brewing to themselves.

'Billy, can we stop off on the way home and grab a pastie supper? I'm bloody starving after all this craic.'

Billy smiles. 'Is the Pope a Catholic?' he replies.

ACKNOWLEDGEMENTS

The book you have just read has been with me in one form or another for more than thirty years and over that period I have gone from periods of cosmic enthusiasm for telling my story to utter dread at the thought of sharing it with the world, of laying my soul bare. But throughout it all, folk always seemed fascinated with my journey and many encouraged me to take the leap. However no man is an island, and I couldn't have done it without the help and support of certain people whom I would like to thank:

James Hodgkinson, Kelly Ellis and the team from John Blake Publishing. Despite my story getting many soul-destroying rejections over the years, the JB team understood the heart of it – that it wasn't just another book about the Troubles – and took my hand to lead me gently through the publishing process.

Margaret Hanbury, of the Hanbury Agency, my agent who got me a book deal within weeks of coming on board (after countless others had turned me away) and has been a constant source of help and support from beginning to end. When she first read the finished book, she called me and the emotion in her voice as she discussed my story touched my heart and soul.

Tom Henry, my writing partner and friend, whose constant help and ongoing support through the last five years has led me to where I am now. He believed in my story from the beginning, even when others didn't, and when I had had enough and was ready to throw the towel in, he encouraged me to stick with it and see it through. Forever in your debt.

This book is dedicated to my dad, and namesake, John Chambers, whose death forty years ago left a hole in my heart and soul that can never be healed, for loving and caring for us and raising us as a single parent. What a journey he set me on. My siblings Mags, Jean and David, for always being there for me and giving me endless unconditional love and support in all that I do. This is also their story. My grandparents, John and Susie Chambers, who loved and cared for us when our world fell to pieces. My aunties, uncles and cousins, especially Jacky, who always engulfed me in love, and Uncle Rab, who was always there for us. Also, my uncle Jim and aunt Maureen, who always cared for us and give us love. My aunt Anne and uncle John. Wee Sam, Linda, Mandy, Joanne, Denise, Karen and Stephen, Leanne and Nichola, for always being there for me and for bringing so much joy and happiness into my shattered childhood. All my friends and family in Belfast and in Glencairn, especially Natalie and Julie and Davey Mc C. Those in London, too, especially John Hibbs, a lifelong friend who has always been there for me and shared so many happy, crazy times with me.

All my friends and followers on Twitter and my blog. Many have been on this journey with me and some have supported and comforted me when darkness threatened to engulf me.

Nick Bradley and Darren Cooper from my London days – you always believed in me, and my story. I'm glad our paths crossed.

My wee cousins Karen and Shannon and all other members of the Chambers clan no longer with us. I love and miss you all every day.

Jay McFall, my wonderful Mod mucker and great friend, for letting me use her photos and for documenting our crazy Mod odyssey.

Gary, my lifelong best friend and soulmate, who has always been there to support me – and to take the mick non-stop. I love him like a brother, and we will always be as thick as thieves. I'm so glad our paths crossed.

My mother-in-law, Janet and late father-in-law, Roy, for always making me feel welcome. Thanks for the best home-made curries in the universe.

My three-legged cat Baby and his sister Fluffy, and our two goldfish, Tiny and Jaws.

Most importantly, my beautiful wife, Simone, and children, Autumn and Jude, who love and care for me every day, and who pick me up when life gets me down. My life would be empty without you and I love you beyond words.

And finally, of course, my mother, Sally McBride.

ABOUT THE AUTHOR

JOHN CHAMBERS was born in Belfast in 1966 and grew up during some of the most turbulent years of the Troubles. He now lives with his wife and children in the north of England, but his heart's desire remains a pastie supper from Beatties chippy on the Shankill Road. In no particular order, his interests include astronomy, quantum mechanics, military history, music, the Mod movement and his mother-in-law's curries.

John can be found blogging at www.belfastchildis.com and tweeting at @bfchild66